Midnight Societ
THE BLACK LAKE

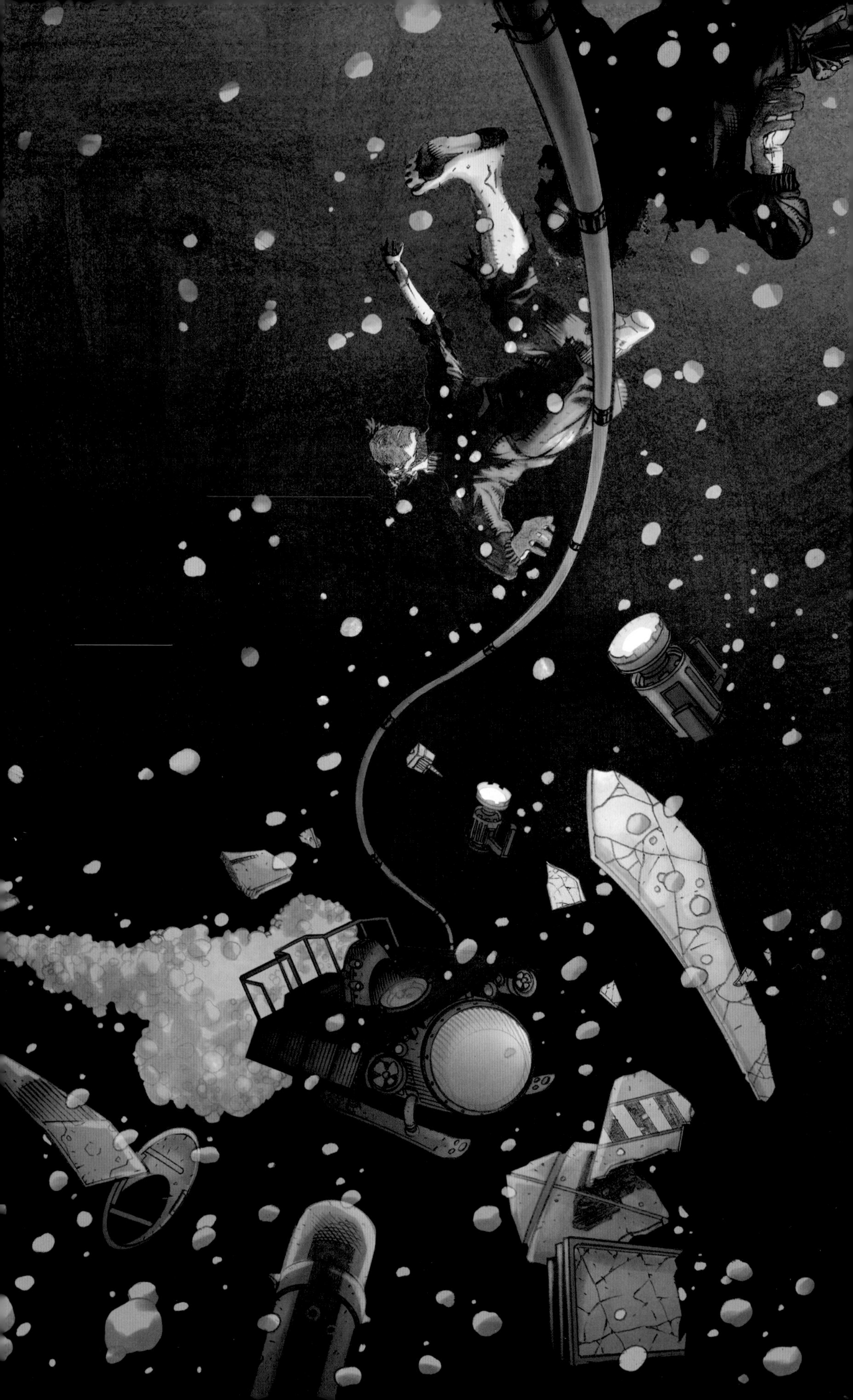

Midnight Society™
THE BLACK LAKE

Story and art
DREW EDWARD JOHNSON

Colors—covers and chapter 1
LIZZY JOHN

Colors—chapters 2 to 4
DANIELE RUDONI

Letters
STEVE DUTRO

SPECIAL THANKS
to Steve Ziolkowski for submarine
designs and vehicle models, Karl Tolson for dialect
consultation, Hart Reickhoff for *Midnight Society*
icon designs, and Shon Bury and Taylor Smith at
Space Goat Productions, Inc.

DARK HORSE BOOKS

For my wife Karen, who made it possible
for me to tell my story. Thank you, Love.
—Drew Edward Johnson

President and Publisher
MIKE RICHARDSON

Editor
PHILIP R. SIMON

Assistant Editor
ROXY POLK

Designer
ETHAN KIMBERLING

Digital Art Technician
CHRISTINA McKENZIE

MIDNIGHT SOCIETY: THE BLACK LAKE

This volume collects issues #1–#4 of the Dark Horse Comics miniseries Midnight Society: The Black Lake, published in 2015.

Published by
Dark Horse Books
A division of Dark Horse Comics, Inc.
10956 SE Main Street
Milwaukie, OR 97222

DarkHorse.com

To find a comics shop in your area, call the Comic Shop Locator Service toll-free at 1-888-266-4226.

First edition: January 2016
ISBN 978-1-61655-825-3

INTRODUCTION

The black lake.

The grass is greener . . .

I've been a big comic book geek since I was a little kid. I've always admired comic artists for their ability to create worlds that I love to live in for a while. The sheer amount of labor involved in the drawing of those worlds is also extremely admirable, and it's something I've always found very difficult to do. Being friends with Drew and watching his process has been very inspirational—and fills me with envy. He does what my little-kid self had fantasies of doing. Granted, I get to draw for a living as well. Being an animation professional for many, many years on a little-known, short-lived show called *The Simpsons* has given me a wonderful career. But still . . . the little kid in me just wants to draw superheroes and stuff . . .

Drew would often set up shop at our studio and draw his pages (his wife Karen also works on the show). I would always drop by to watch and see the pages evolve and be impressed by what I saw being drawn. Dang! He gets to draw comics!

The opportunities in the art business to do your *own* stuff can be rare, and what you hold in your hands is one such opportunity. When an artist gets to do his or her own stuff, it's worth sitting up and taking notice—and this one has been a long time coming. The work is gorgeous. The obsidian blacks, tapering lines, and feathering so sharp you can lacerate your eyeballs on it, and coloring so juicy you need to go on a diet afterward. This is cool stuff.

Envious.

Enjoy!

—**Paul Wee**

Burbank, California, 2015

Born and raised in Honolulu, Hawaii, Paul Wee grew up obsessed with comic books, science fiction, art, and monsters. Moving from Hawaii to Los Angeles in 1984, he found a city full of the cool stuff he was looking for and promptly began studying art at Otis/Parsons, the California Art Institute, Associates in Art, and the LA Academy of Figurative Art. He also found a great many Jedi Masters to study with, including Glenn Vilppu, Mark Westermoe, Steve Huston, and John Watkiss. He's taught figure drawing for many years and exhibits and sells his own art and self-published books and products at San Diego Comic-Con and other shows. Paul has also won an Emmy Award and worked on an obscure, short-lived television series called The Simpsons *for a really long time.*

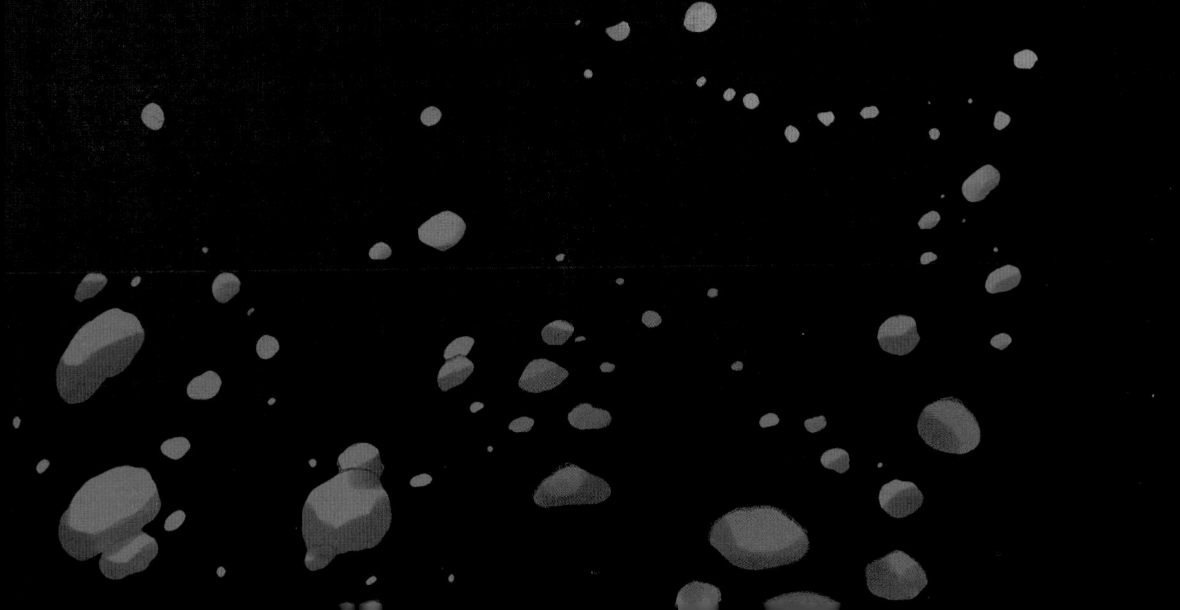

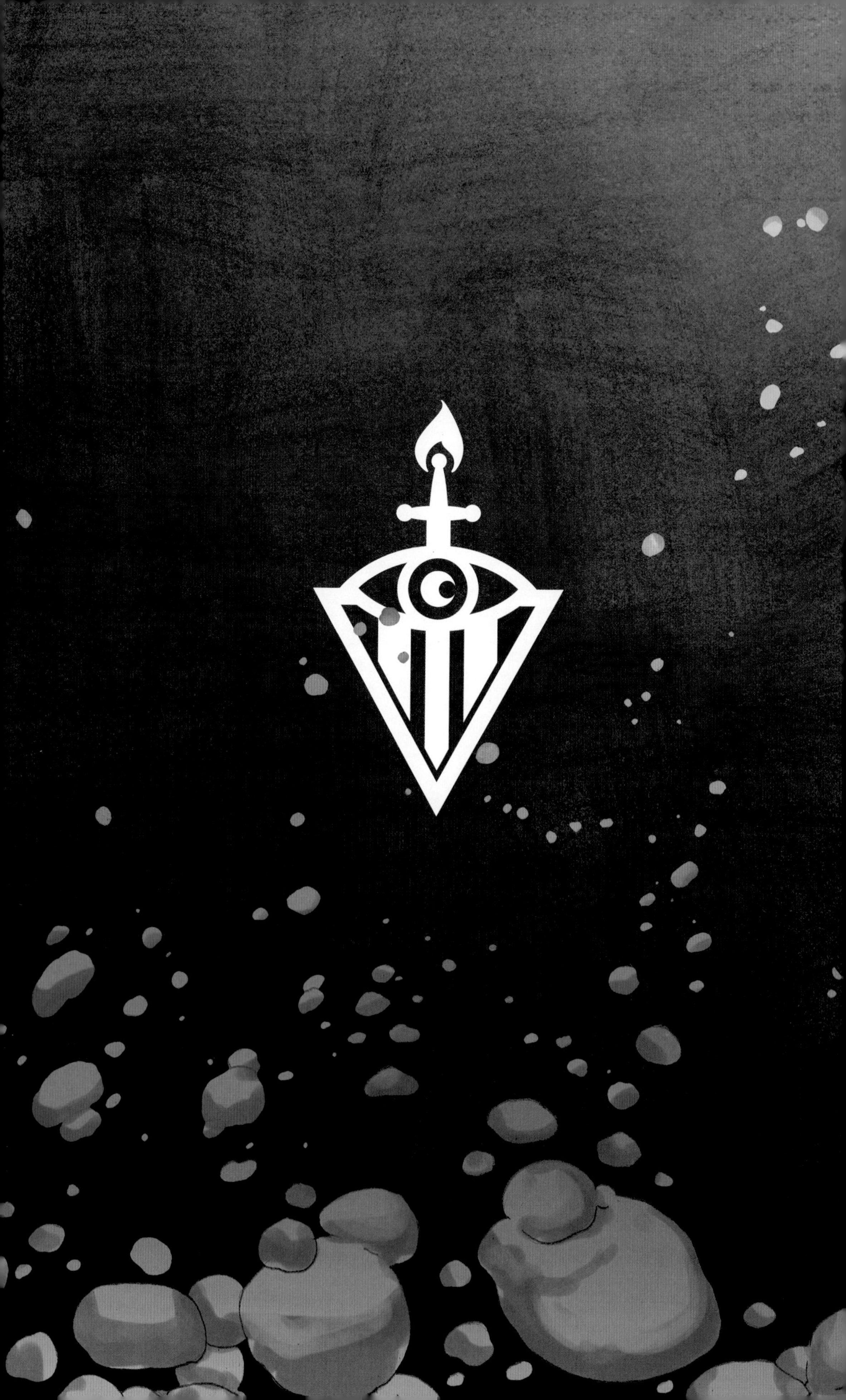

CHAPTER ONE

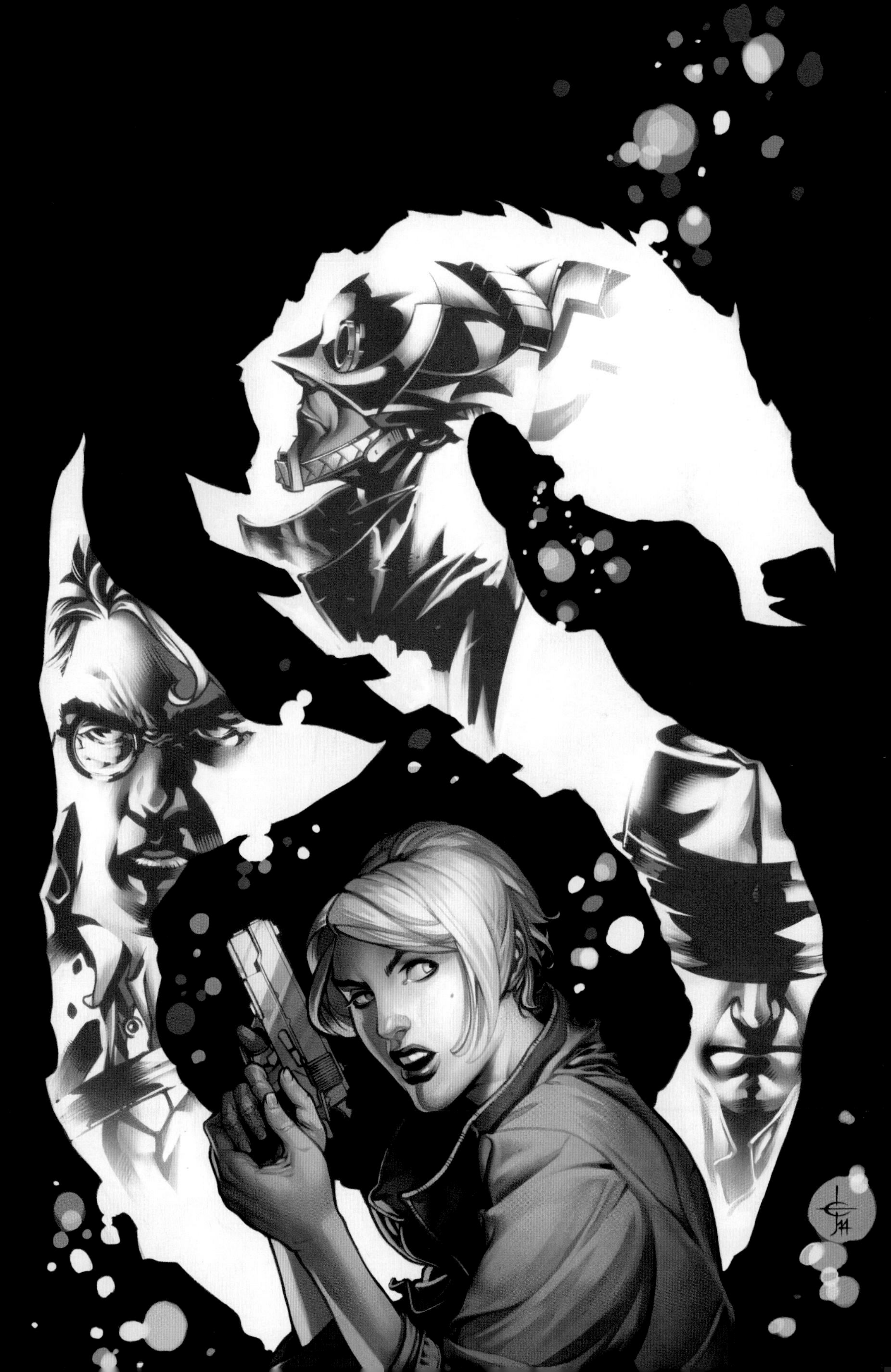

"I fly past a long-blind leviathan who sinks below me and disappears as I rise higher. Before I break the surface, I scramble to remember *anything* about myself."

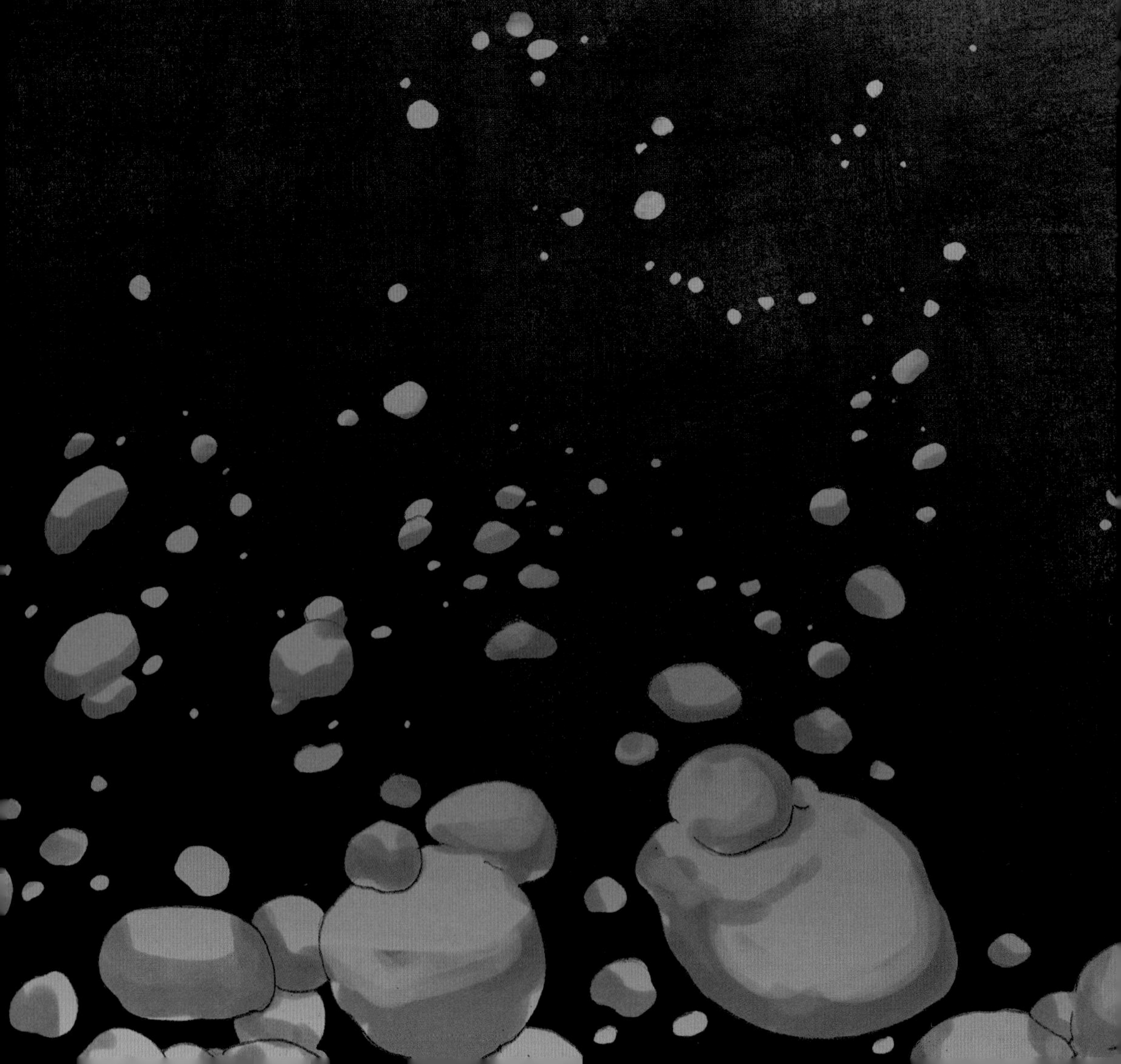

1.

In Which We Meet Two Celebrated Adventurers With A Problem Of Ethics, And A Young Woman Takes An Urgent Job At Four O'Clock In The Morning.

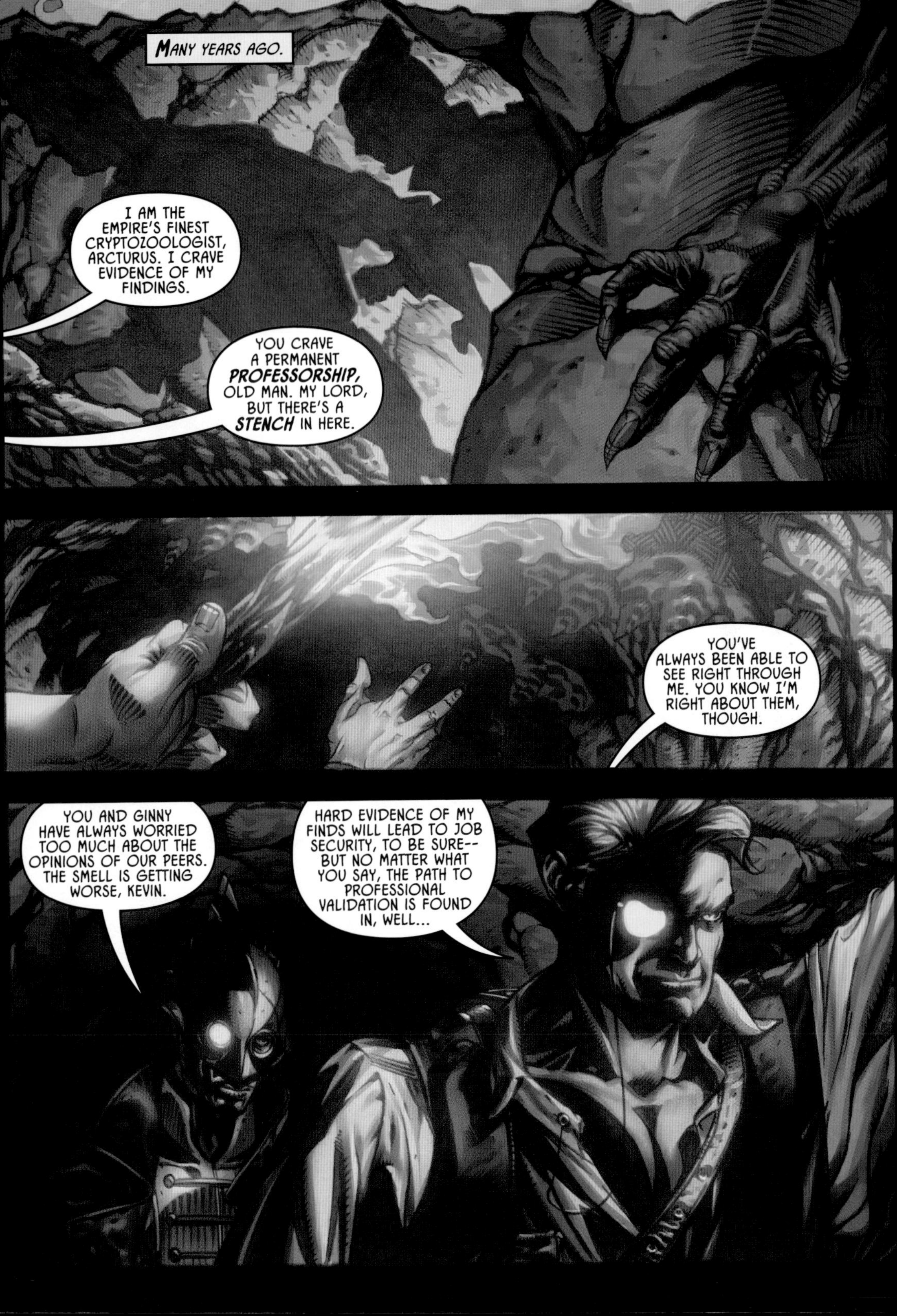
MANY YEARS AGO.
I AM THE EMPIRE'S FINEST CRYPTOZOOLOGIST, ARCTURUS. I CRAVE EVIDENCE OF MY FINDINGS.
YOU CRAVE A PERMANENT PROFESSORSHIP, OLD MAN. MY LORD, BUT THERE'S A STENCH IN HERE.
YOU'VE ALWAYS BEEN ABLE TO SEE RIGHT THROUGH ME. YOU KNOW I'M RIGHT ABOUT THEM, THOUGH.
YOU AND GINNY HAVE ALWAYS WORRIED TOO MUCH ABOUT THE OPINIONS OF OUR PEERS. THE SMELL IS GETTING WORSE, KEVIN.
HARD EVIDENCE OF MY FINDS WILL LEAD TO JOB SECURITY, TO BE SURE-- BUT NO MATTER WHAT YOU SAY, THE PATH TO PROFESSIONAL VALIDATION IS FOUND IN, WELL...

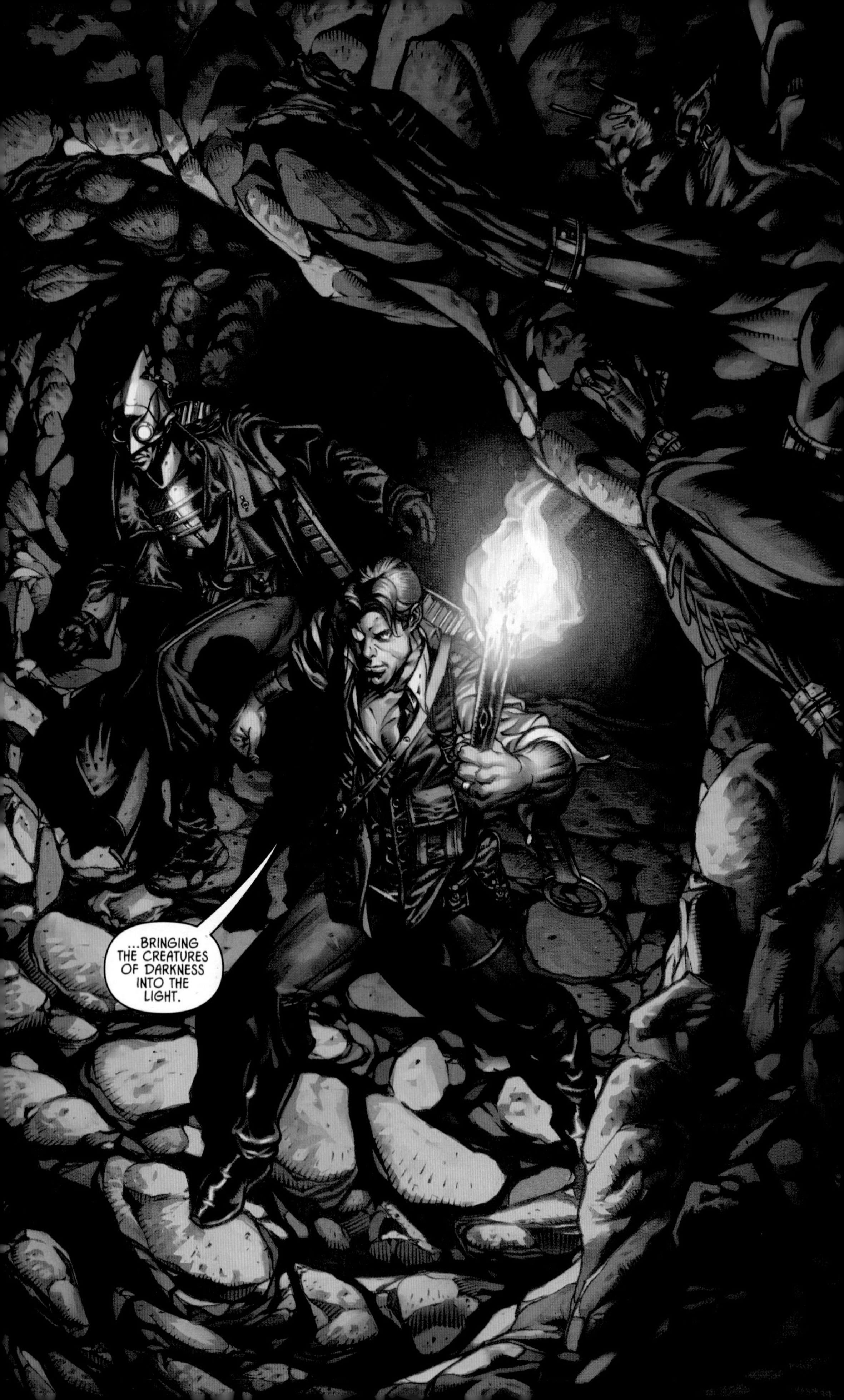
...BRINGING THE CREATURES OF DARKNESS INTO THE LIGHT.

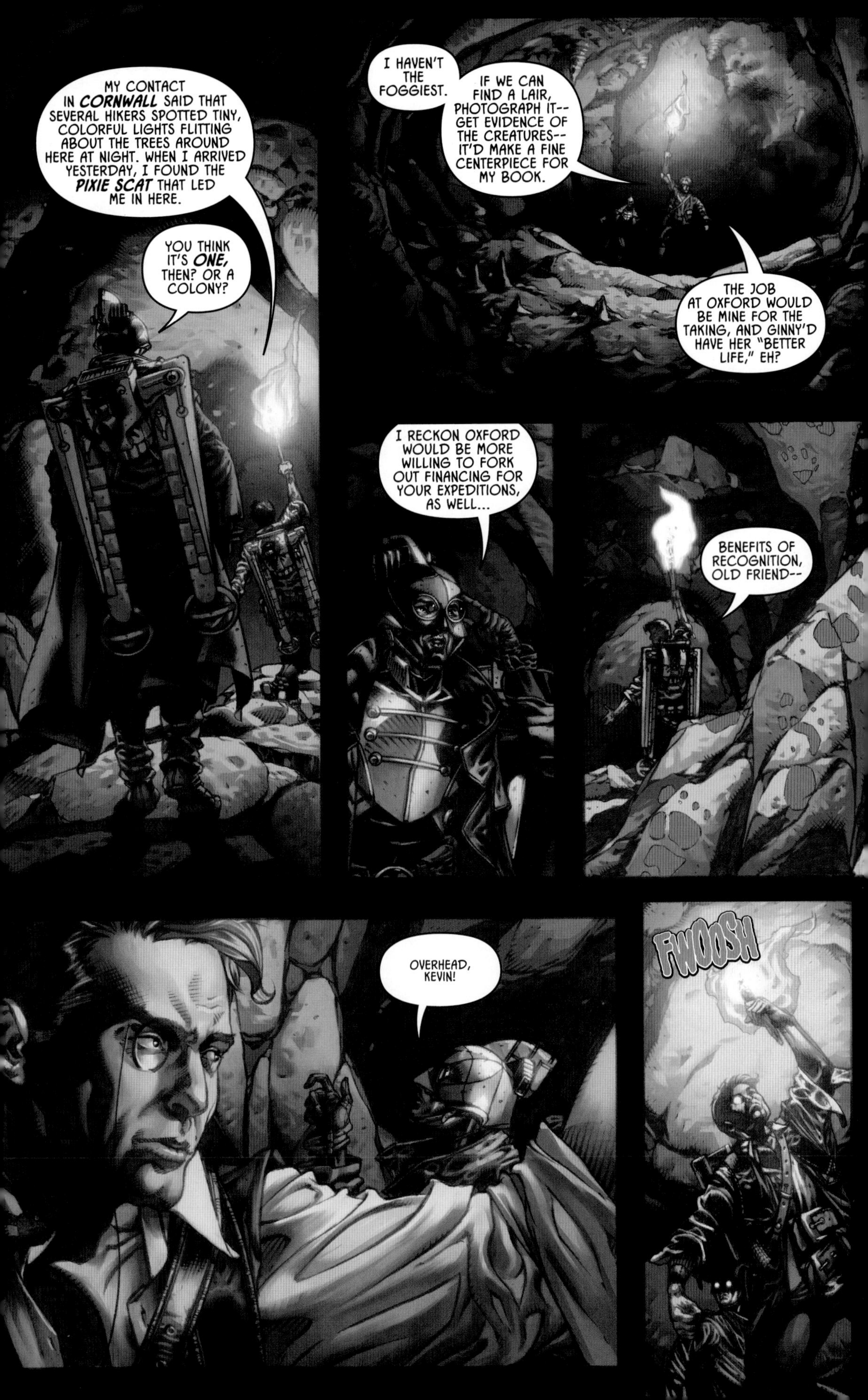
MY CONTACT IN CORNWALL SAID THAT SEVERAL HIKERS SPOTTED TINY, COLORFUL LIGHTS FLITTING ABOUT THE TREES AROUND HERE AT NIGHT. WHEN I ARRIVED YESTERDAY, I FOUND THE PIXIE SCAT THAT LED ME IN HERE.
YOU THINK IT'S ONE, THEN? OR A COLONY?
I HAVEN'T THE FOGGIEST.
IF WE CAN FIND A LAIR, PHOTOGRAPH IT--GET EVIDENCE OF THE CREATURES--IT'D MAKE A FINE CENTERPIECE FOR MY BOOK.
THE JOB AT OXFORD WOULD BE MINE FOR THE TAKING, AND GINNY'D HAVE HER "BETTER LIFE," EH?
I RECKON OXFORD WOULD BE MORE WILLING TO FORK OUT FINANCING FOR YOUR EXPEDITIONS, AS WELL...
BENEFITS OF RECOGNITION, OLD FRIEND--
OVERHEAD, KEVIN!
FWOOSH

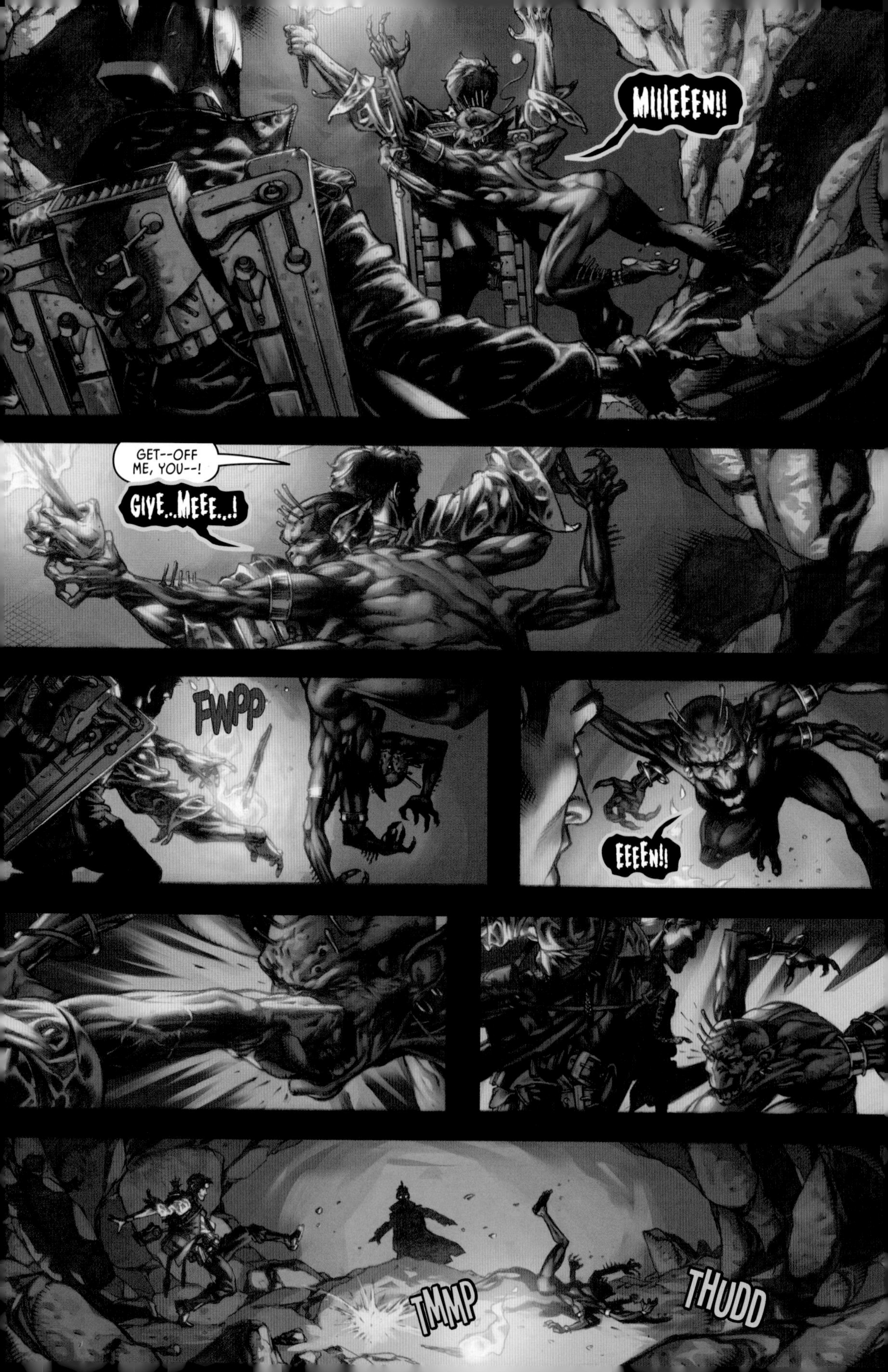

MIIIEEEN!!
GET--OFF ME, YOU--!
GIVE..MEEE...!
FWPP
EEEEN!!
TMMP
THUDD

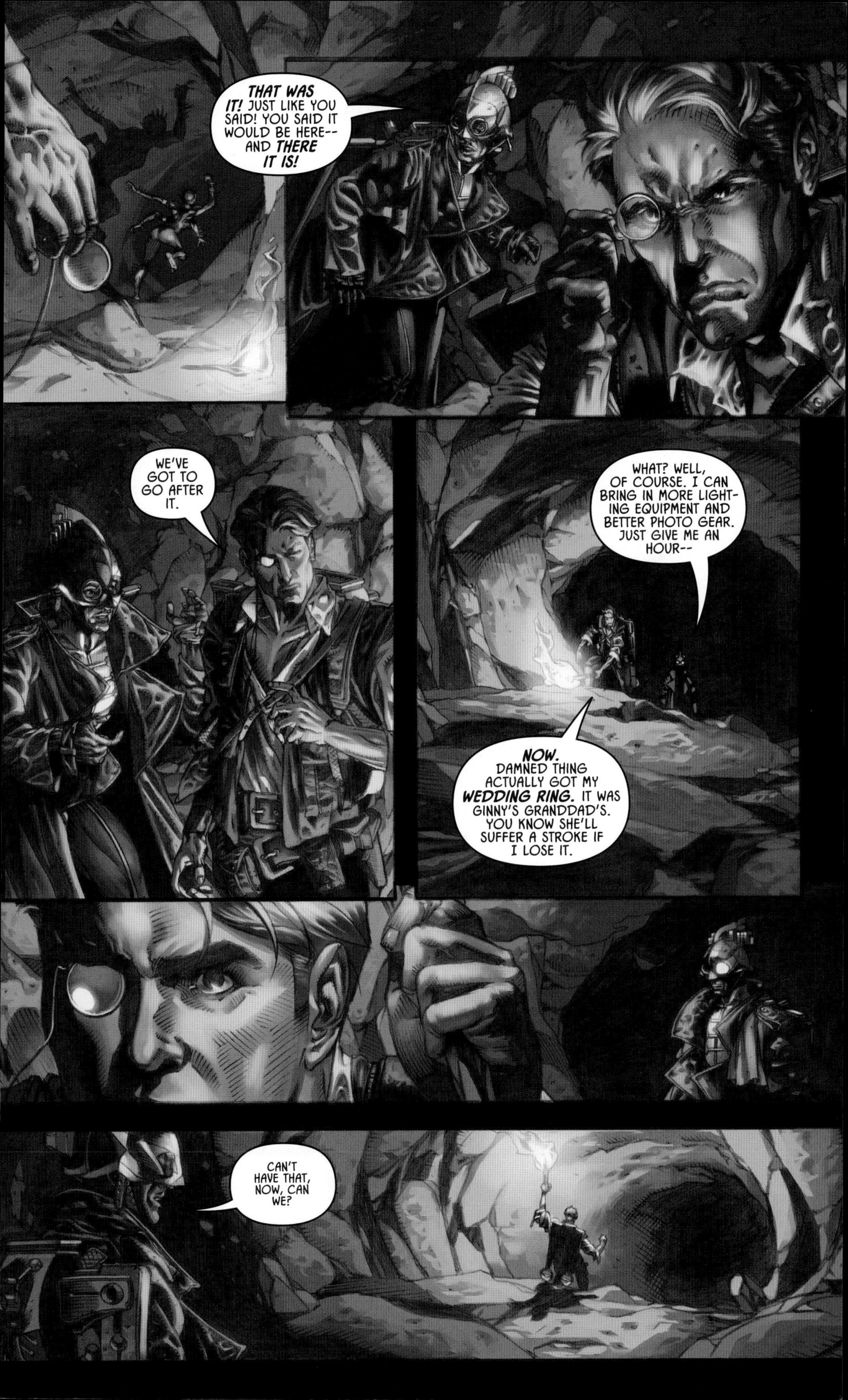

THAT WAS IT! JUST LIKE YOU SAID! YOU SAID IT WOULD BE HERE-- AND THERE IT IS!
WE'VE GOT TO GO AFTER IT.
WHAT? WELL, OF COURSE. I CAN BRING IN MORE LIGHTING EQUIPMENT AND BETTER PHOTO GEAR. JUST GIVE ME AN HOUR--
NOW. DAMNED THING ACTUALLY GOT MY WEDDING RING. IT WAS GINNY'S GRANDDAD'S. YOU KNOW SHE'LL SUFFER A STROKE IF I LOSE IT.
CAN'T HAVE THAT, NOW, CAN WE?

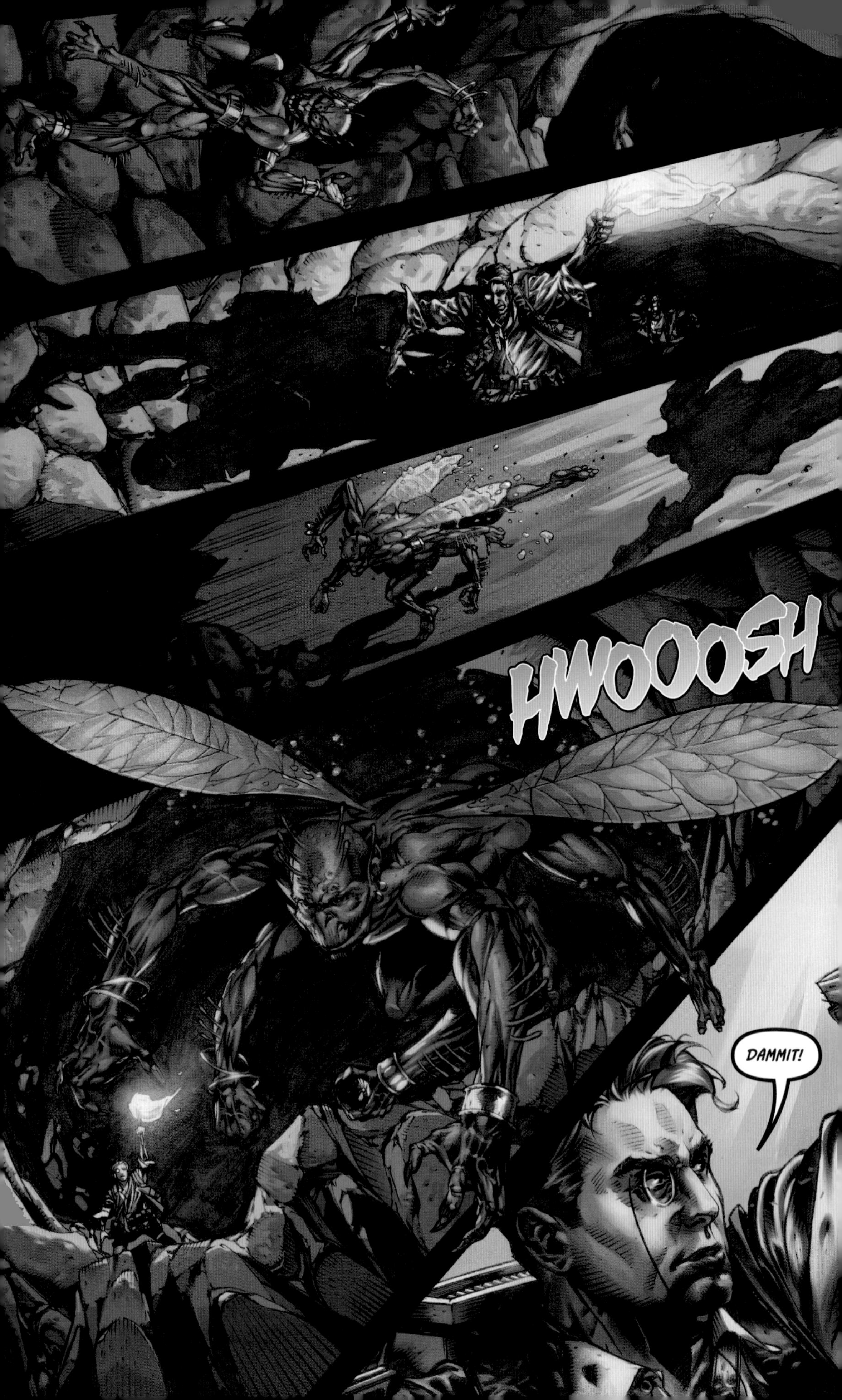
HWOOOSH
DAMMIT!

YOU FORGET YOU'RE WEARING ONE OF MY WING PACKS, THICKIE?
CHOK
WSSHH
YOU HAVEN'T CALLED ME THAT SINCE WE WERE BOARDERS!
YOU HAVEN'T ACTED THIS *THICK* SINCE THEN, OLD BOY!
SKASH
NO!!!

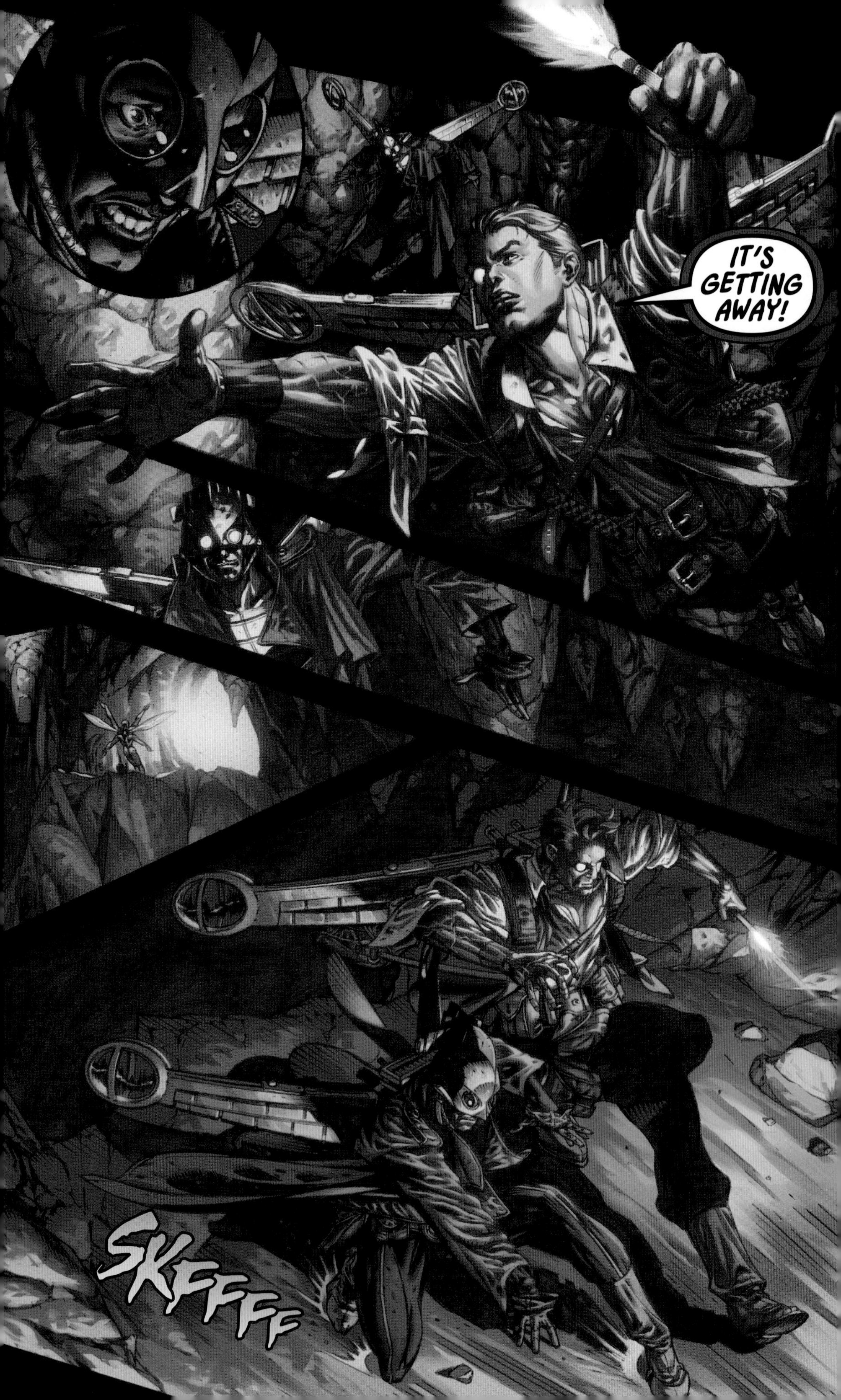
IT'S GETTING AWAY!
SKEFFFF

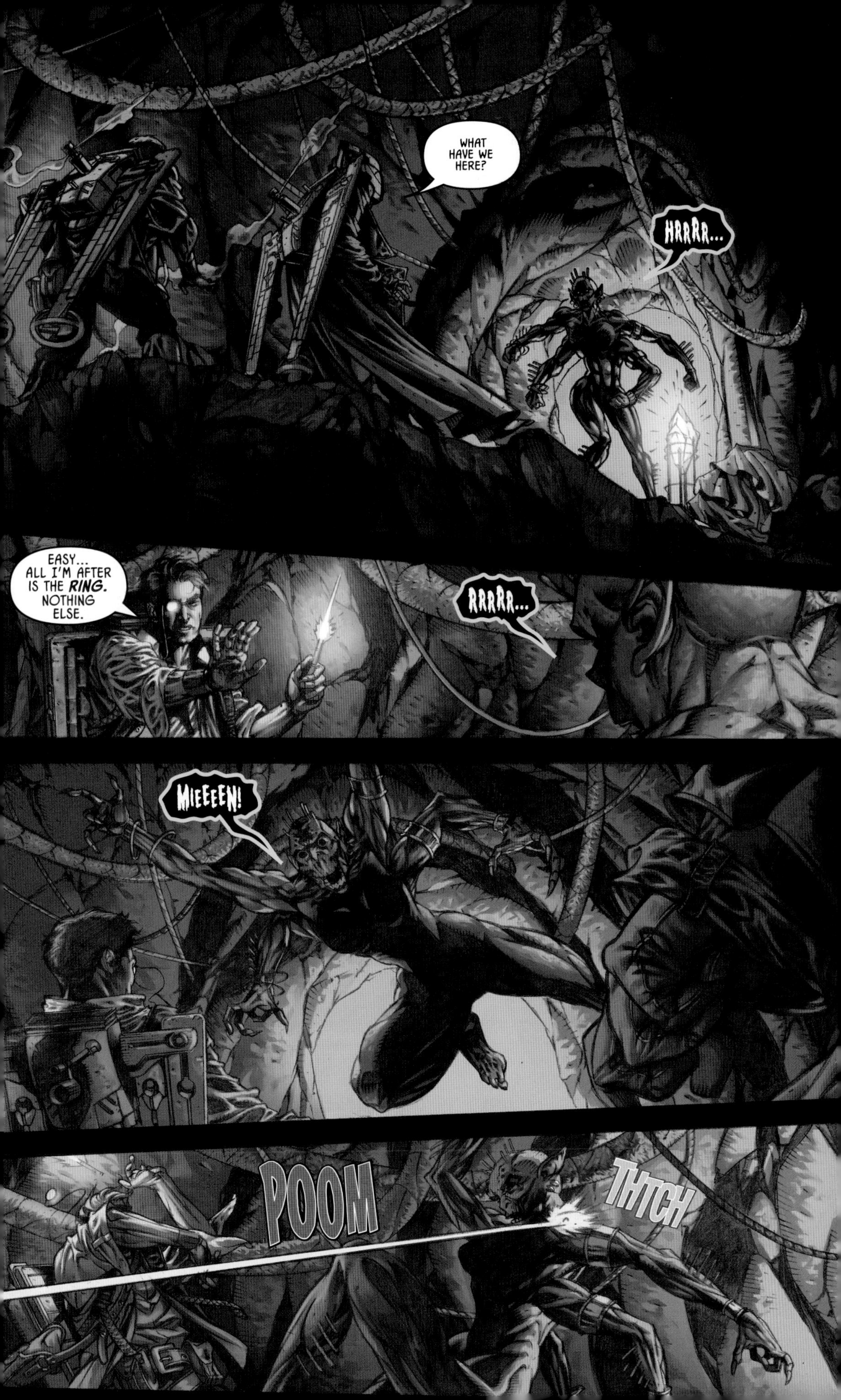
WHAT HAVE WE HERE?
HRRRR...
EASY... ALL I'M AFTER IS THE **RING.** NOTHING ELSE.
RRRRR...
MIEEEEN!
POOM
THTCH

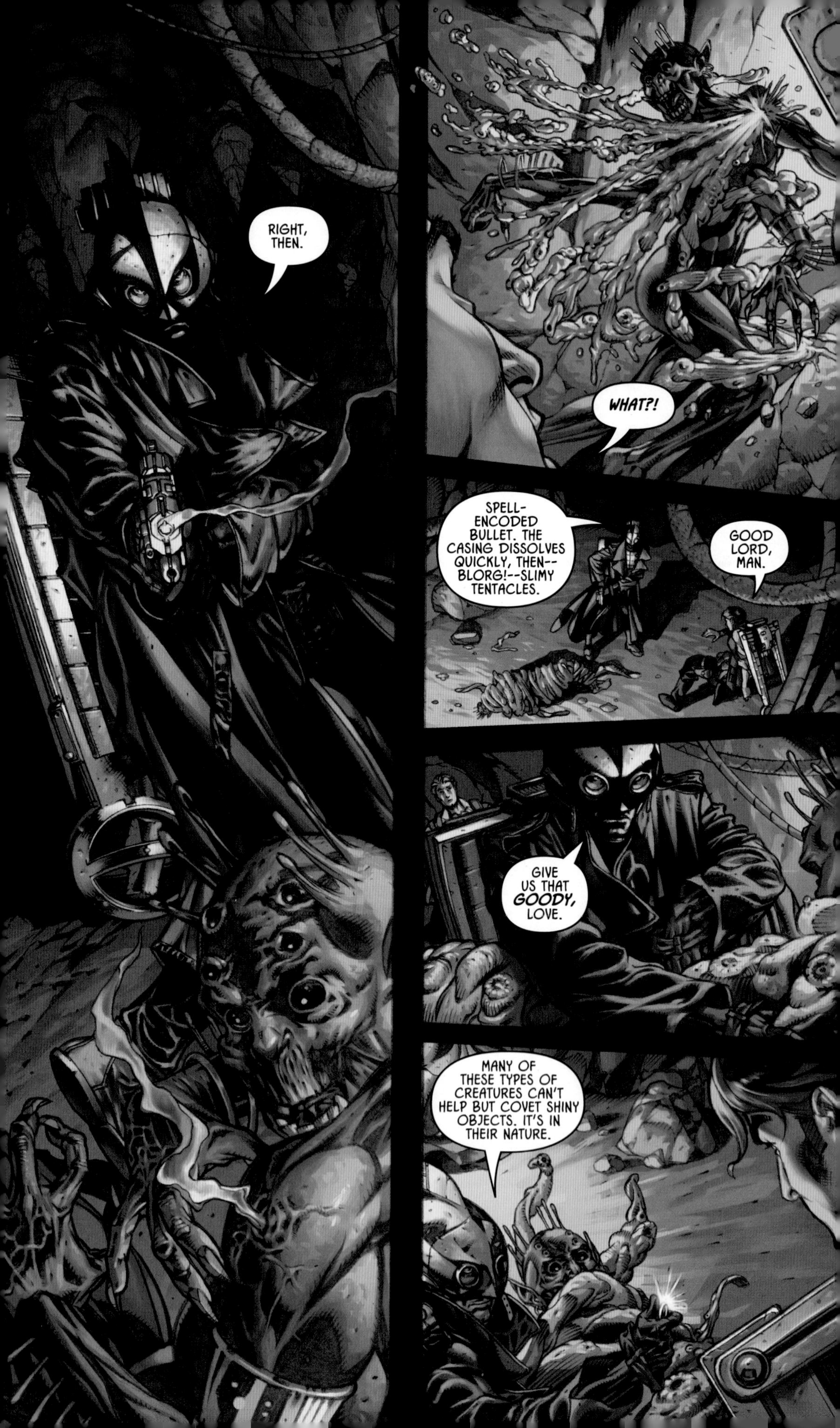

RIGHT, THEN.
WHAT?!
SPELL-ENCODED BULLET. THE CASING DISSOLVES QUICKLY, THEN--BLORG!--SLIMY TENTACLES.
GOOD LORD, MAN.
GIVE US THAT *GOODY,* LOVE.
MANY OF THESE TYPES OF CREATURES CAN'T HELP BUT COVET SHINY OBJECTS. IT'S IN THEIR NATURE.

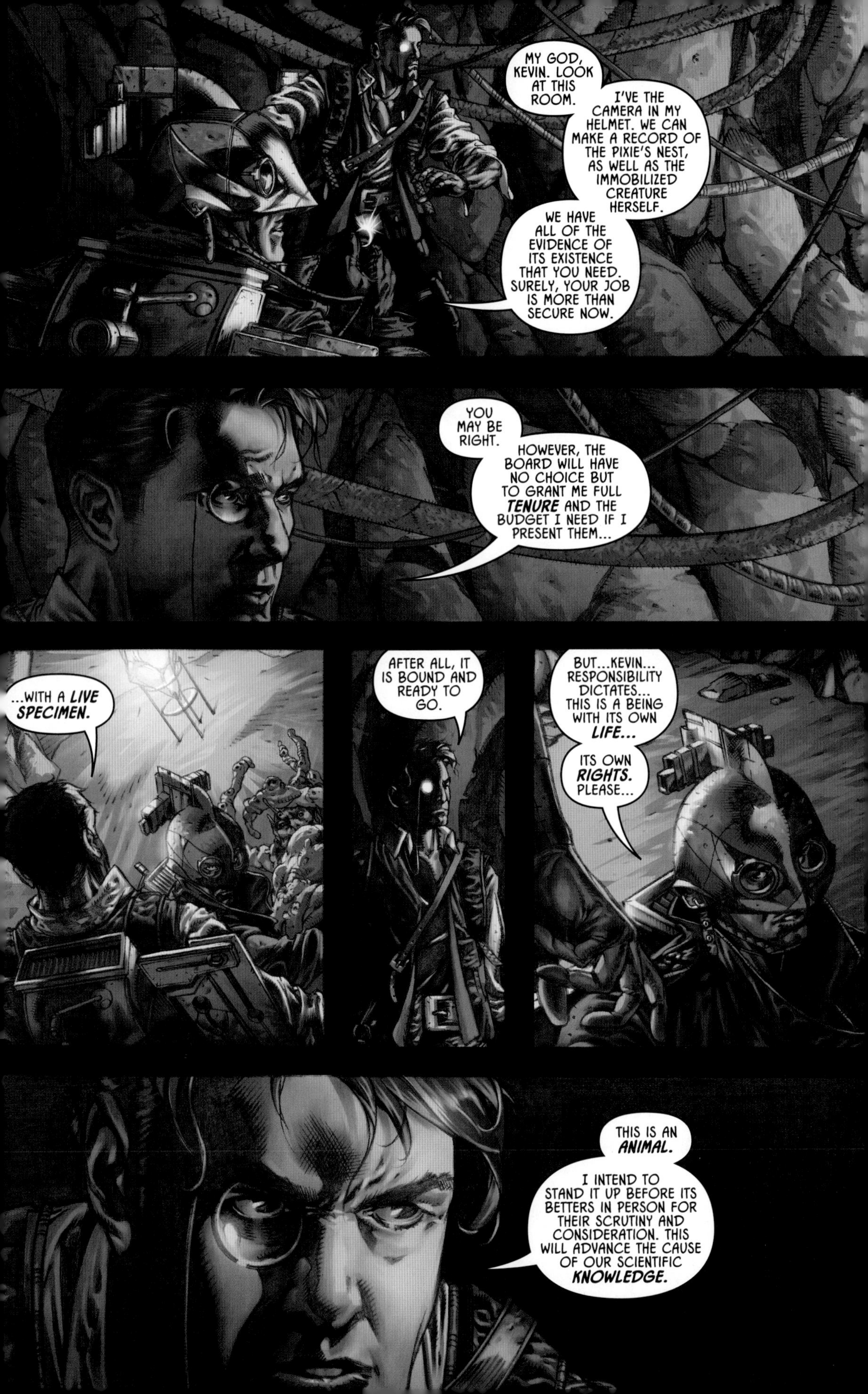

MY GOD, KEVIN. LOOK AT THIS ROOM.
I'VE THE CAMERA IN MY HELMET. WE CAN MAKE A RECORD OF THE PIXIE'S NEST, AS WELL AS THE IMMOBILIZED CREATURE HERSELF.
WE HAVE ALL OF THE EVIDENCE OF ITS EXISTENCE THAT YOU NEED. SURELY, YOUR JOB IS MORE THAN SECURE NOW.
YOU MAY BE RIGHT.
HOWEVER, THE BOARD WILL HAVE NO CHOICE BUT TO GRANT ME FULL ***TENURE*** AND THE BUDGET I NEED IF I PRESENT THEM...
...WITH A ***LIVE SPECIMEN.***
AFTER ALL, IT IS BOUND AND READY TO GO.
BUT...KEVIN... RESPONSIBILITY DICTATES... THIS IS A BEING WITH ITS OWN ***LIFE...***
ITS OWN ***RIGHTS.*** PLEASE...
THIS IS AN ***ANIMAL.***
I INTEND TO STAND IT UP BEFORE ITS BETTERS IN PERSON FOR THEIR SCRUTINY AND CONSIDERATION. THIS WILL ADVANCE THE CAUSE OF OUR SCIENTIFIC ***KNOWLEDGE.***

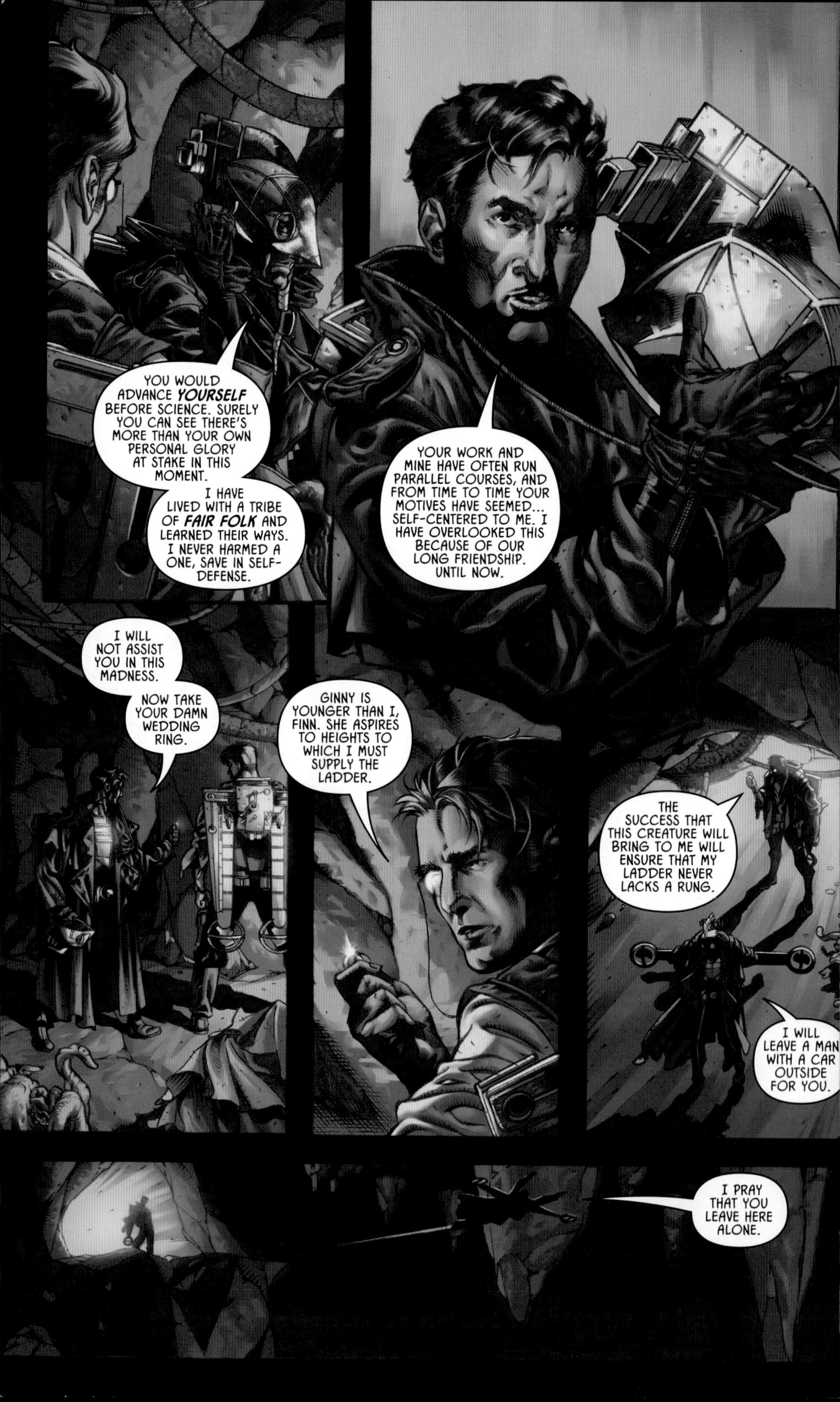
YOU WOULD ADVANCE YOURSELF BEFORE SCIENCE. SURELY YOU CAN SEE THERE'S MORE THAN YOUR OWN PERSONAL GLORY AT STAKE IN THIS MOMENT.
I HAVE LIVED WITH A TRIBE OF FAIR FOLK AND LEARNED THEIR WAYS. I NEVER HARMED A ONE, SAVE IN SELF-DEFENSE.
YOUR WORK AND MINE HAVE OFTEN RUN PARALLEL COURSES, AND FROM TIME TO TIME YOUR MOTIVES HAVE SEEMED... SELF-CENTERED TO ME. I HAVE OVERLOOKED THIS BECAUSE OF OUR LONG FRIENDSHIP. UNTIL NOW.
I WILL NOT ASSIST YOU IN THIS MADNESS.
NOW TAKE YOUR DAMN WEDDING RING.
GINNY IS YOUNGER THAN I, FINN. SHE ASPIRES TO HEIGHTS TO WHICH I MUST SUPPLY THE LADDER.
THE SUCCESS THAT THIS CREATURE WILL BRING TO ME WILL ENSURE THAT MY LADDER NEVER LACKS A RUNG.
I WILL LEAVE A MAN WITH A CAR OUTSIDE FOR YOU.
I PRAY THAT YOU LEAVE HERE ALONE.

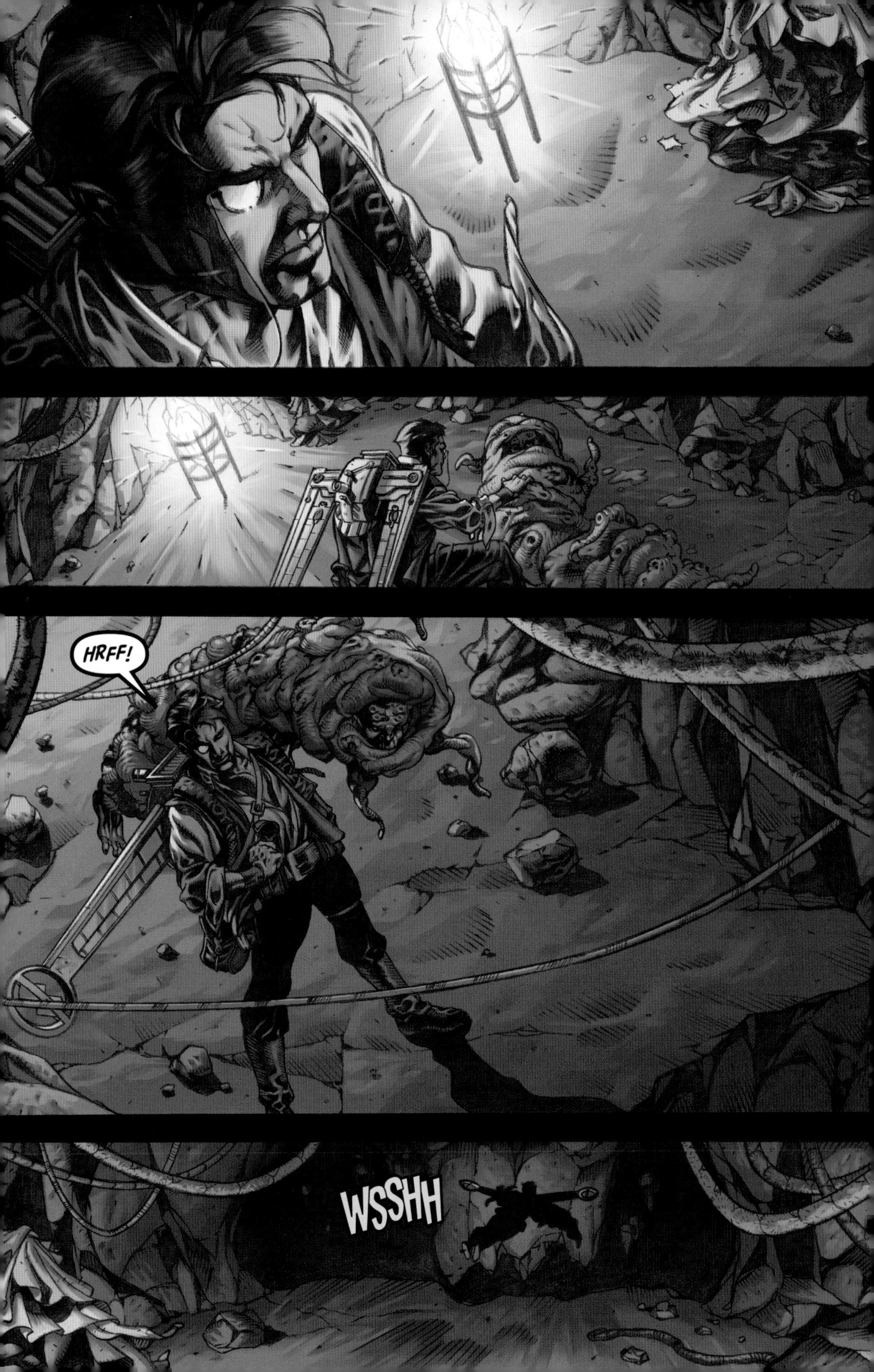
HRFF!
WSSHH

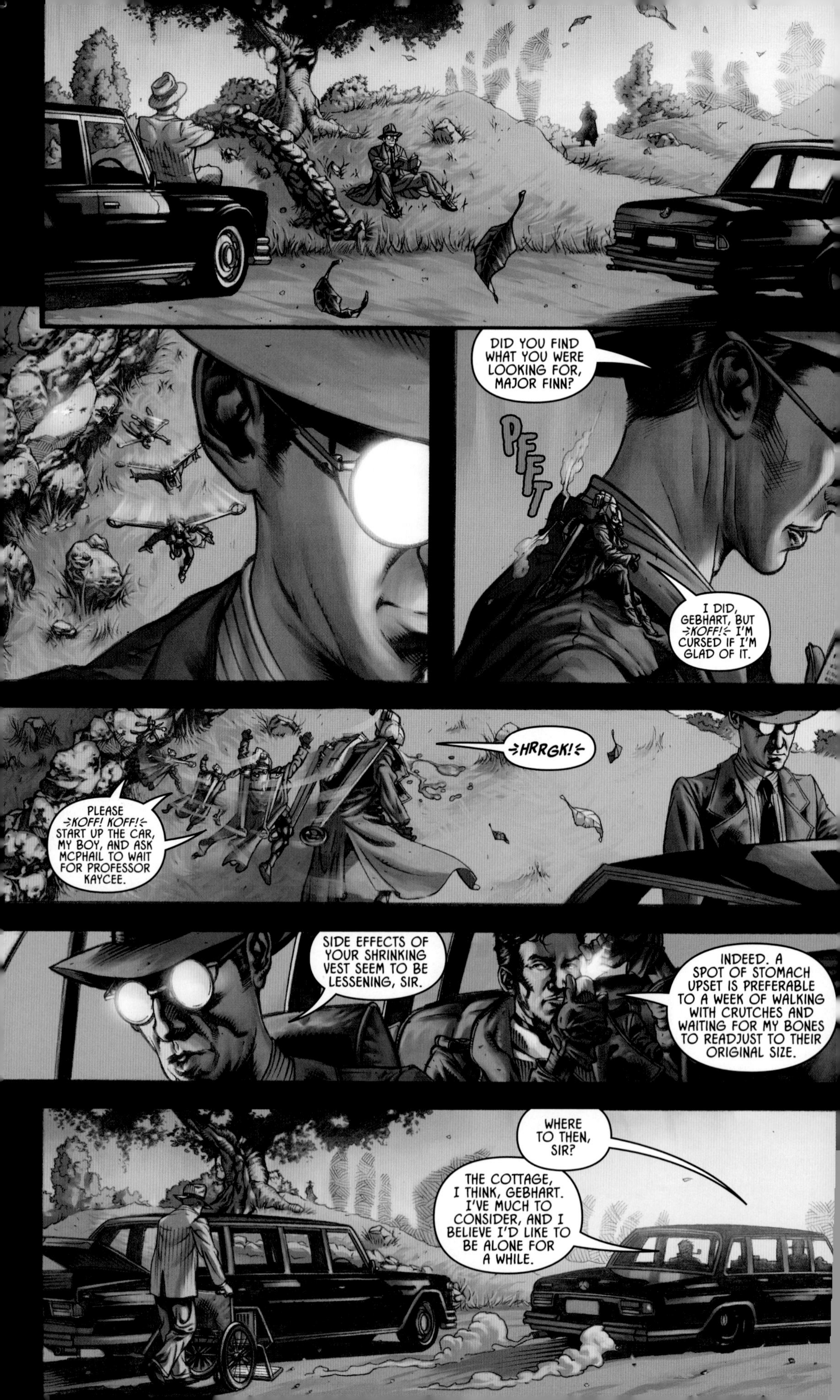
DID YOU FIND WHAT YOU WERE LOOKING FOR, MAJOR FINN?
PFFT
I DID, GEBHART, BUT *KOFF!* I'M CURSED IF I'M GLAD OF IT.
HRRGK!
PLEASE *KOFF! KOFF!* START UP THE CAR, MY BOY, AND ASK MCPHAIL TO WAIT FOR PROFESSOR KAYCEE.
SIDE EFFECTS OF YOUR SHRINKING VEST SEEM TO BE LESSENING, SIR.
INDEED. A SPOT OF STOMACH UPSET IS PREFERABLE TO A WEEK OF WALKING WITH CRUTCHES AND WAITING FOR MY BONES TO READJUST TO THEIR ORIGINAL SIZE.
WHERE TO THEN, SIR?
THE COTTAGE, I THINK, GEBHART. I'VE MUCH TO CONSIDER, AND I BELIEVE I'D LIKE TO BE ALONE FOR A WHILE.

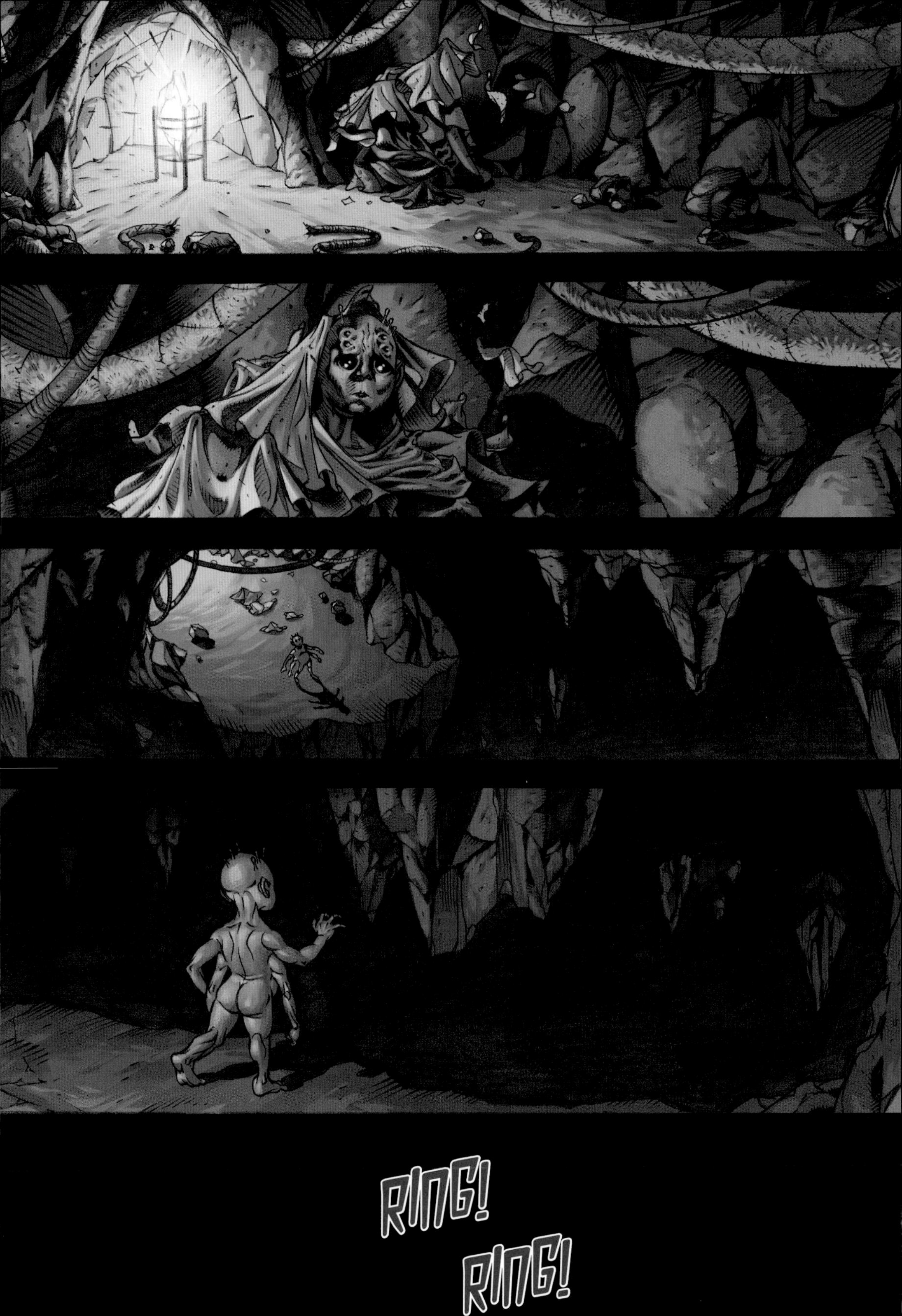
RING!
RING!

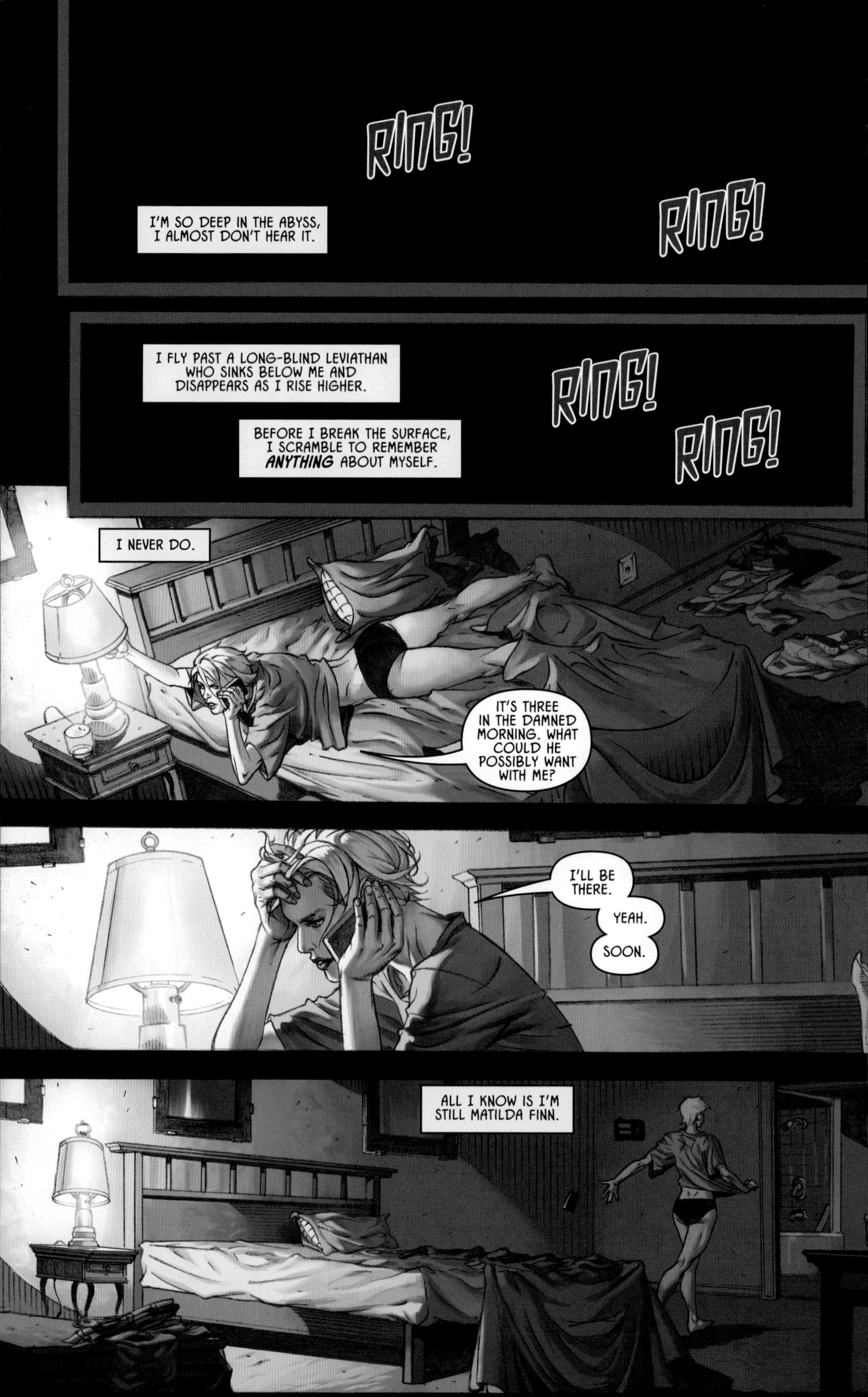
RING!
I'M SO DEEP IN THE ABYSS, I ALMOST DON'T HEAR IT.
RING!
I FLY PAST A LONG-BLIND LEVIATHAN WHO SINKS BELOW ME AND DISAPPEARS AS I RISE HIGHER.
RING!
BEFORE I BREAK THE SURFACE, I SCRAMBLE TO REMEMBER *ANYTHING* ABOUT MYSELF.
RING!
I NEVER DO.
IT'S THREE IN THE DAMNED MORNING. WHAT COULD HE POSSIBLY WANT WITH ME?
I'LL BE THERE.
YEAH.
SOON.
ALL I KNOW IS I'M STILL MATILDA FINN.

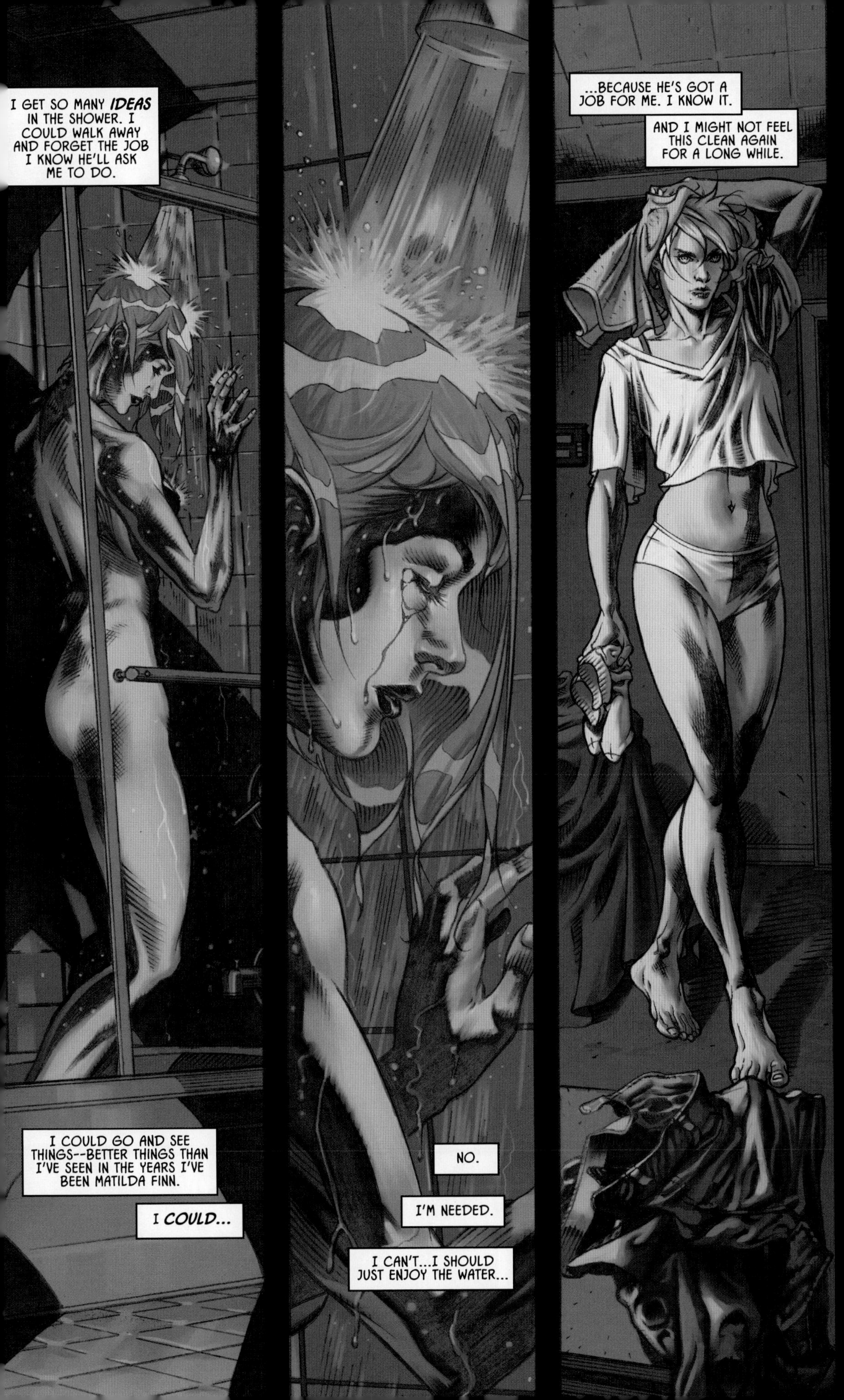
I GET SO MANY IDEAS IN THE SHOWER. I COULD WALK AWAY AND FORGET THE JOB I KNOW HE'LL ASK ME TO DO.
I COULD GO AND SEE THINGS--BETTER THINGS THAN I'VE SEEN IN THE YEARS I'VE BEEN MATILDA FINN.
I COULD...
NO.
I'M NEEDED.
I CAN'T...I SHOULD JUST ENJOY THE WATER...
...BECAUSE HE'S GOT A JOB FOR ME. I KNOW IT.
AND I MIGHT NOT FEEL THIS CLEAN AGAIN FOR A LONG WHILE.

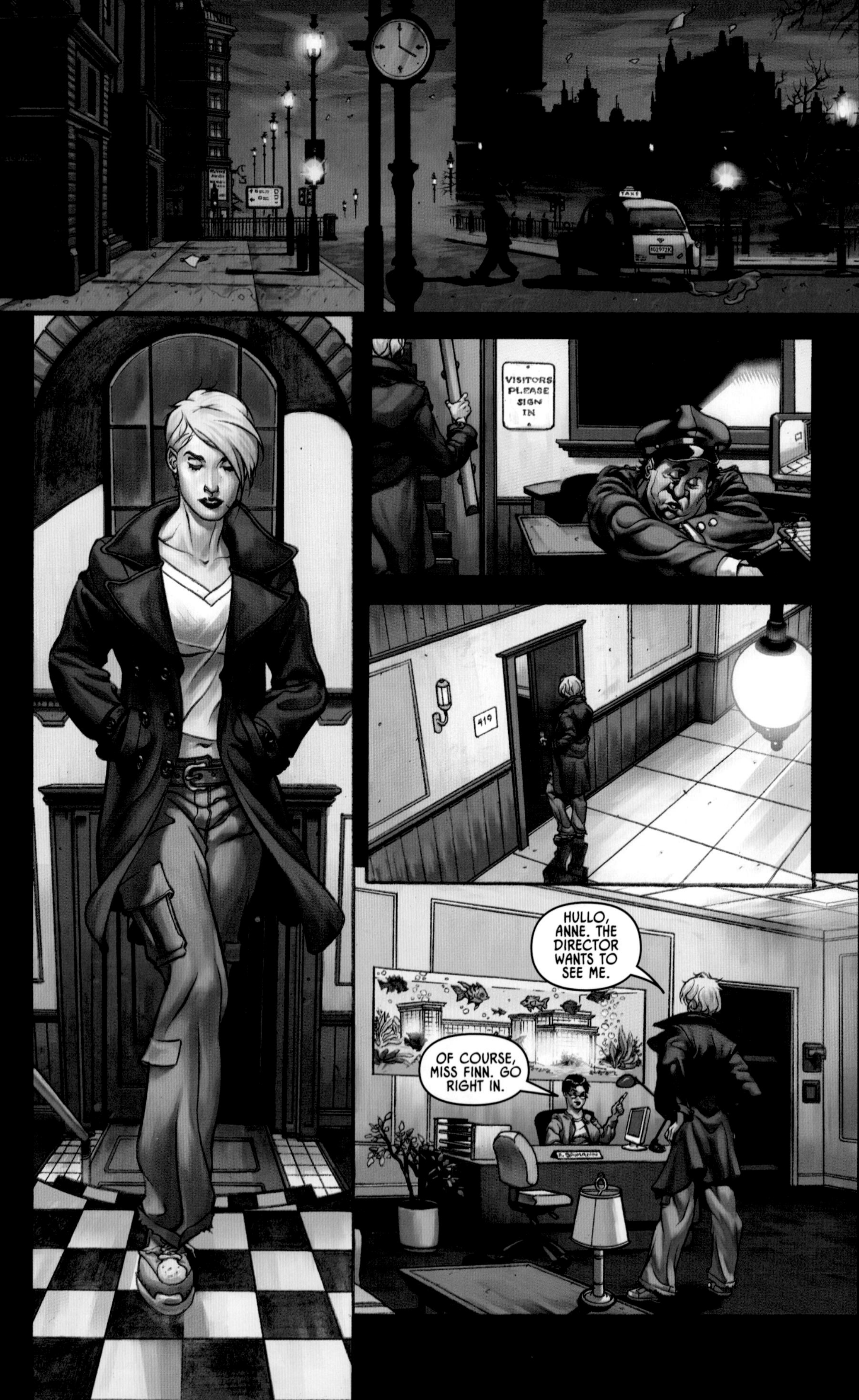

VISITORS PLEASE SIGN IN
419
HULLO, ANNE. THE DIRECTOR WANTS TO SEE ME.
OF COURSE, MISS FINN. GO RIGHT IN.

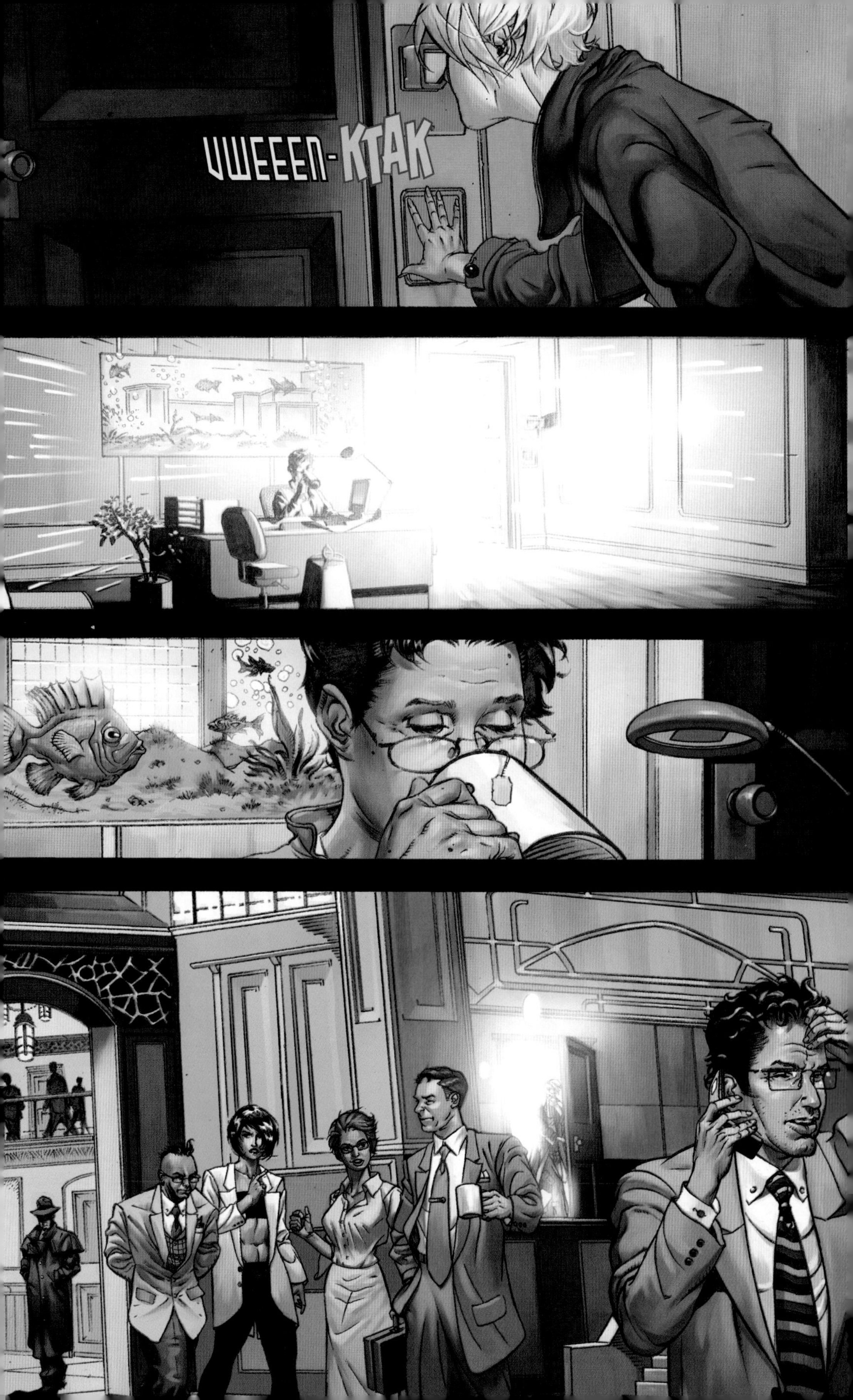
VWEEEN-KTAK

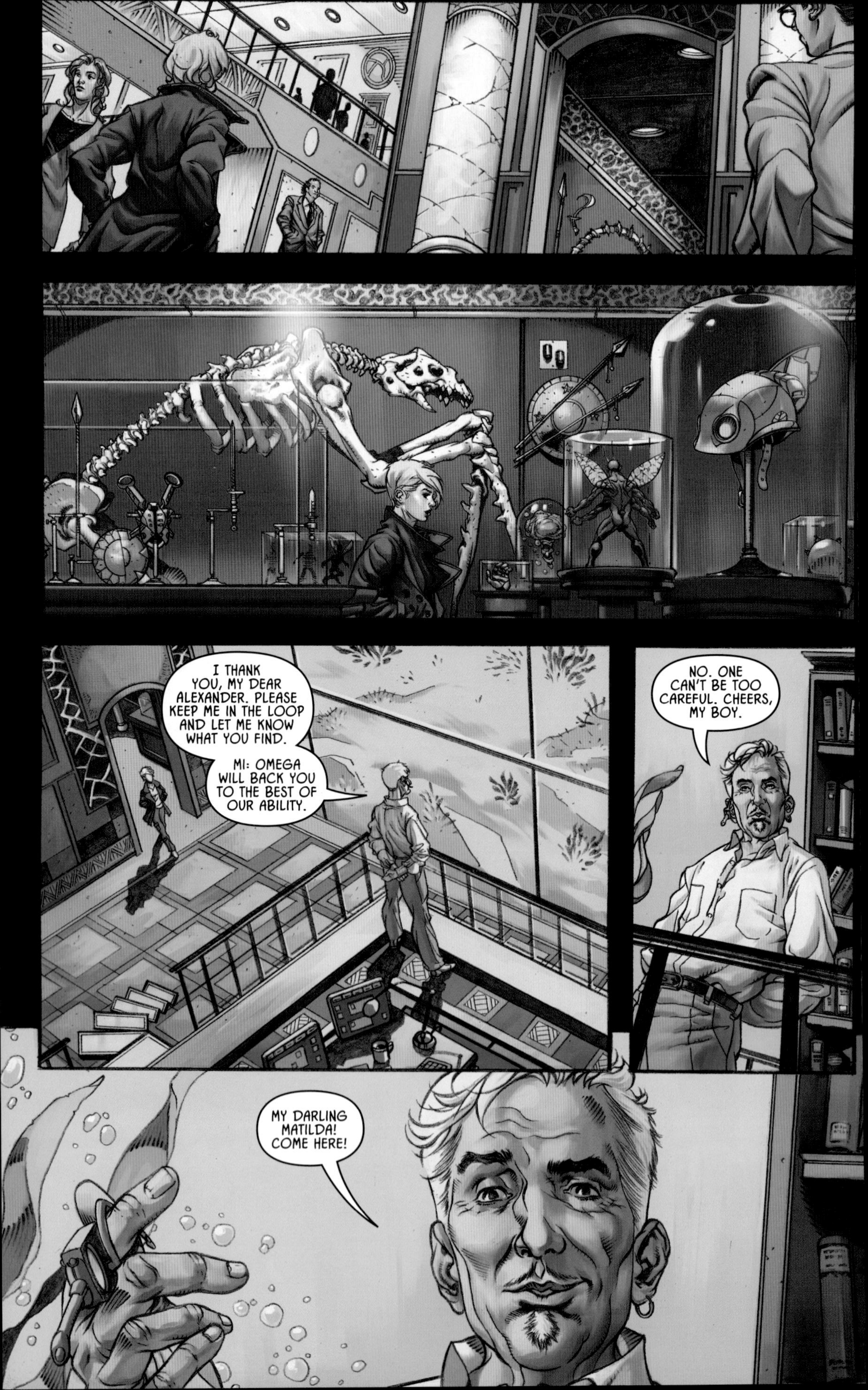
I THANK YOU, MY DEAR ALEXANDER. PLEASE KEEP ME IN THE LOOP AND LET ME KNOW WHAT YOU FIND.
MI: OMEGA WILL BACK YOU TO THE BEST OF OUR ABILITY.
NO. ONE CAN'T BE TOO CAREFUL. CHEERS, MY BOY.
MY DARLING MATILDA! COME HERE!

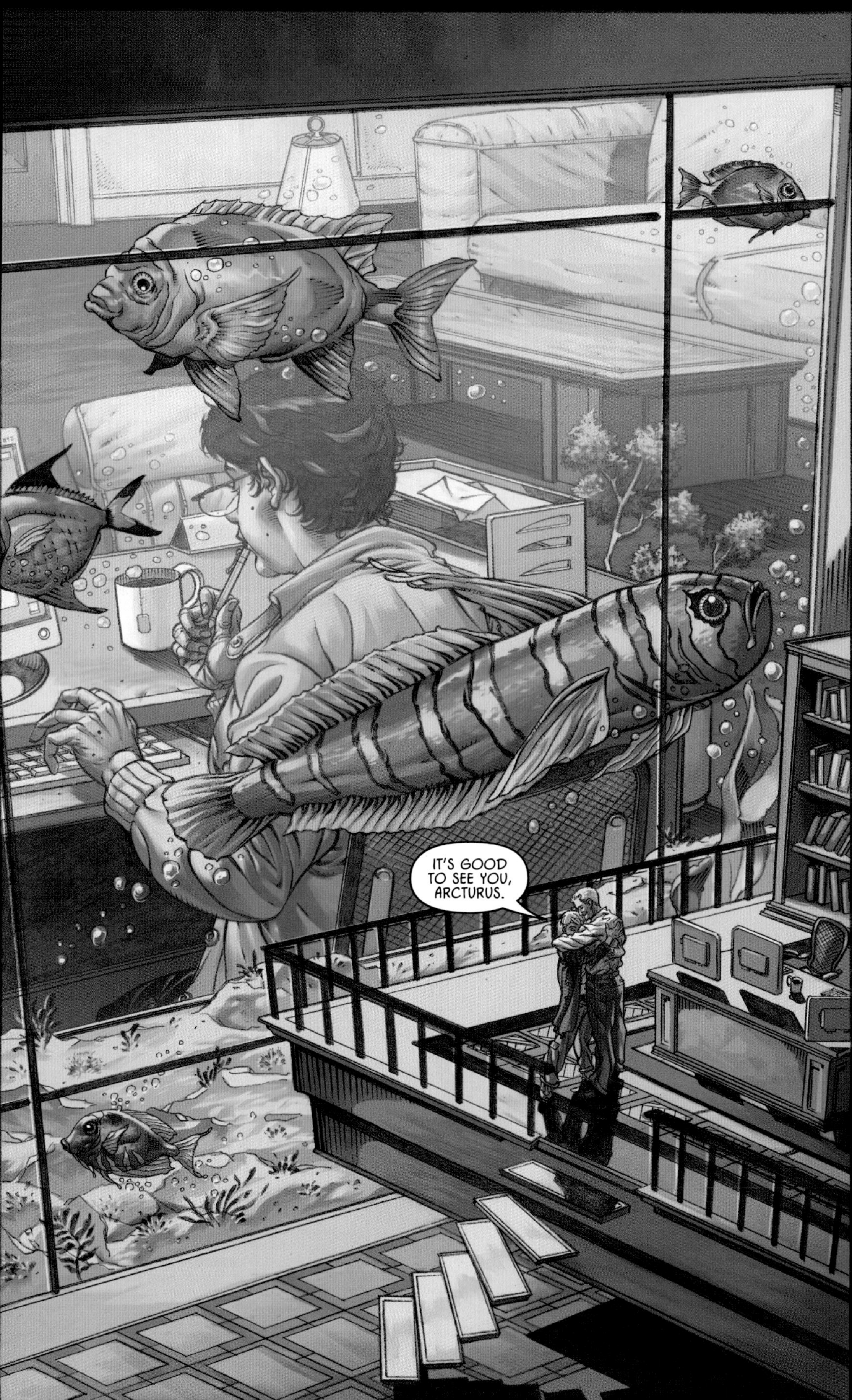
IT'S GOOD TO SEE YOU, ARCTURUS.

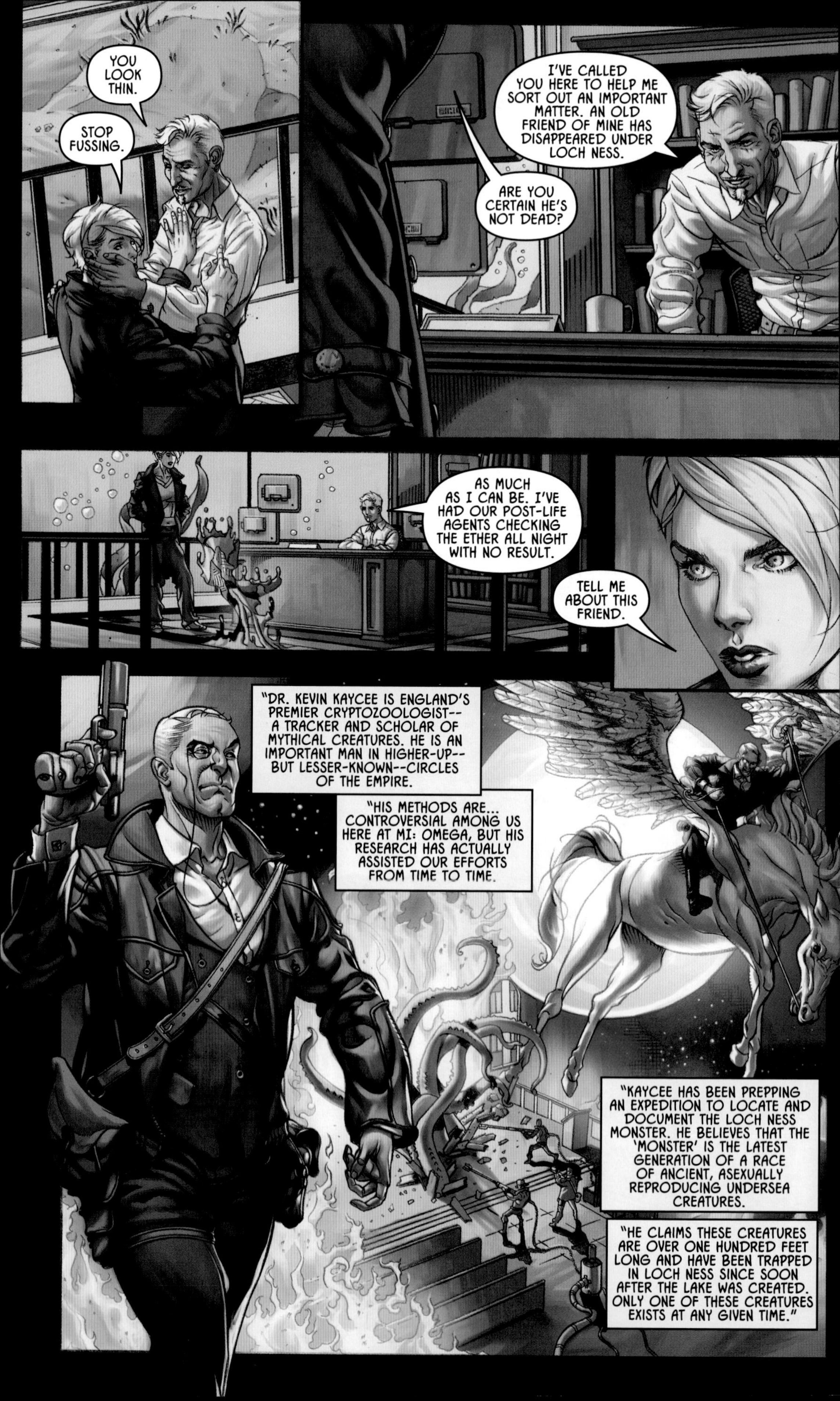
YOU LOOK THIN.
STOP FUSSING.
I'VE CALLED YOU HERE TO HELP ME SORT OUT AN IMPORTANT MATTER. AN OLD FRIEND OF MINE HAS DISAPPEARED UNDER LOCH NESS.
ARE YOU CERTAIN HE'S NOT DEAD?
AS MUCH AS I CAN BE. I'VE HAD OUR POST-LIFE AGENTS CHECKING THE ETHER ALL NIGHT WITH NO RESULT.
TELL ME ABOUT THIS FRIEND.
"DR. KEVIN KAYCEE IS ENGLAND'S PREMIER CRYPTOZOOLOGIST-- A TRACKER AND SCHOLAR OF MYTHICAL CREATURES. HE IS AN IMPORTANT MAN IN HIGHER-UP-- BUT LESSER-KNOWN--CIRCLES OF THE EMPIRE.
"HIS METHODS ARE... CONTROVERSIAL AMONG US HERE AT MI: OMEGA, BUT HIS RESEARCH HAS ACTUALLY ASSISTED OUR EFFORTS FROM TIME TO TIME.
"KAYCEE HAS BEEN PREPPING AN EXPEDITION TO LOCATE AND DOCUMENT THE LOCH NESS MONSTER. HE BELIEVES THAT THE 'MONSTER' IS THE LATEST GENERATION OF A RACE OF ANCIENT, ASEXUALLY REPRODUCING UNDERSEA CREATURES.
"HE CLAIMS THESE CREATURES ARE OVER ONE HUNDRED FEET LONG AND HAVE BEEN TRAPPED IN LOCH NESS SINCE SOON AFTER THE LAKE WAS CREATED. ONLY ONE OF THESE CREATURES EXISTS AT ANY GIVEN TIME."

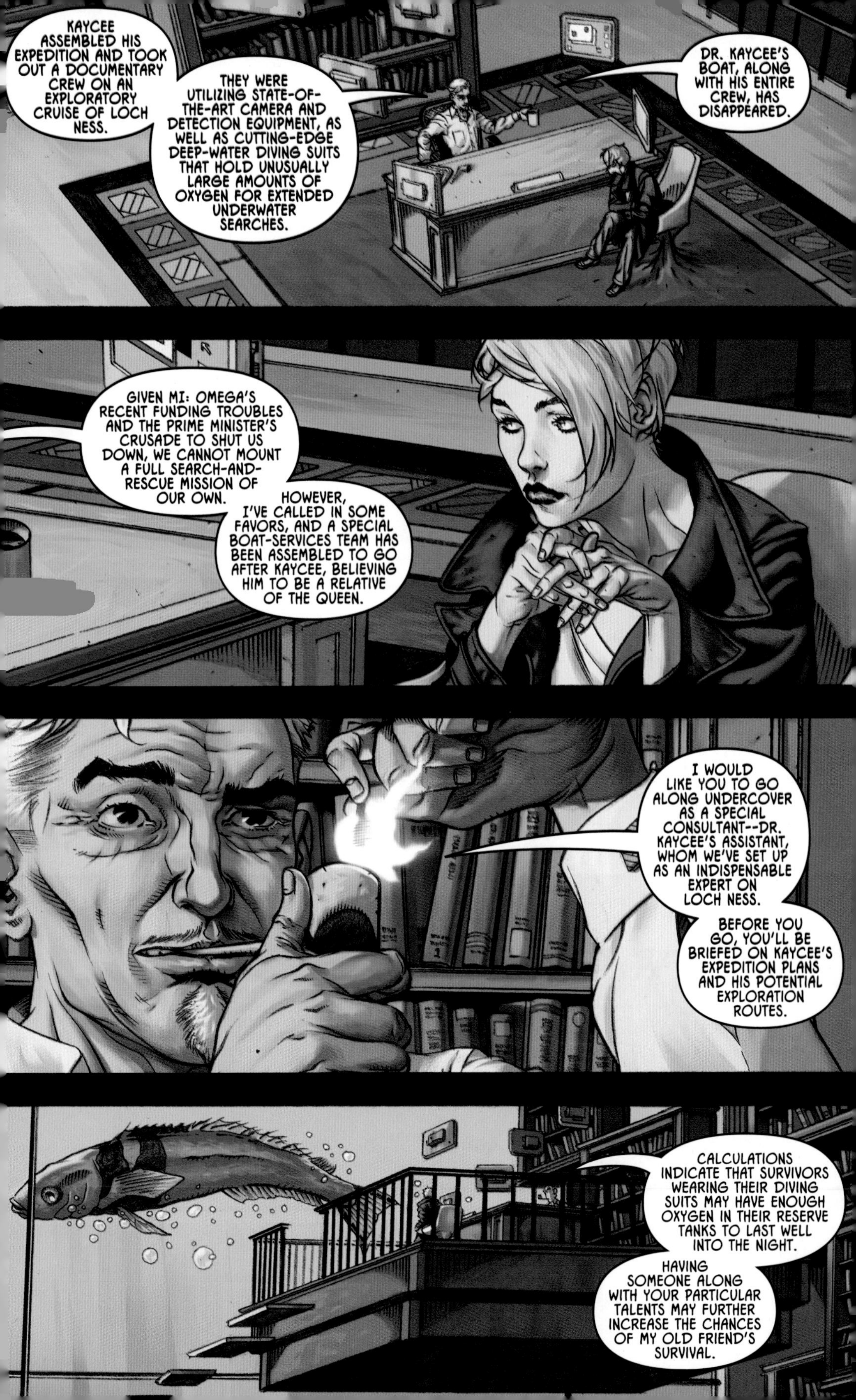
KAYCEE ASSEMBLED HIS EXPEDITION AND TOOK OUT A DOCUMENTARY CREW ON AN EXPLORATORY CRUISE OF LOCH NESS.
THEY WERE UTILIZING STATE-OF-THE-ART CAMERA AND DETECTION EQUIPMENT, AS WELL AS CUTTING-EDGE DEEP-WATER DIVING SUITS THAT HOLD UNUSUALLY LARGE AMOUNTS OF OXYGEN FOR EXTENDED UNDERWATER SEARCHES.
DR. KAYCEE'S BOAT, ALONG WITH HIS ENTIRE CREW, HAS DISAPPEARED.
GIVEN MI: OMEGA'S RECENT FUNDING TROUBLES AND THE PRIME MINISTER'S CRUSADE TO SHUT US DOWN, WE CANNOT MOUNT A FULL SEARCH-AND-RESCUE MISSION OF OUR OWN.
HOWEVER, I'VE CALLED IN SOME FAVORS, AND A SPECIAL BOAT-SERVICES TEAM HAS BEEN ASSEMBLED TO GO AFTER KAYCEE, BELIEVING HIM TO BE A RELATIVE OF THE QUEEN.
I WOULD LIKE YOU TO GO ALONG UNDERCOVER AS A SPECIAL CONSULTANT--DR. KAYCEE'S ASSISTANT, WHOM WE'VE SET UP AS AN INDISPENSABLE EXPERT ON LOCH NESS.
BEFORE YOU GO, YOU'LL BE BRIEFED ON KAYCEE'S EXPEDITION PLANS AND HIS POTENTIAL EXPLORATION ROUTES.
CALCULATIONS INDICATE THAT SURVIVORS WEARING THEIR DIVING SUITS MAY HAVE ENOUGH OXYGEN IN THEIR RESERVE TANKS TO LAST WELL INTO THE NIGHT.
HAVING SOMEONE ALONG WITH YOUR PARTICULAR TALENTS MAY FURTHER INCREASE THE CHANCES OF MY OLD FRIEND'S SURVIVAL.

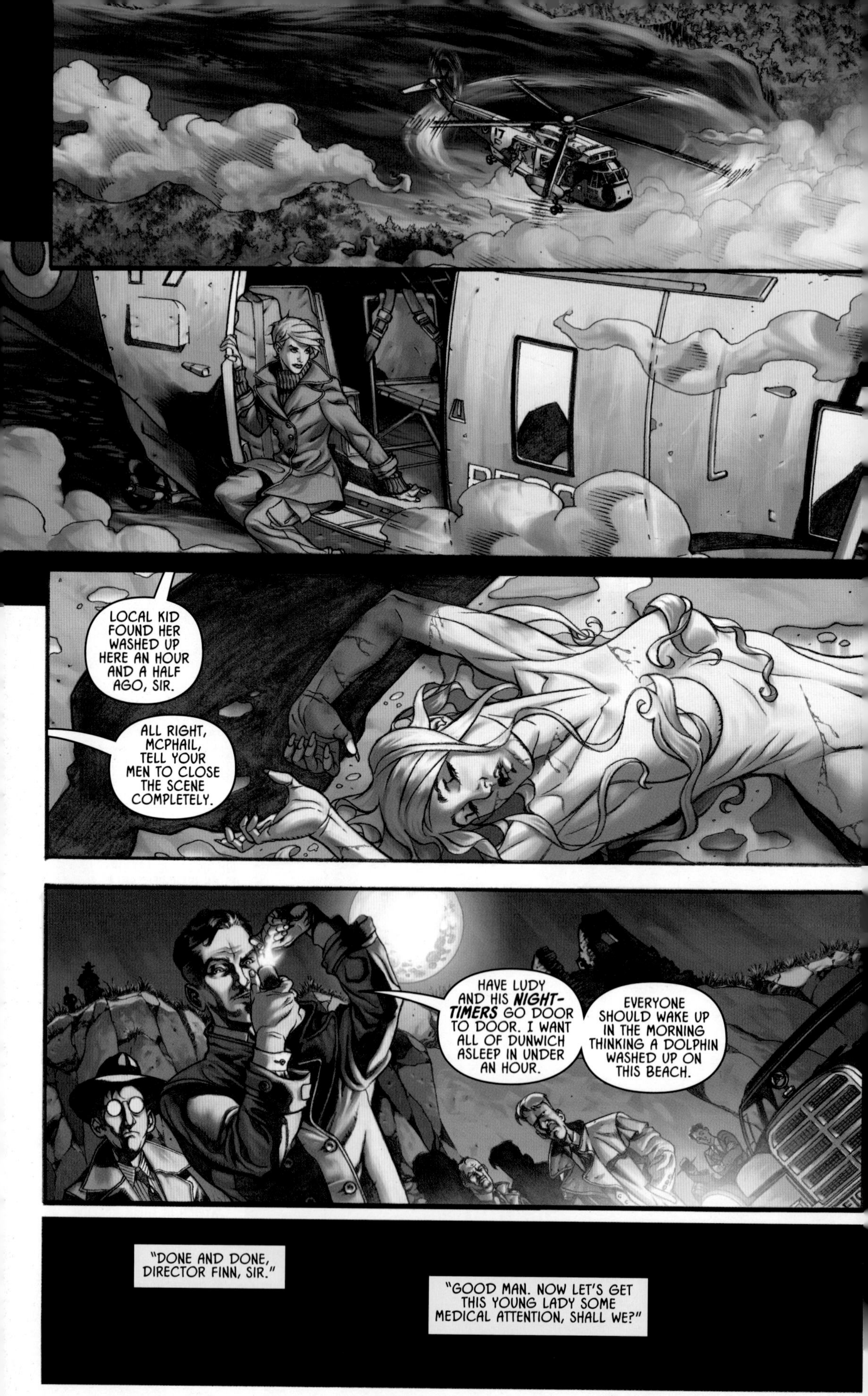
LOCAL KID FOUND HER WASHED UP HERE AN HOUR AND A HALF AGO, SIR.
ALL RIGHT, MCPHAIL, TELL YOUR MEN TO CLOSE THE SCENE COMPLETELY.
HAVE LUDY AND HIS NIGHT-TIMERS GO DOOR TO DOOR. I WANT ALL OF DUNWICH ASLEEP IN UNDER AN HOUR.
EVERYONE SHOULD WAKE UP IN THE MORNING THINKING A DOLPHIN WASHED UP ON THIS BEACH.
"DONE AND DONE, DIRECTOR FINN, SIR."
"GOOD MAN. NOW LET'S GET THIS YOUNG LADY SOME MEDICAL ATTENTION, SHALL WE?"

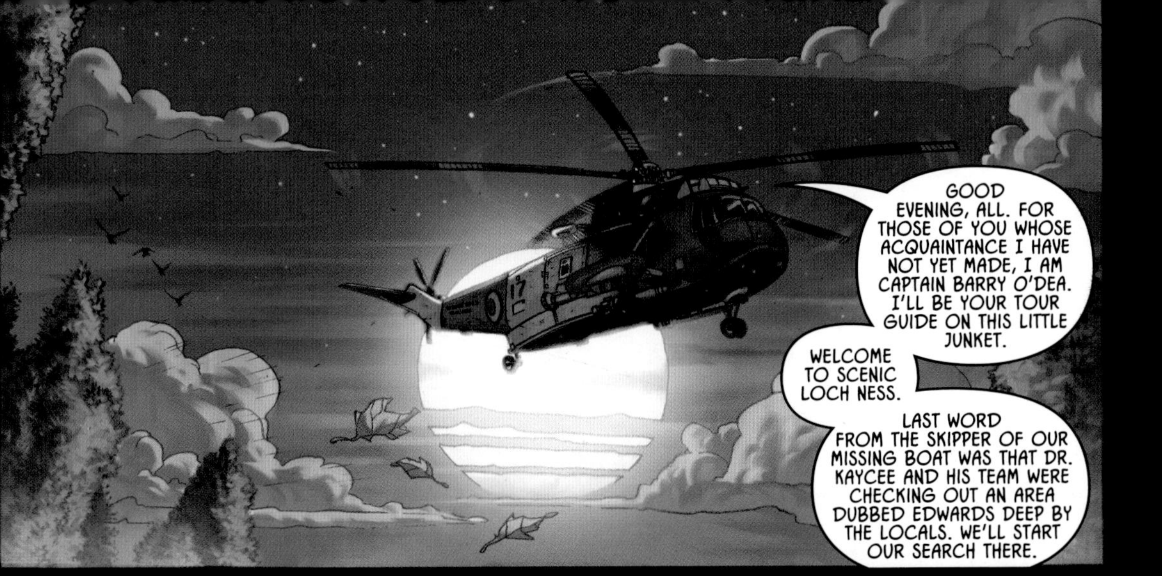
GOOD EVENING, ALL. FOR THOSE OF YOU WHOSE ACQUAINTANCE I HAVE NOT YET MADE, I AM CAPTAIN BARRY O'DEA. I'LL BE YOUR TOUR GUIDE ON THIS LITTLE JUNKET.
WELCOME TO SCENIC LOCH NESS.
LAST WORD FROM THE SKIPPER OF OUR MISSING BOAT WAS THAT DR. KAYCEE AND HIS TEAM WERE CHECKING OUT AN AREA DUBBED EDWARDS DEEP BY THE LOCALS. WE'LL START OUR SEARCH THERE.

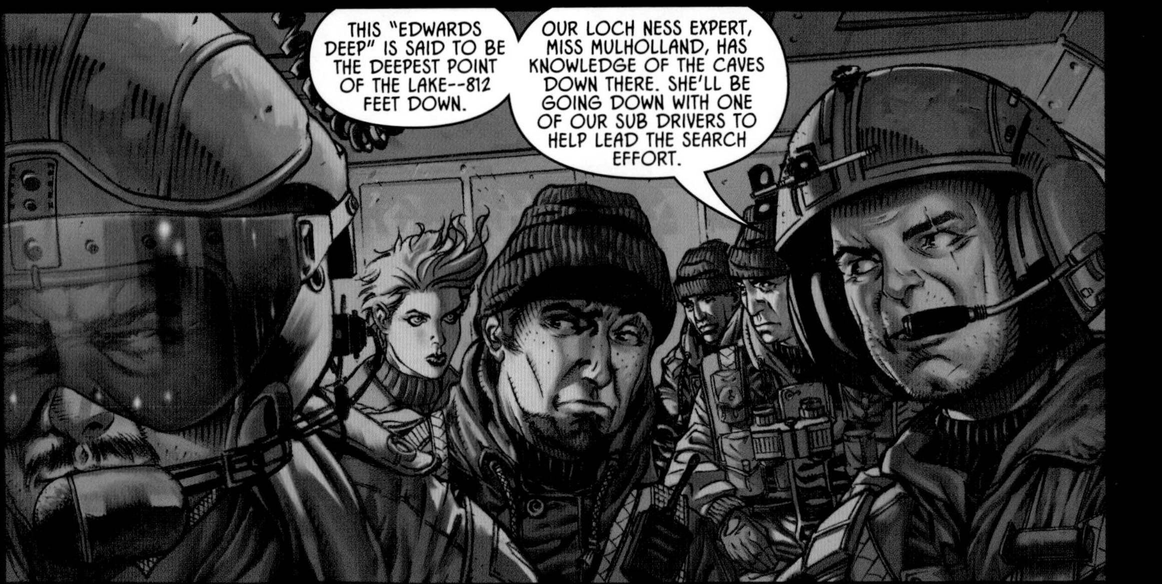
THIS "EDWARDS DEEP" IS SAID TO BE THE DEEPEST POINT OF THE LAKE--812 FEET DOWN.
OUR LOCH NESS EXPERT, MISS MULHOLLAND, HAS KNOWLEDGE OF THE CAVES DOWN THERE. SHE'LL BE GOING DOWN WITH ONE OF OUR SUB DRIVERS TO HELP LEAD THE SEARCH EFFORT.

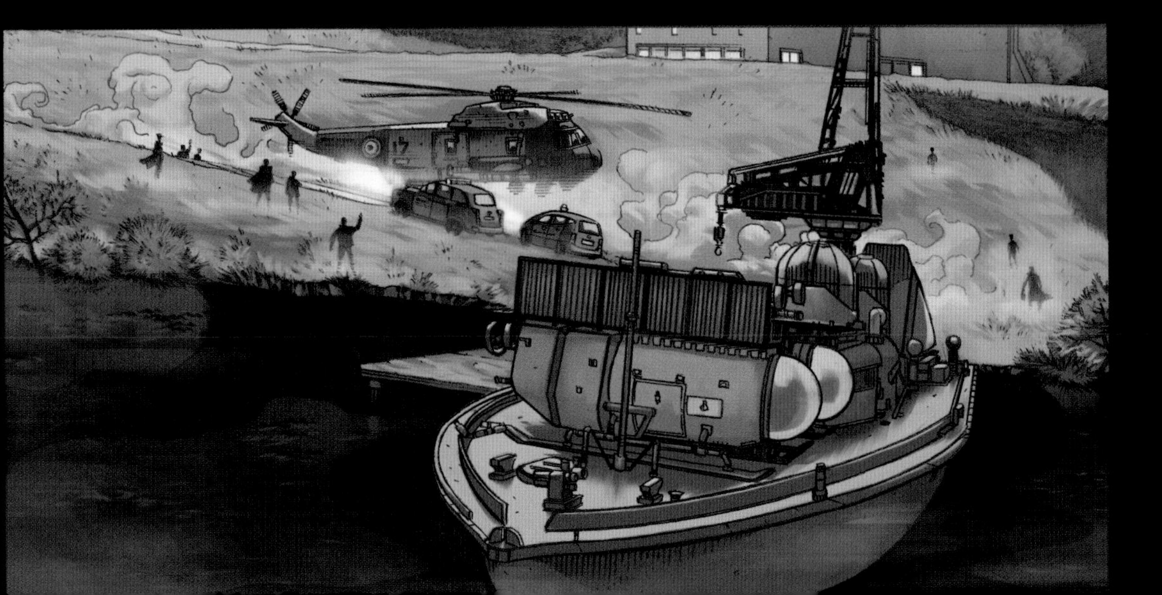

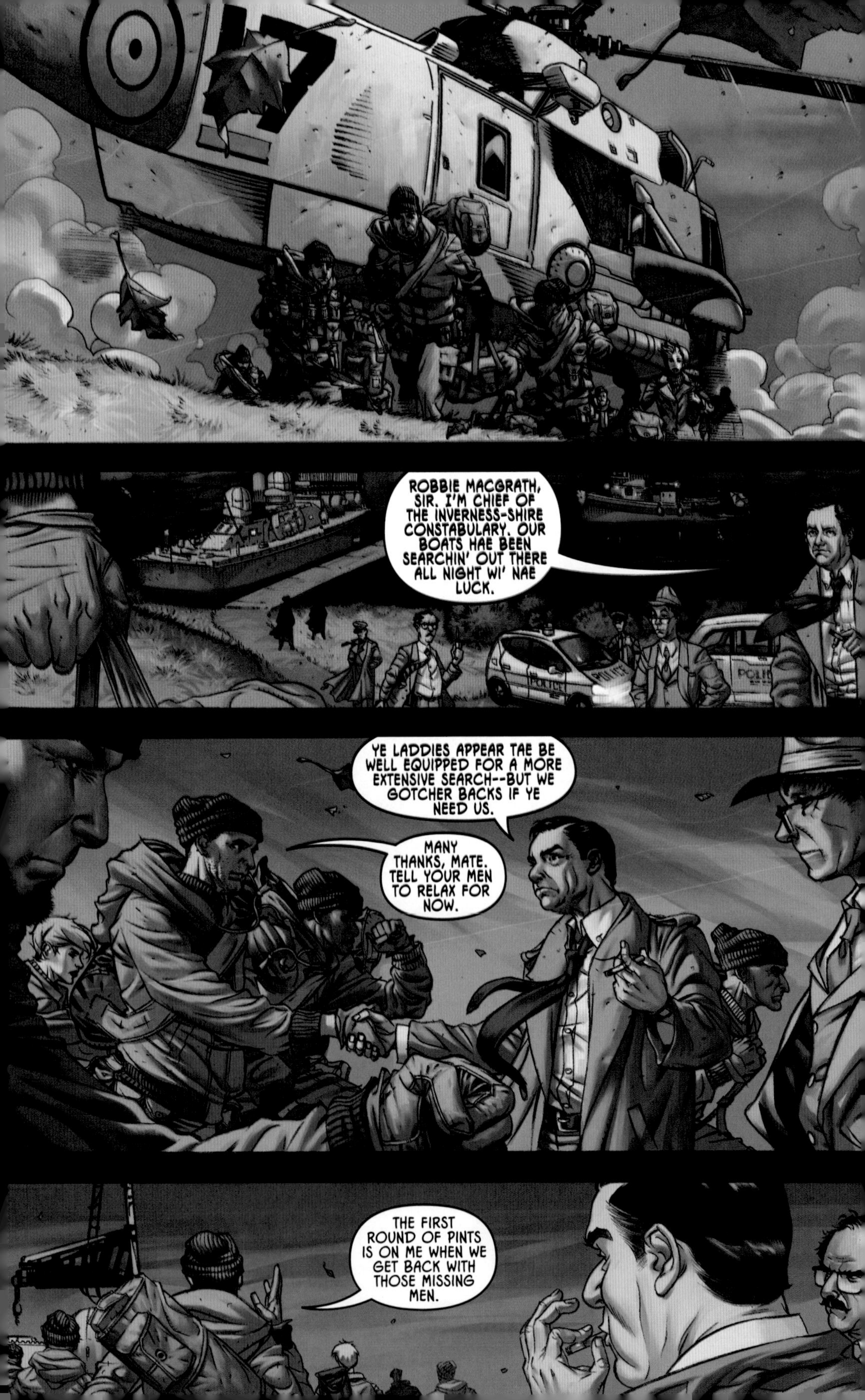
ROBBIE MACGRATH, SIR. I'M CHIEF OF THE INVERNESS-SHIRE CONSTABULARY. OUR BOATS HAE BEEN SEARCHIN' OUT THERE ALL NIGHT WI' NAE LUCK.
YE LADDIES APPEAR TAE BE WELL EQUIPPED FOR A MORE EXTENSIVE SEARCH--BUT WE GOTCHER BACKS IF YE NEED US.
MANY THANKS, MATE. TELL YOUR MEN TO RELAX FOR NOW.
THE FIRST ROUND OF PINTS IS ON ME WHEN WE GET BACK WITH THOSE MISSING MEN.

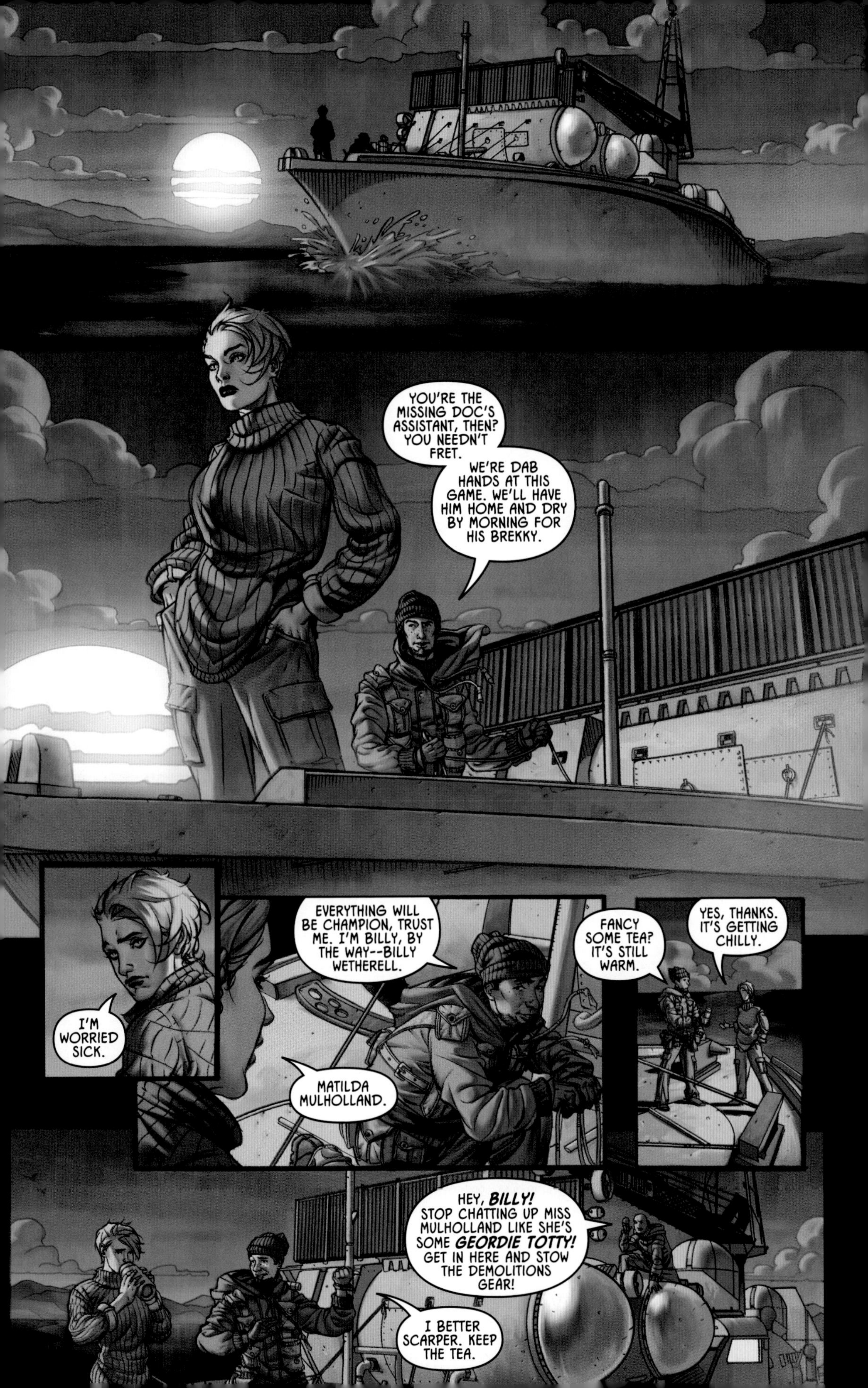
YOU'RE THE MISSING DOC'S ASSISTANT, THEN? YOU NEEDN'T FRET.
WE'RE DAB HANDS AT THIS GAME. WE'LL HAVE HIM HOME AND DRY BY MORNING FOR HIS BREKKY.
I'M WORRIED SICK.
EVERYTHING WILL BE CHAMPION, TRUST ME. I'M BILLY, BY THE WAY--BILLY WETHERELL.
MATILDA MULHOLLAND.
FANCY SOME TEA? IT'S STILL WARM.
YES, THANKS. IT'S GETTING CHILLY.
HEY, BILLY! STOP CHATTING UP MISS MULHOLLAND LIKE SHE'S SOME GEORDIE TOTTY! GET IN HERE AND STOW THE DEMOLITIONS GEAR!
I BETTER SCARPER. KEEP THE TEA.

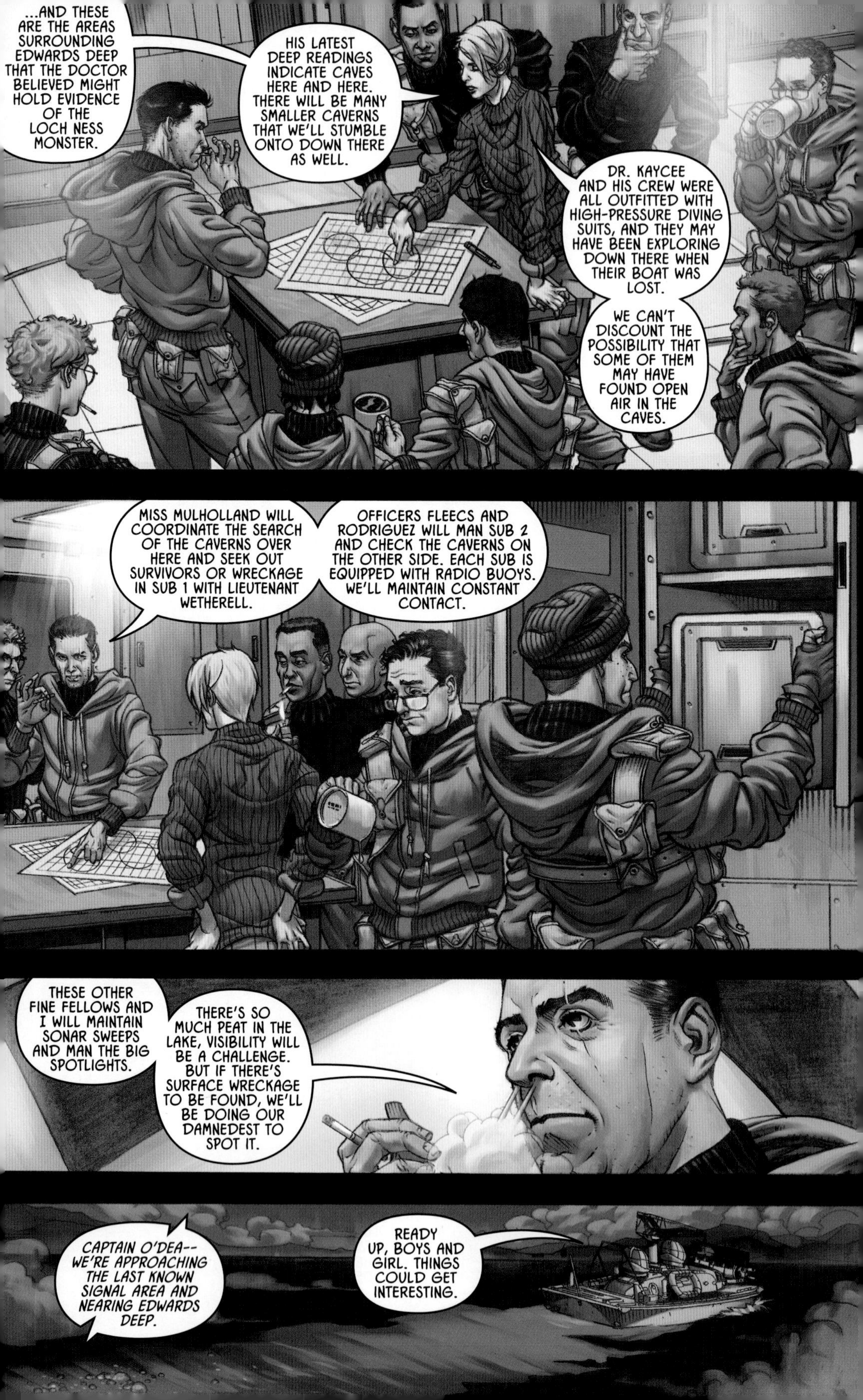
...AND THESE ARE THE AREAS SURROUNDING EDWARDS DEEP THAT THE DOCTOR BELIEVED MIGHT HOLD EVIDENCE OF THE LOCH NESS MONSTER.
HIS LATEST DEEP READINGS INDICATE CAVES HERE AND HERE. THERE WILL BE MANY SMALLER CAVERNS THAT WE'LL STUMBLE ONTO DOWN THERE AS WELL.
DR. KAYCEE AND HIS CREW WERE ALL OUTFITTED WITH HIGH-PRESSURE DIVING SUITS, AND THEY MAY HAVE BEEN EXPLORING DOWN THERE WHEN THEIR BOAT WAS LOST.
WE CAN'T DISCOUNT THE POSSIBILITY THAT SOME OF THEM MAY HAVE FOUND OPEN AIR IN THE CAVES.
MISS MULHOLLAND WILL COORDINATE THE SEARCH OF THE CAVERNS OVER HERE AND SEEK OUT SURVIVORS OR WRECKAGE IN SUB 1 WITH LIEUTENANT WETHERELL.
OFFICERS FLEECS AND RODRIGUEZ WILL MAN SUB 2 AND CHECK THE CAVERNS ON THE OTHER SIDE. EACH SUB IS EQUIPPED WITH RADIO BUOYS. WE'LL MAINTAIN CONSTANT CONTACT.
THESE OTHER FINE FELLOWS AND I WILL MAINTAIN SONAR SWEEPS AND MAN THE BIG SPOTLIGHTS.
THERE'S SO MUCH PEAT IN THE LAKE, VISIBILITY WILL BE A CHALLENGE. BUT IF THERE'S SURFACE WRECKAGE TO BE FOUND, WE'LL BE DOING OUR DAMNEDEST TO SPOT IT.
CAPTAIN O'DEA-- WE'RE APPROACHING THE LAST KNOWN SIGNAL AREA AND NEARING EDWARDS DEEP.
READY UP, BOYS AND GIRL. THINGS COULD GET INTERESTING.

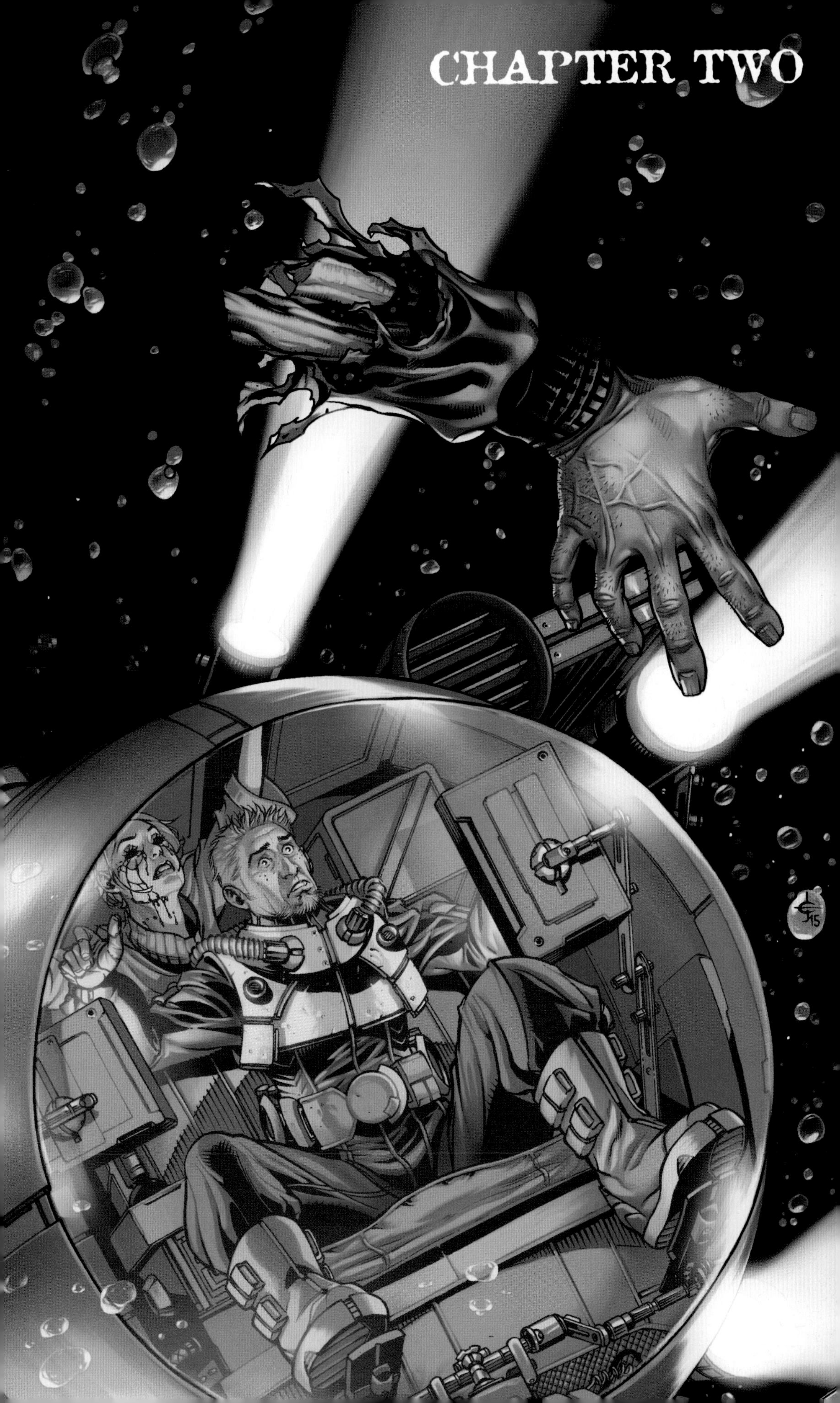
CHAPTER TWO

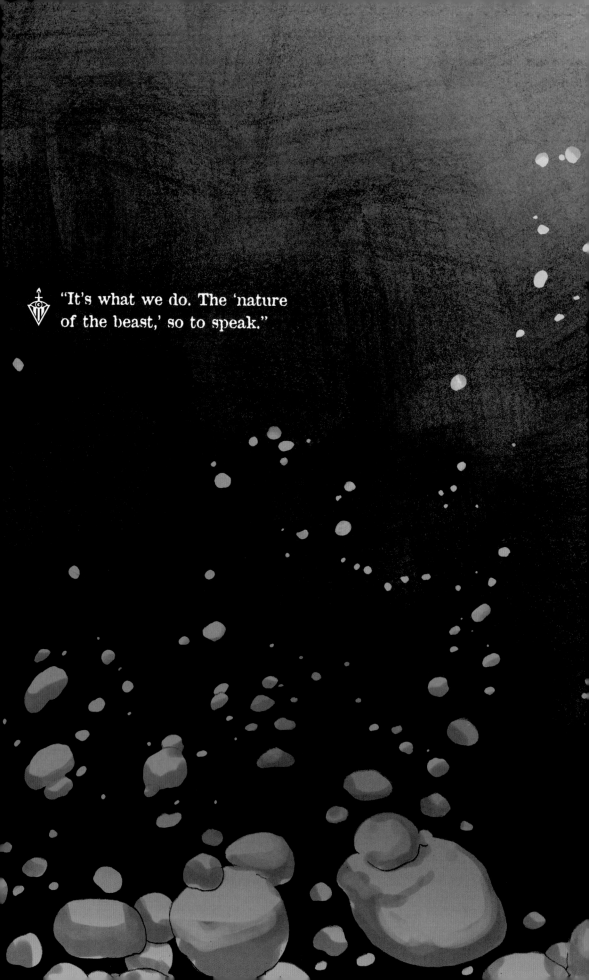

"It's what we do. The 'nature of the beast,' so to speak."

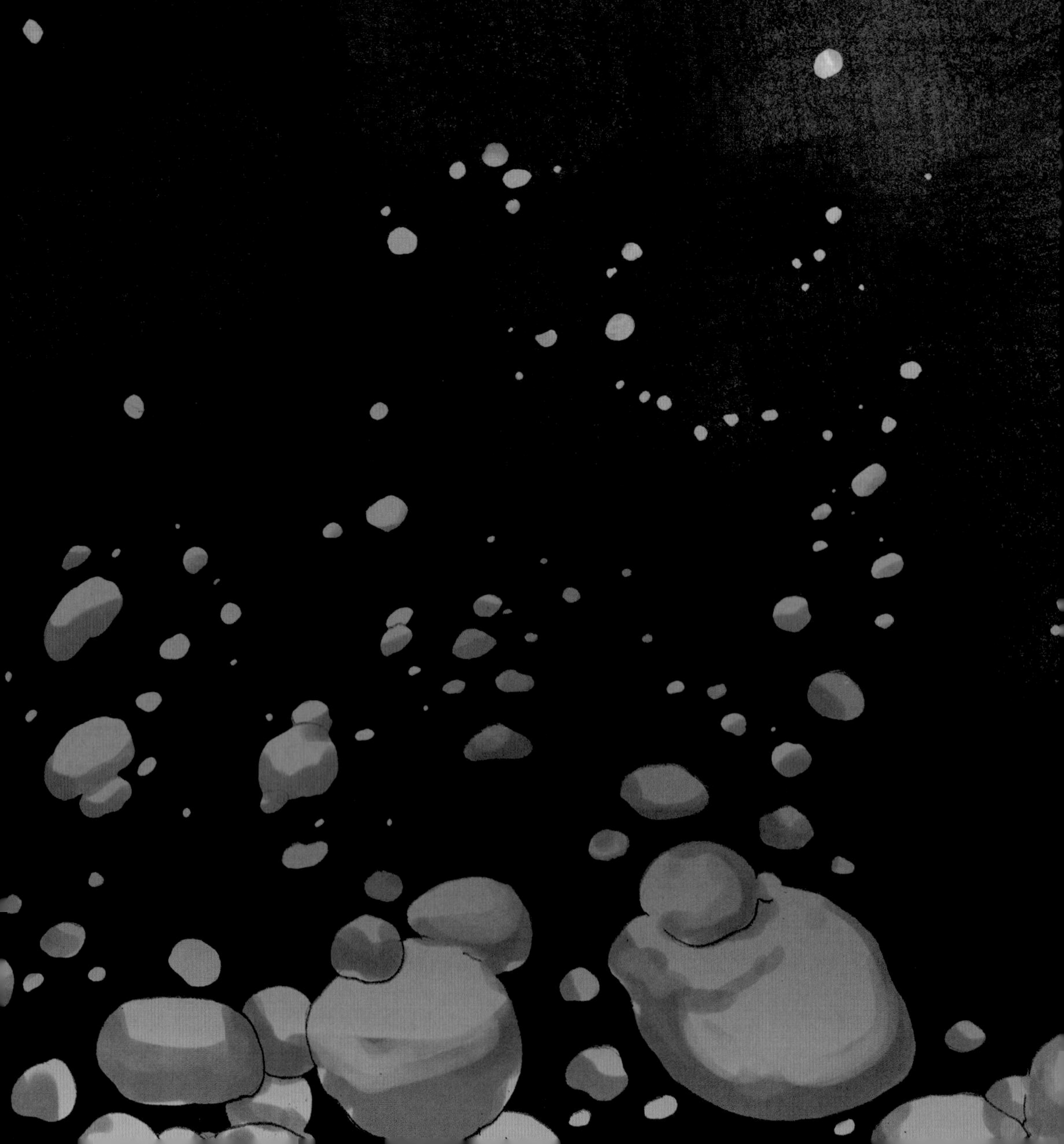

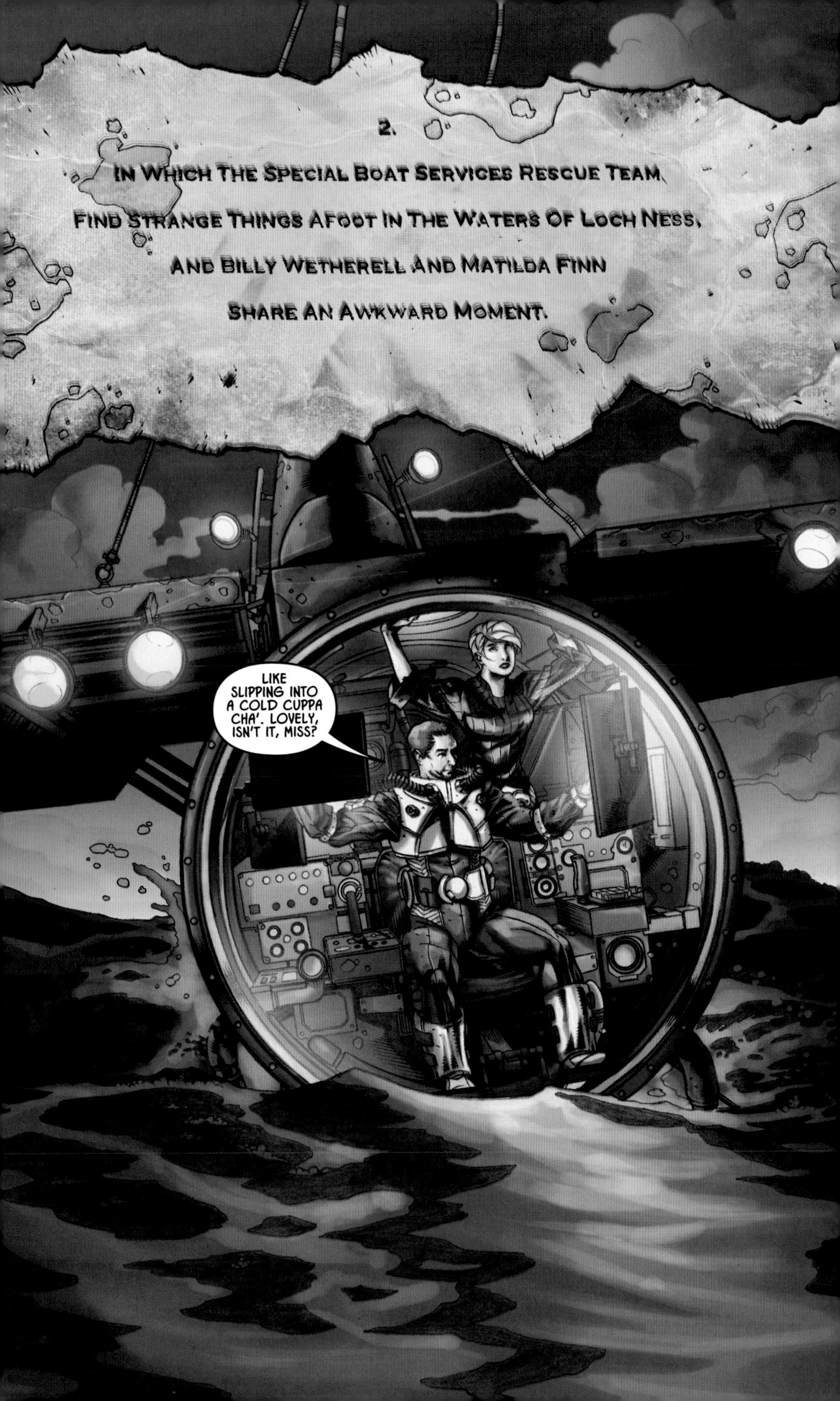
2.
In Which The Special Boat Services Rescue Team
Find Strange Things Afoot In The Waters Of Loch Ness,
And Billy Wetherell And Matilda Finn
Share An Awkward Moment.
LIKE SLIPPING INTO A COLD CUPPA CHA'. LOVELY, ISN'T IT, MISS?

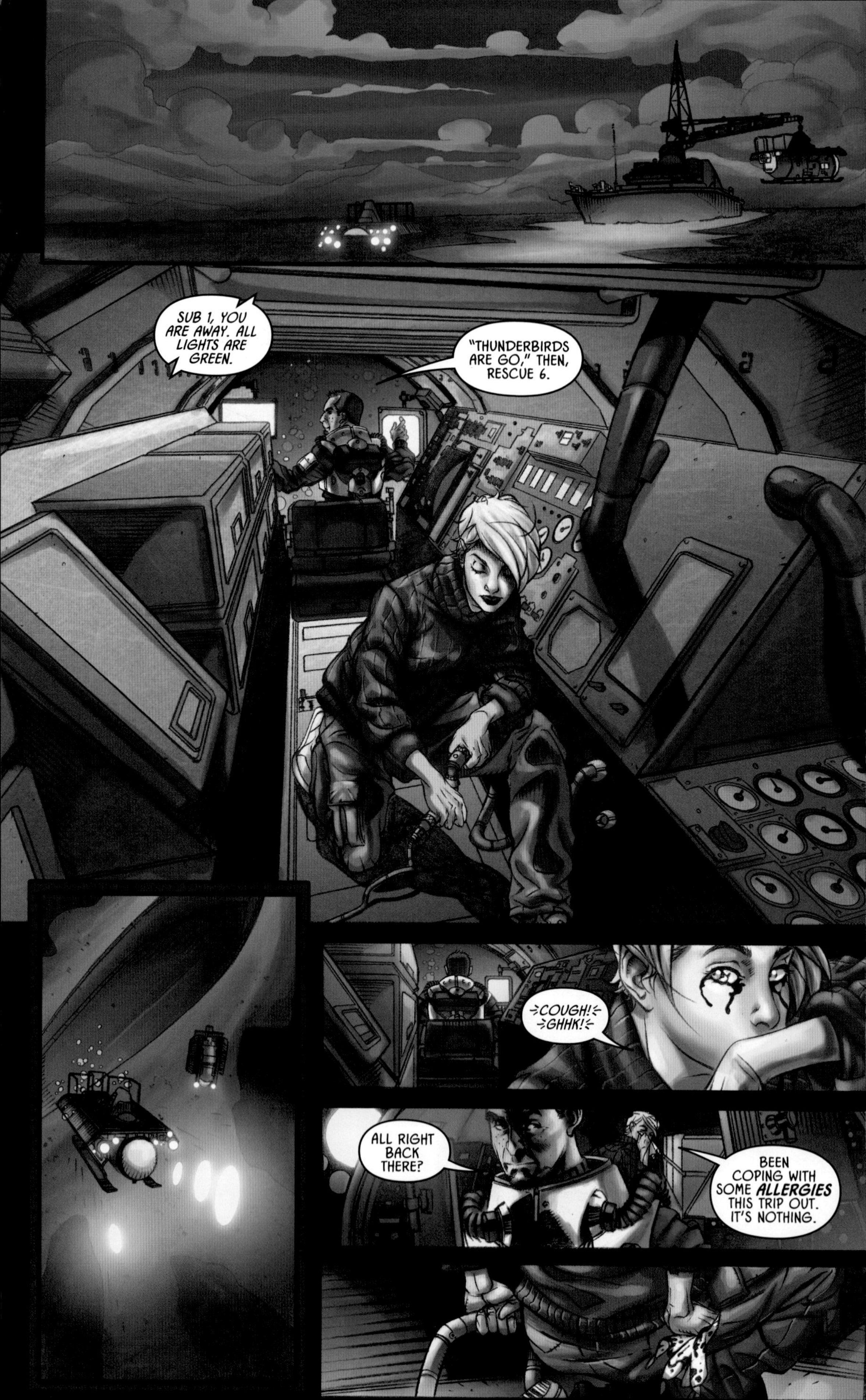
SUB 1, YOU ARE AWAY. ALL LIGHTS ARE GREEN.
"THUNDERBIRDS ARE GO," THEN, RESCUE 6.
COUGH! GHHK!
ALL RIGHT BACK THERE?
BEEN COPING WITH SOME ALLERGIES THIS TRIP OUT. IT'S NOTHING.

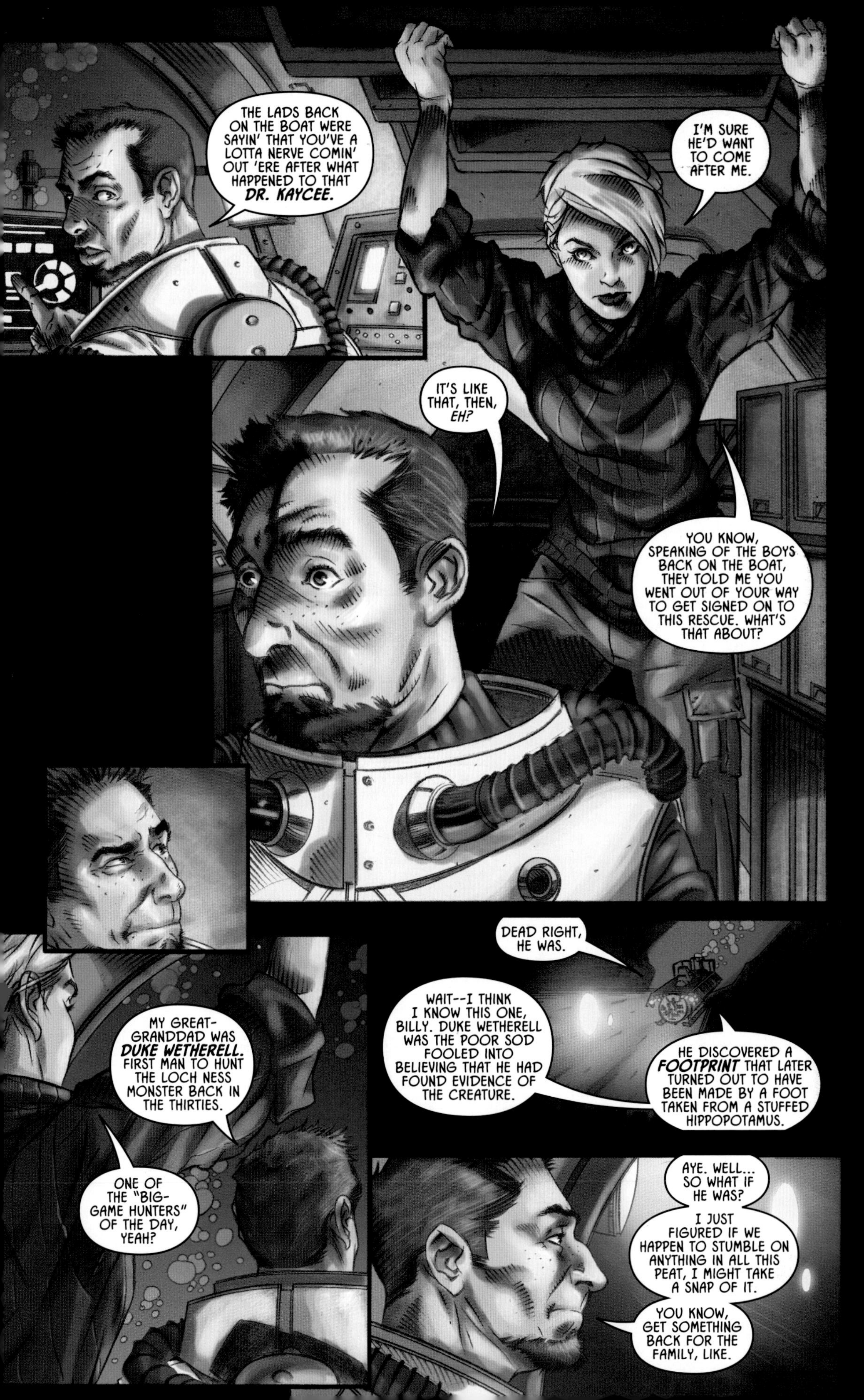
THE LADS BACK ON THE BOAT WERE SAYIN' THAT YOU'VE A LOTTA NERVE COMIN' OUT 'ERE AFTER WHAT HAPPENED TO THAT DR. KAYCEE.
I'M SURE HE'D WANT TO COME AFTER ME.
IT'S LIKE THAT, THEN, EH?
YOU KNOW, SPEAKING OF THE BOYS BACK ON THE BOAT, THEY TOLD ME YOU WENT OUT OF YOUR WAY TO GET SIGNED ON TO THIS RESCUE. WHAT'S THAT ABOUT?
MY GREAT-GRANDDAD WAS DUKE WETHERELL. FIRST MAN TO HUNT THE LOCH NESS MONSTER BACK IN THE THIRTIES.
ONE OF THE "BIG-GAME HUNTERS" OF THE DAY, YEAH?
DEAD RIGHT, HE WAS.
WAIT--I THINK I KNOW THIS ONE, BILLY. DUKE WETHERELL WAS THE POOR SOD FOOLED INTO BELIEVING THAT HE HAD FOUND EVIDENCE OF THE CREATURE.
HE DISCOVERED A FOOTPRINT THAT LATER TURNED OUT TO HAVE BEEN MADE BY A FOOT TAKEN FROM A STUFFED HIPPOPOTAMUS.
AYE. WELL... SO WHAT IF HE WAS?
I JUST FIGURED IF WE HAPPEN TO STUMBLE ON ANYTHING IN ALL THIS PEAT, I MIGHT TAKE A SNAP OF IT.
YOU KNOW, GET SOMETHING BACK FOR THE FAMILY, LIKE.

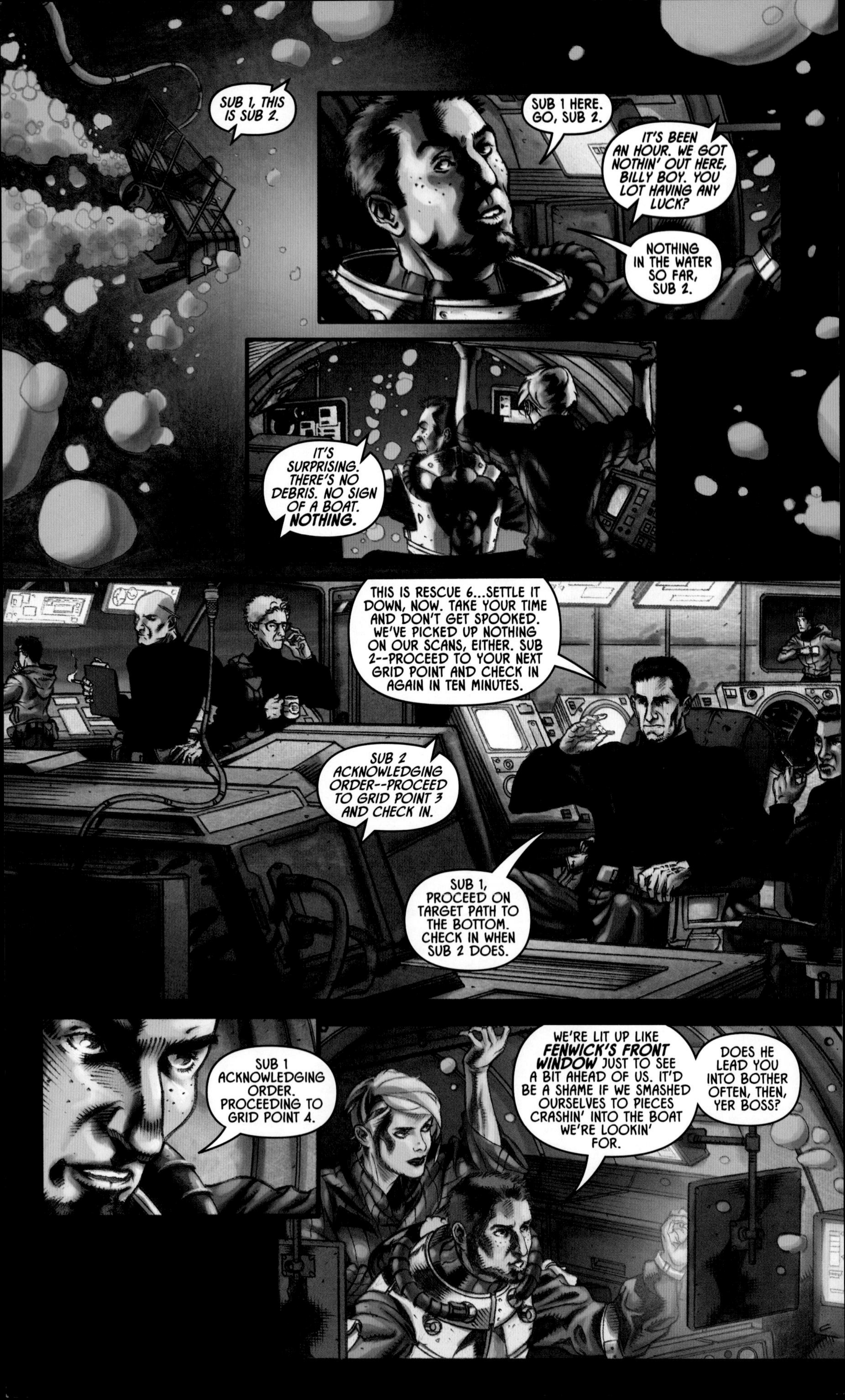
SUB 1, THIS IS SUB 2.
SUB 1 HERE. GO, SUB 2.
IT'S BEEN AN HOUR. WE GOT NOTHIN' OUT HERE, BILLY BOY. YOU LOT HAVING ANY LUCK?
NOTHING IN THE WATER SO FAR, SUB 2.
IT'S SURPRISING. THERE'S NO DEBRIS. NO SIGN OF A BOAT. NOTHING.
THIS IS RESCUE 6...SETTLE IT DOWN, NOW. TAKE YOUR TIME AND DON'T GET SPOOKED. WE'VE PICKED UP NOTHING ON OUR SCANS, EITHER. SUB 2--PROCEED TO YOUR NEXT GRID POINT AND CHECK IN AGAIN IN TEN MINUTES.
SUB 2 ACKNOWLEDGING ORDER--PROCEED TO GRID POINT 3 AND CHECK IN.
SUB 1, PROCEED ON TARGET PATH TO THE BOTTOM. CHECK IN WHEN SUB 2 DOES.
SUB 1 ACKNOWLEDGING ORDER. PROCEEDING TO GRID POINT 4.
WE'RE LIT UP LIKE FENWICK'S FRONT WINDOW JUST TO SEE A BIT AHEAD OF US. IT'D BE A SHAME IF WE SMASHED OURSELVES TO PIECES CRASHIN' INTO THE BOAT WE'RE LOOKIN' FOR.
DOES HE LEAD YOU INTO BOTHER OFTEN, THEN, YER BOSS?

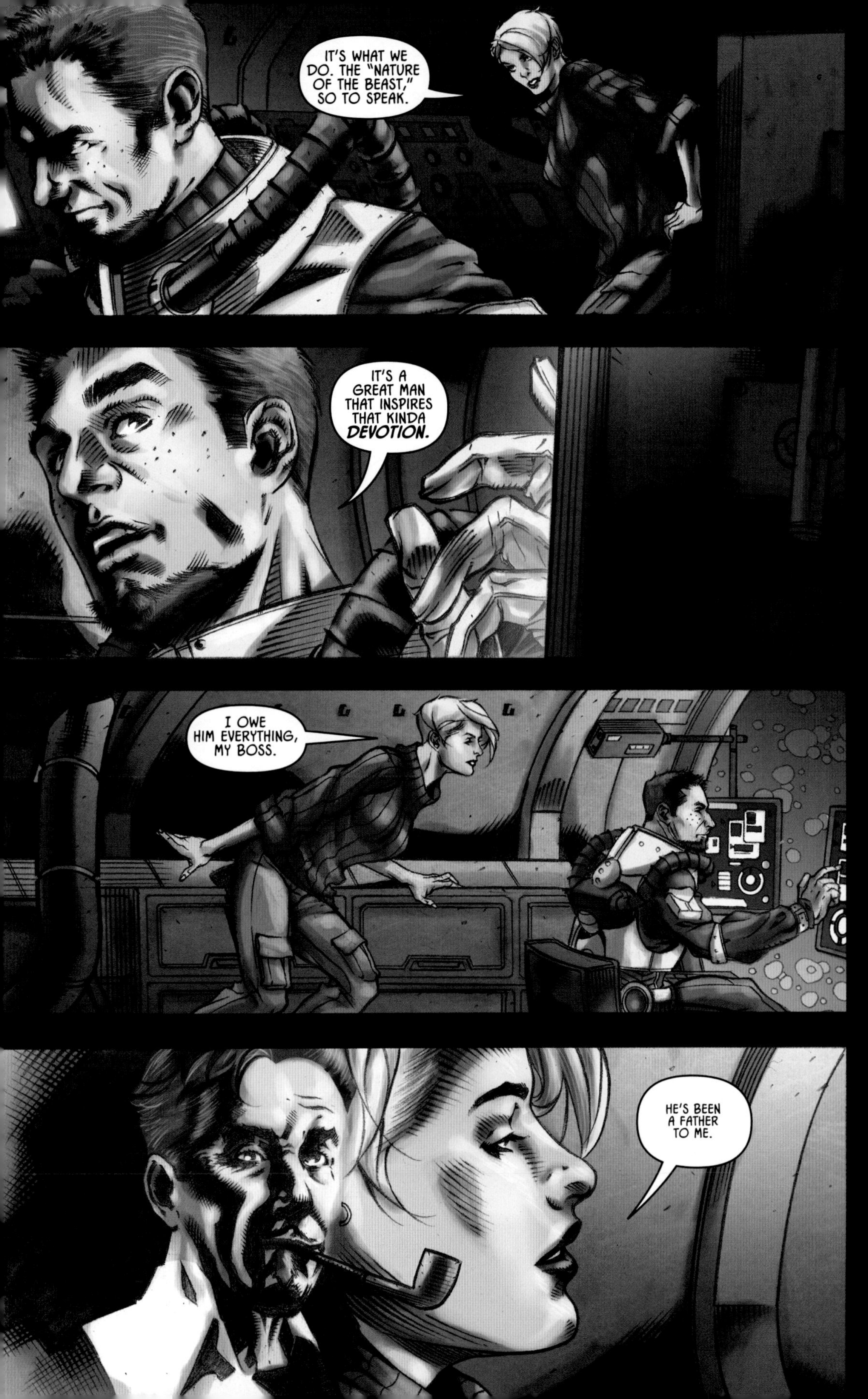
IT'S WHAT WE DO. THE "NATURE OF THE BEAST," SO TO SPEAK.
IT'S A GREAT MAN THAT INSPIRES THAT KINDA *DEVOTION.*
I OWE HIM EVERYTHING, MY BOSS.
HE'S BEEN A FATHER TO ME.

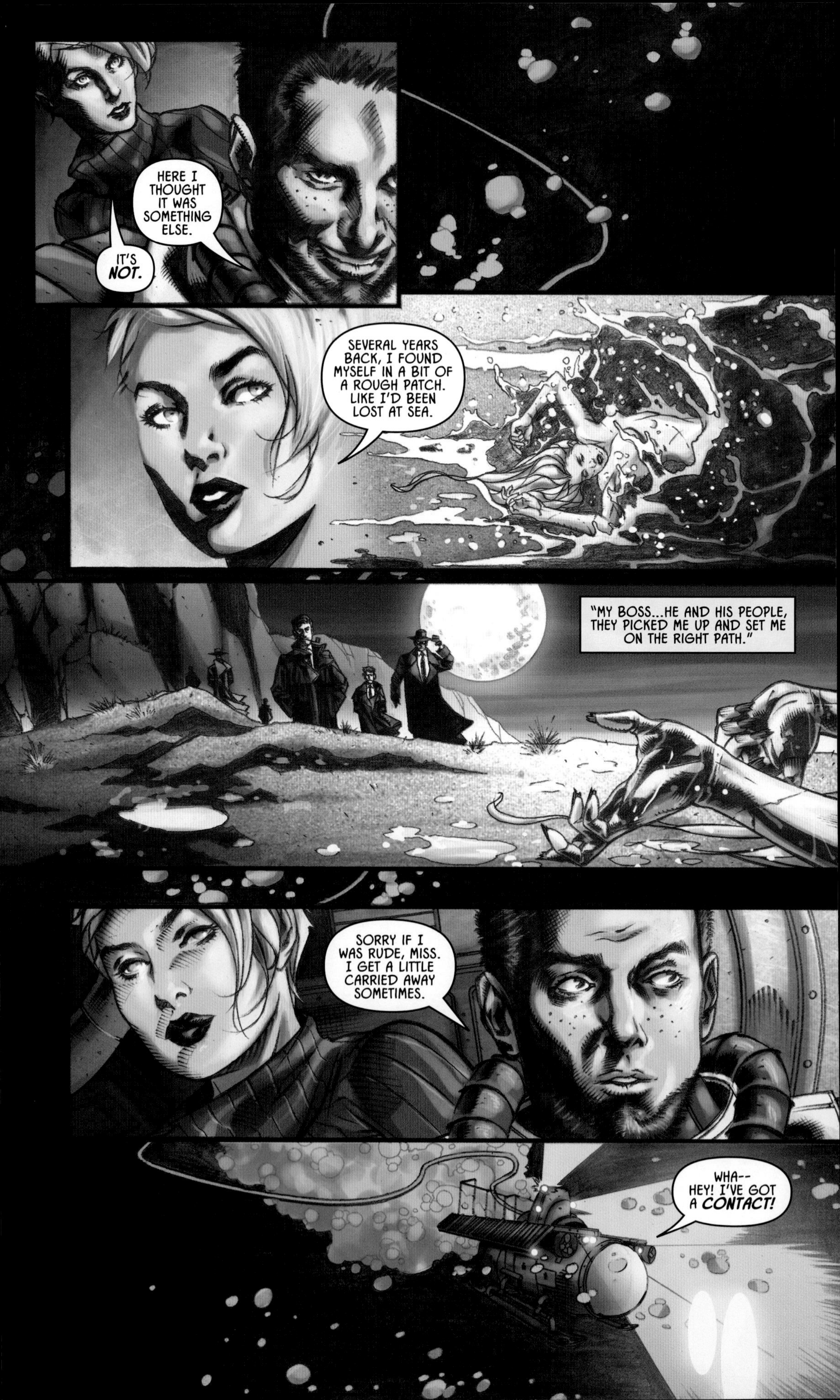
HERE I THOUGHT IT WAS SOMETHING ELSE.
IT'S NOT.
SEVERAL YEARS BACK, I FOUND MYSELF IN A BIT OF A ROUGH PATCH. LIKE I'D BEEN LOST AT SEA.
"MY BOSS...HE AND HIS PEOPLE, THEY PICKED ME UP AND SET ME ON THE RIGHT PATH."
SORRY IF I WAS RUDE, MISS. I GET A LITTLE CARRIED AWAY SOMETIMES.
WHA-- HEY! I'VE GOT A CONTACT!

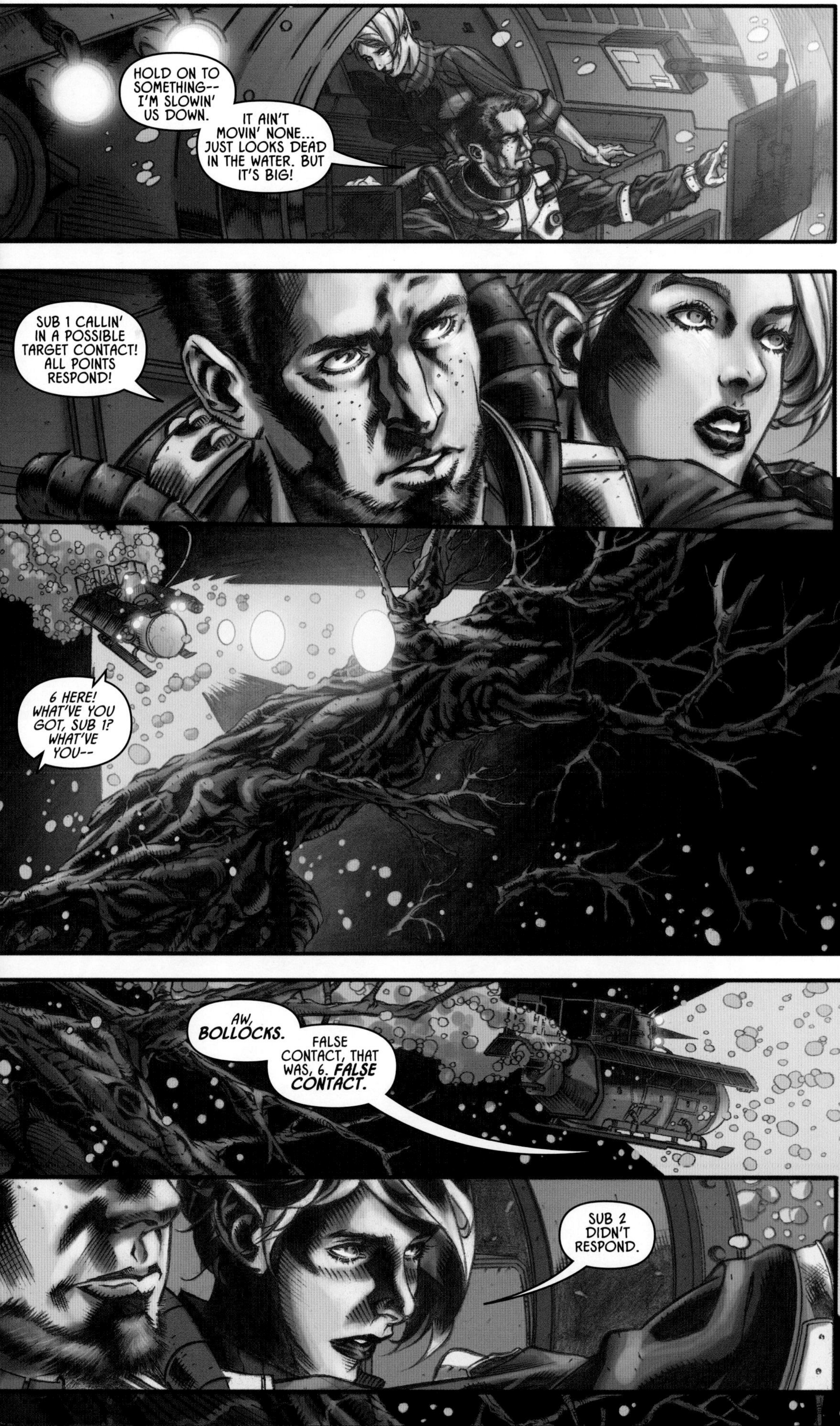
HOLD ON TO SOMETHING-- I'M SLOWIN' US DOWN.
IT AIN'T MOVIN' NONE... JUST LOOKS DEAD IN THE WATER. BUT IT'S BIG!
SUB 1 CALLIN' IN A POSSIBLE TARGET CONTACT! ALL POINTS RESPOND!
6 HERE! WHAT'VE YOU GOT, SUB 1? WHAT'VE YOU--
AW, BOLLOCKS.
FALSE CONTACT, THAT WAS, 6. FALSE CONTACT.
SUB 2 DIDN'T RESPOND.

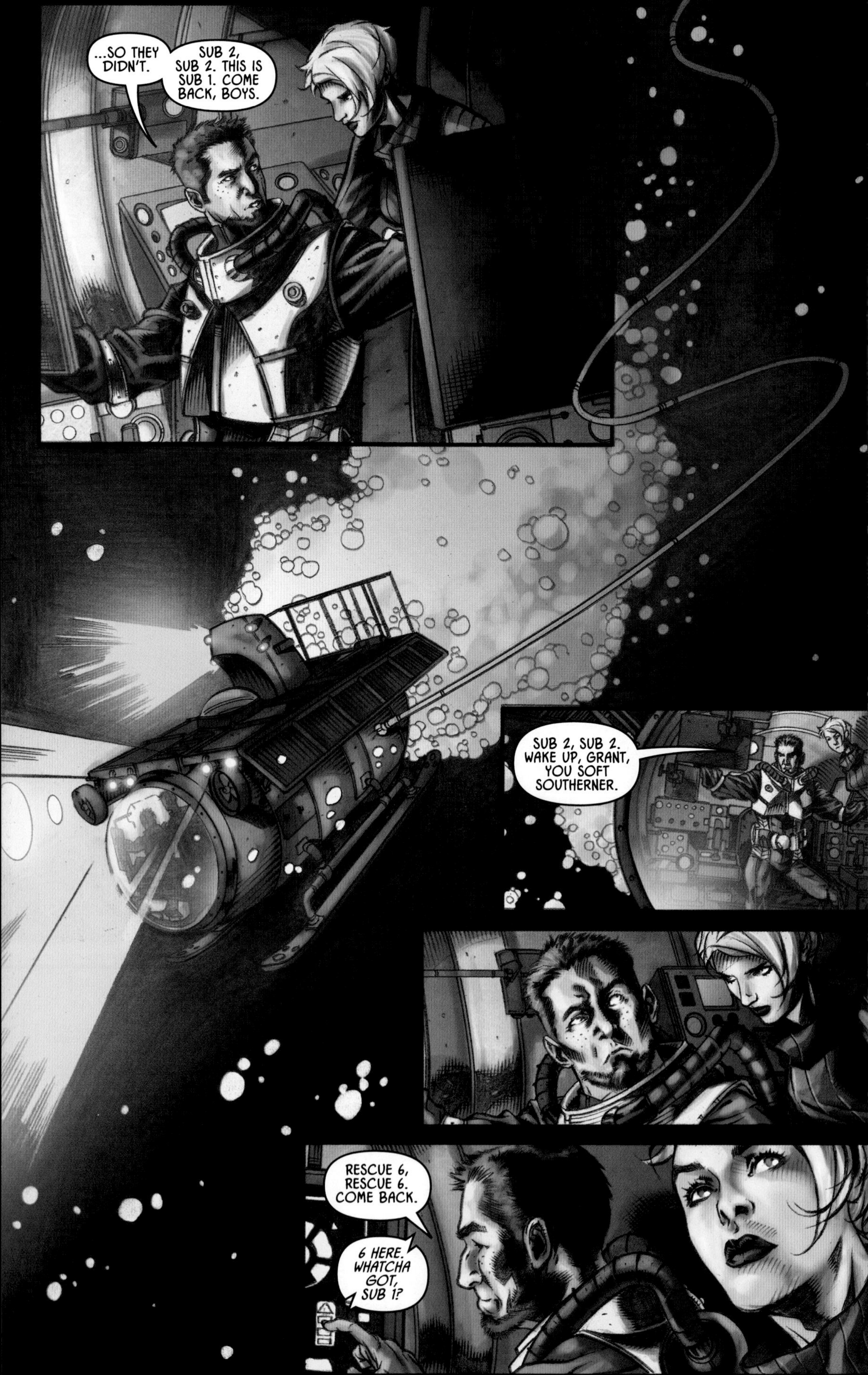
...SO THEY DIDN'T.
SUB 2, SUB 2. THIS IS SUB 1. COME BACK, BOYS.
SUB 2, SUB 2. WAKE UP, GRANT, YOU SOFT SOUTHERNER.
RESCUE 6, RESCUE 6. COME BACK.
6 HERE. WHATCHA GOT, SUB 1?

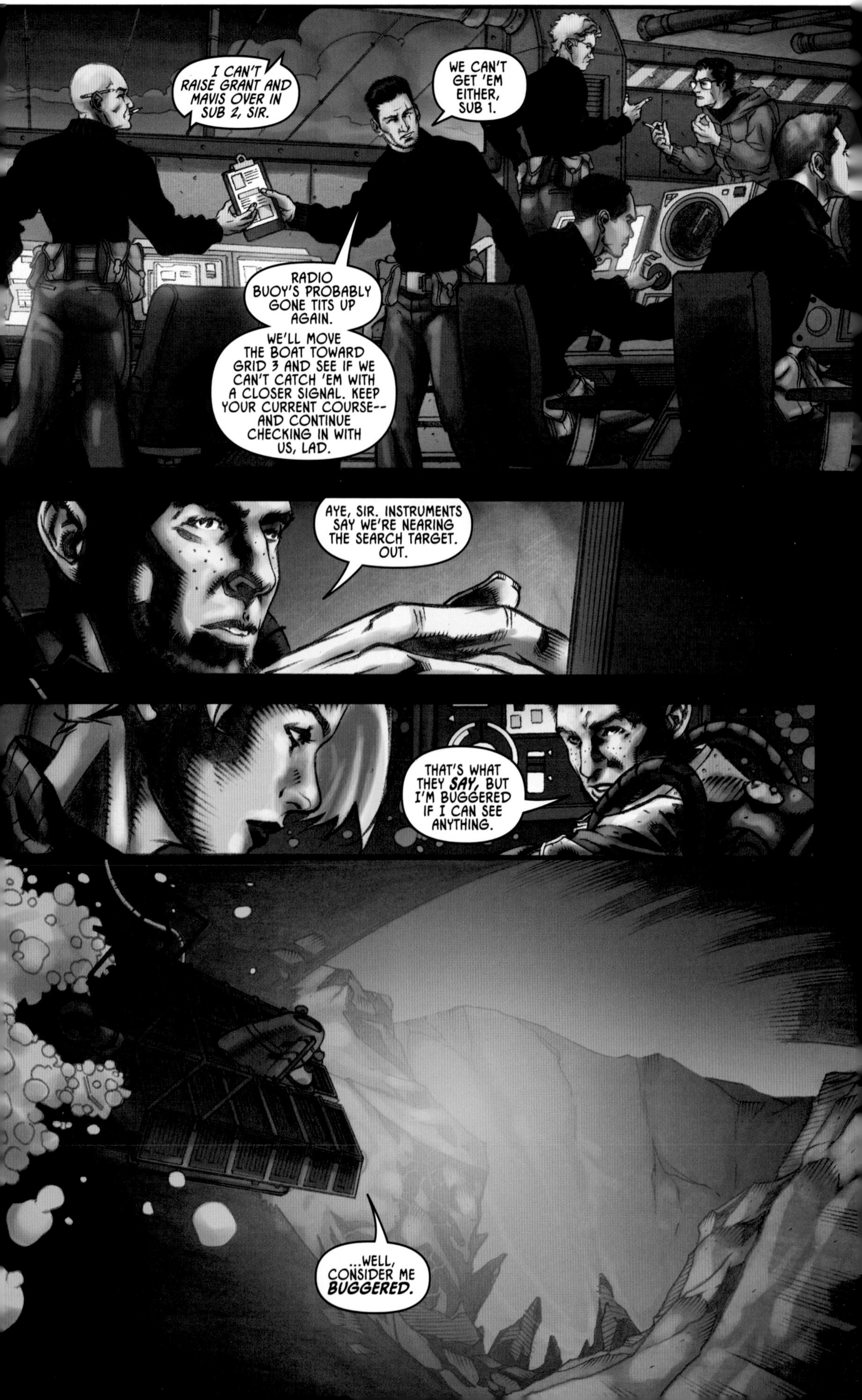
I CAN'T RAISE GRANT AND MAVIS OVER IN SUB 2, SIR.
WE CAN'T GET 'EM EITHER, SUB 1.
RADIO BUOY'S PROBABLY GONE TITS UP AGAIN.
WE'LL MOVE THE BOAT TOWARD GRID 3 AND SEE IF WE CAN'T CATCH 'EM WITH A CLOSER SIGNAL. KEEP YOUR CURRENT COURSE-- AND CONTINUE CHECKING IN WITH US, LAD.
AYE, SIR. INSTRUMENTS SAY WE'RE NEARING THE SEARCH TARGET. OUT.
THAT'S WHAT THEY SAY, BUT I'M BUGGERED IF I CAN SEE ANYTHING.
...WELL, CONSIDER ME BUGGERED.

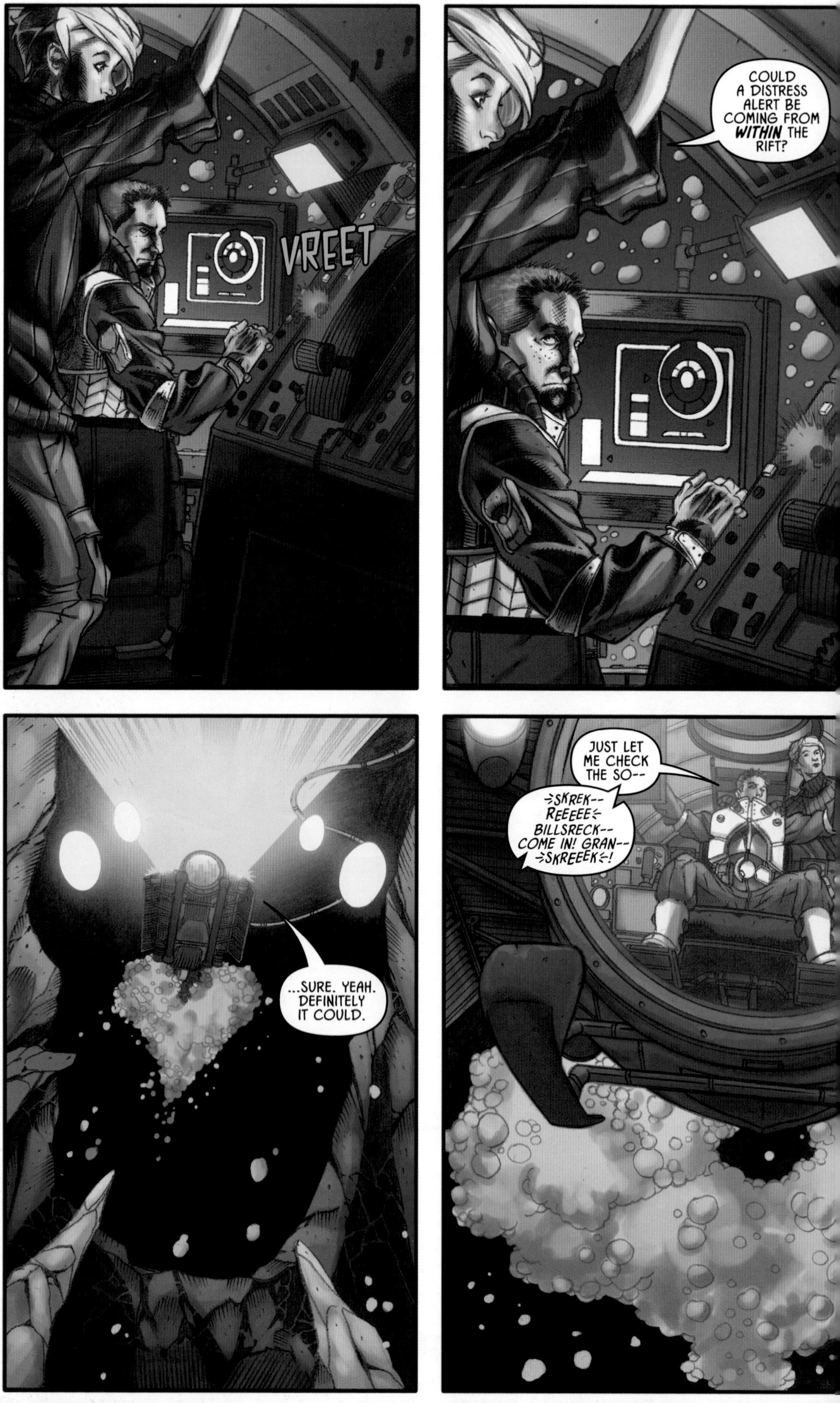
VREET
COULD A DISTRESS ALERT BE COMING FROM WITHIN THE RIFT?
...SURE. YEAH. DEFINITELY IT COULD.
JUST LET ME CHECK THE SO--
⇒SKREK-- REEEEE⇐ BILLSRECK-- COME IN! GRAN-- ⇒SKREEEK⇐!

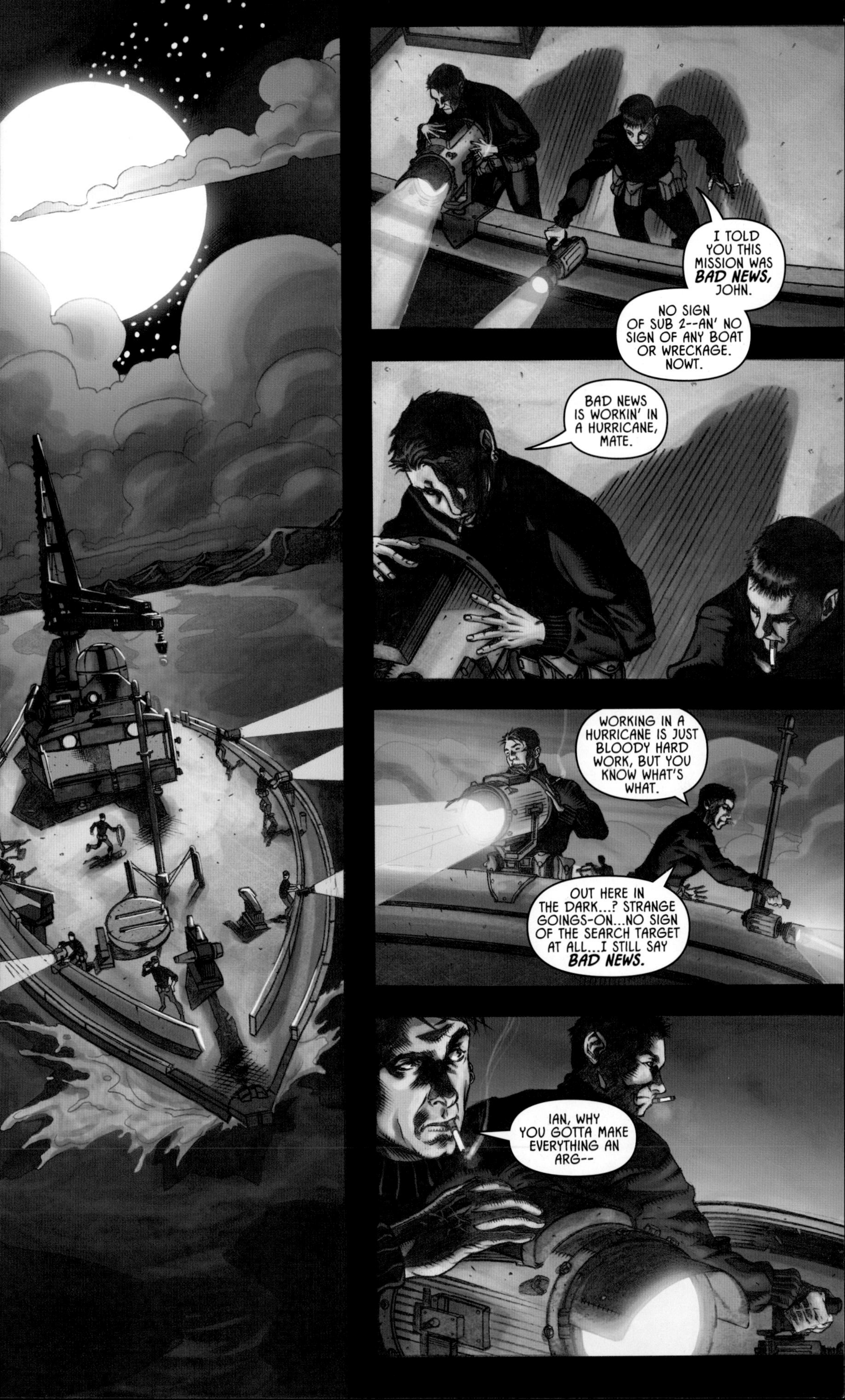
I TOLD YOU THIS MISSION WAS BAD NEWS, JOHN.
NO SIGN OF SUB 2--AN' NO SIGN OF ANY BOAT OR WRECKAGE. NOWT.
BAD NEWS IS WORKIN' IN A HURRICANE, MATE.
WORKING IN A HURRICANE IS JUST BLOODY HARD WORK, BUT YOU KNOW WHAT'S WHAT.
OUT HERE IN THE DARK...? STRANGE GOINGS-ON...NO SIGN OF THE SEARCH TARGET AT ALL...I STILL SAY BAD NEWS.
IAN, WHY YOU GOTTA MAKE EVERYTHING AN ARG--

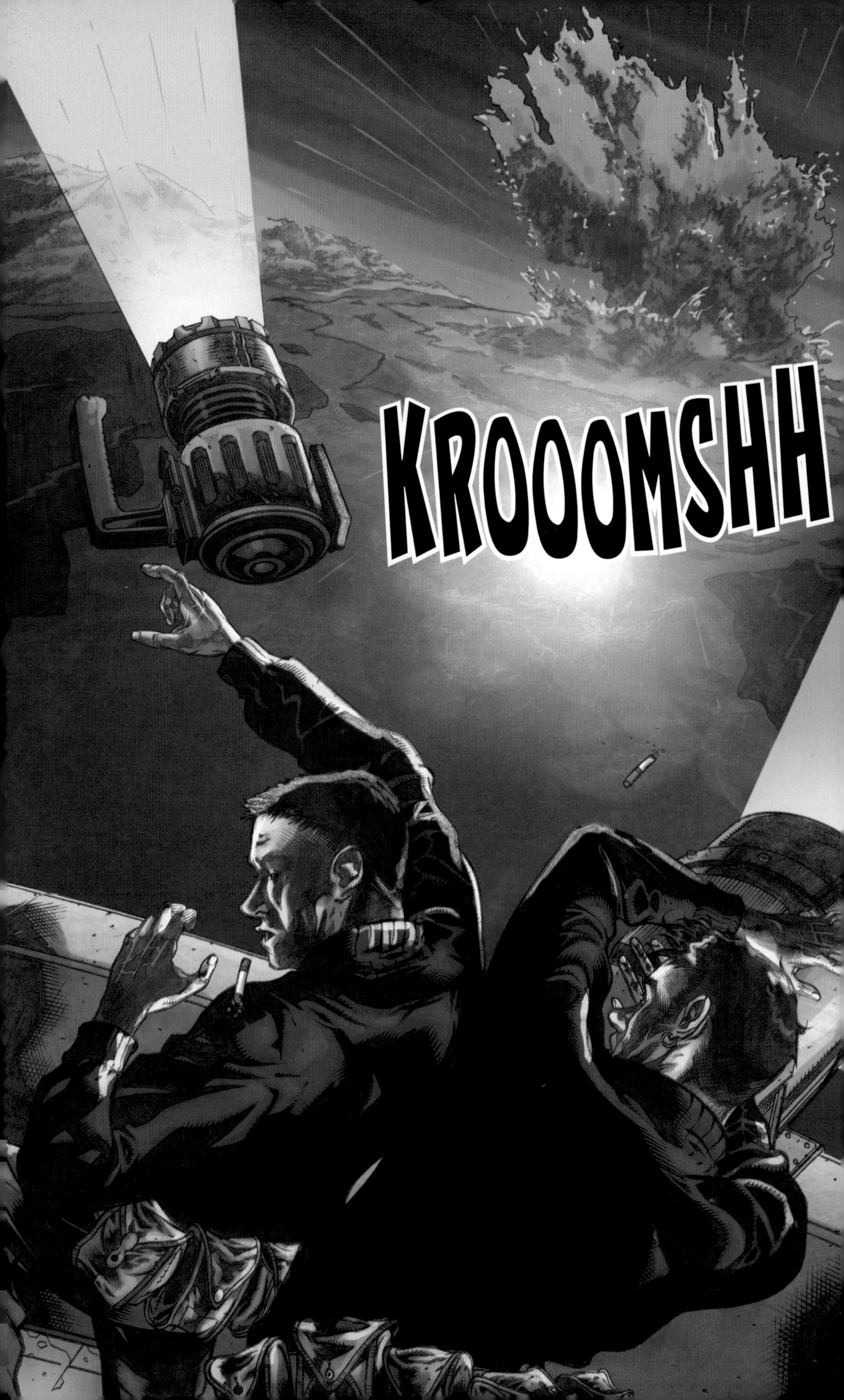
KROOOMSHH

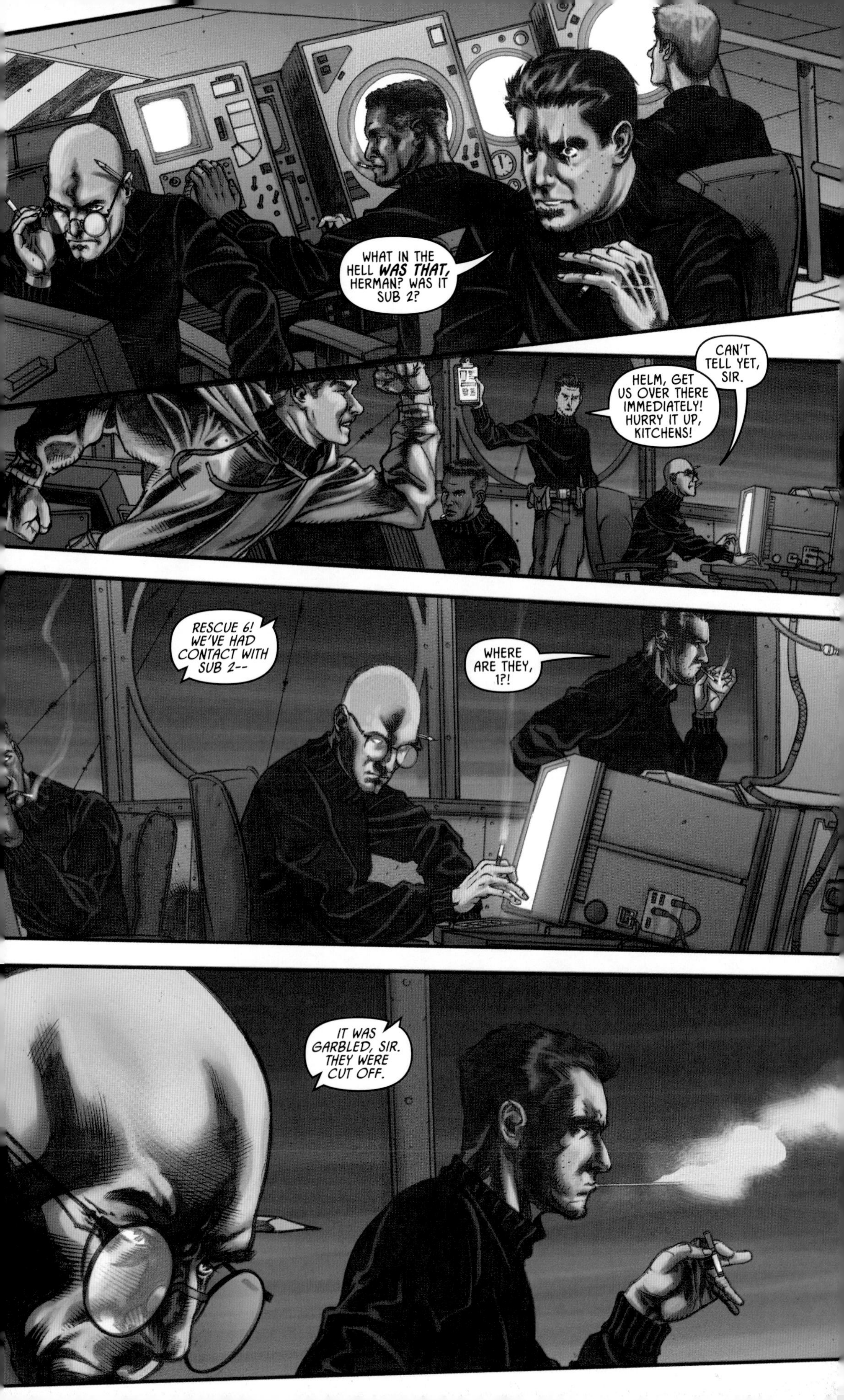
WHAT IN THE HELL **WAS THAT,** HERMAN? WAS IT SUB 2?
CAN'T TELL YET, SIR.
HELM, GET US OVER THERE IMMEDIATELY! HURRY IT UP, KITCHENS!
RESCUE 6! WE'VE HAD CONTACT WITH SUB 2--
WHERE ARE THEY, 1?!
IT WAS GARBLED, SIR. THEY WERE CUT OFF.

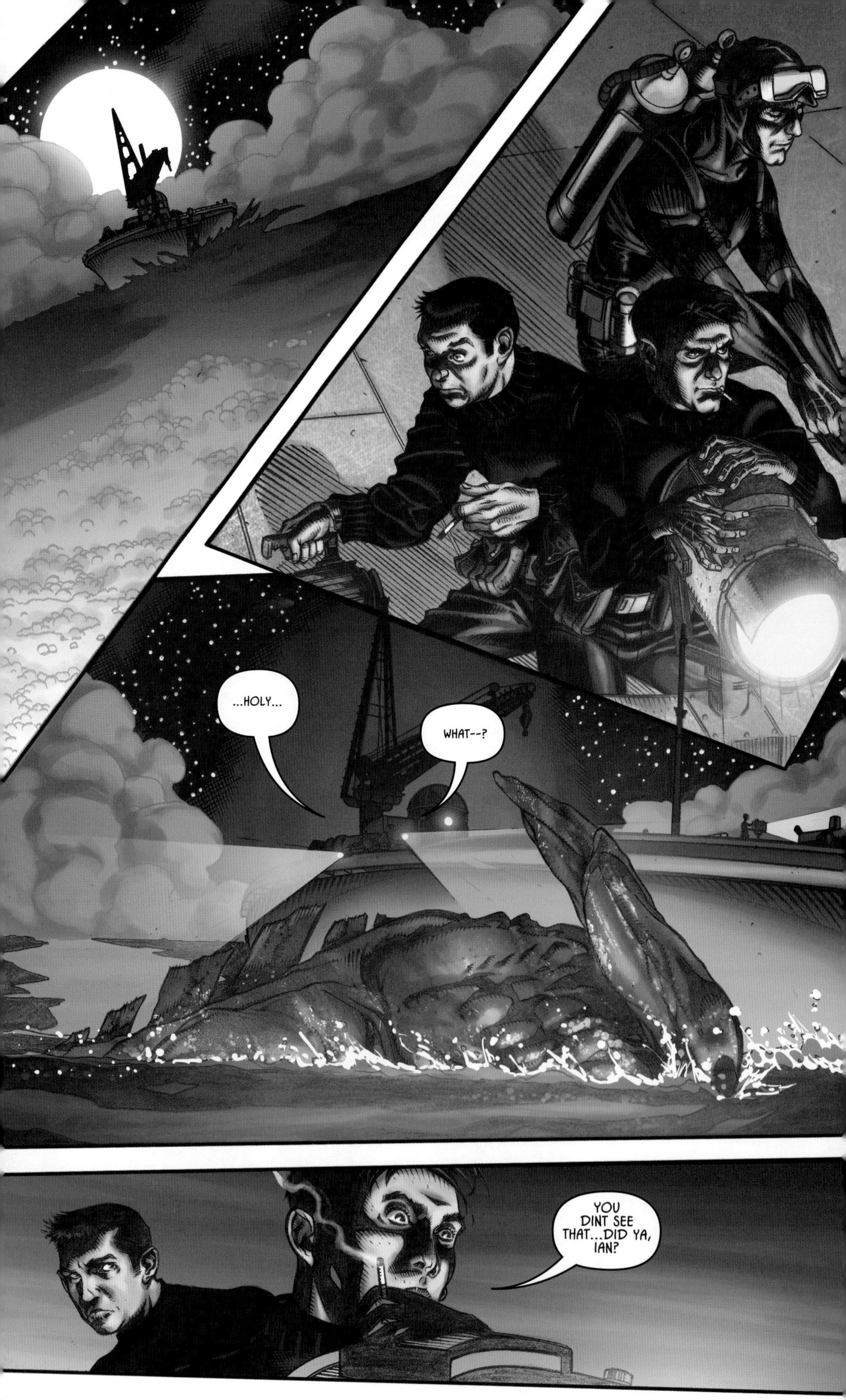
...HOLY...
WHAT--?
YOU DINT SEE THAT...DID YA, IAN?

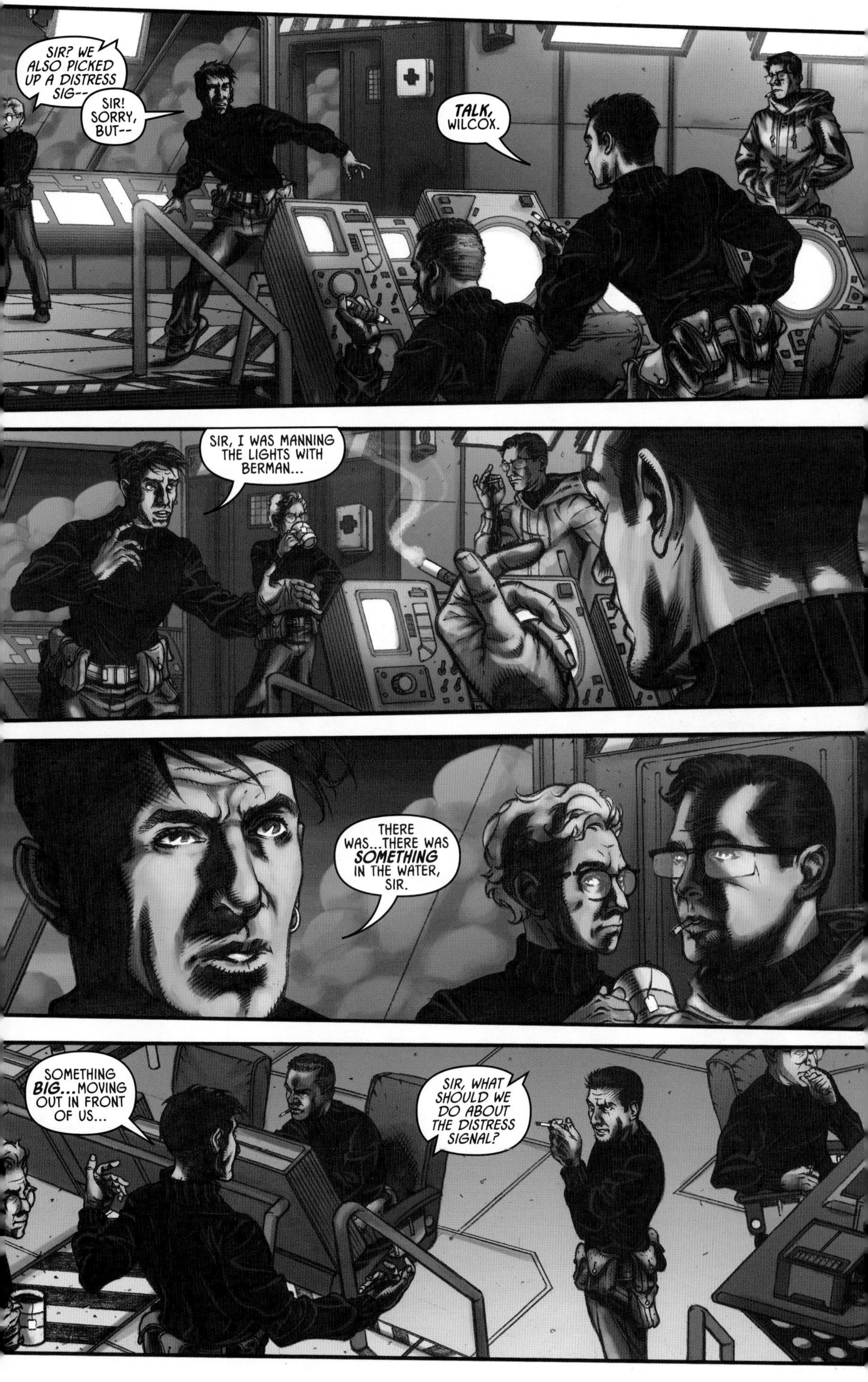
SIR? WE ALSO PICKED UP A DISTRESS SIG--
SIR! SORRY, BUT--
TALK, WILCOX.
SIR, I WAS MANNING THE LIGHTS WITH BERMAN...
THERE WAS...THERE WAS SOMETHING IN THE WATER, SIR.
SOMETHING BIG...MOVING OUT IN FRONT OF US...
SIR, WHAT SHOULD WE DO ABOUT THE DISTRESS SIGNAL?

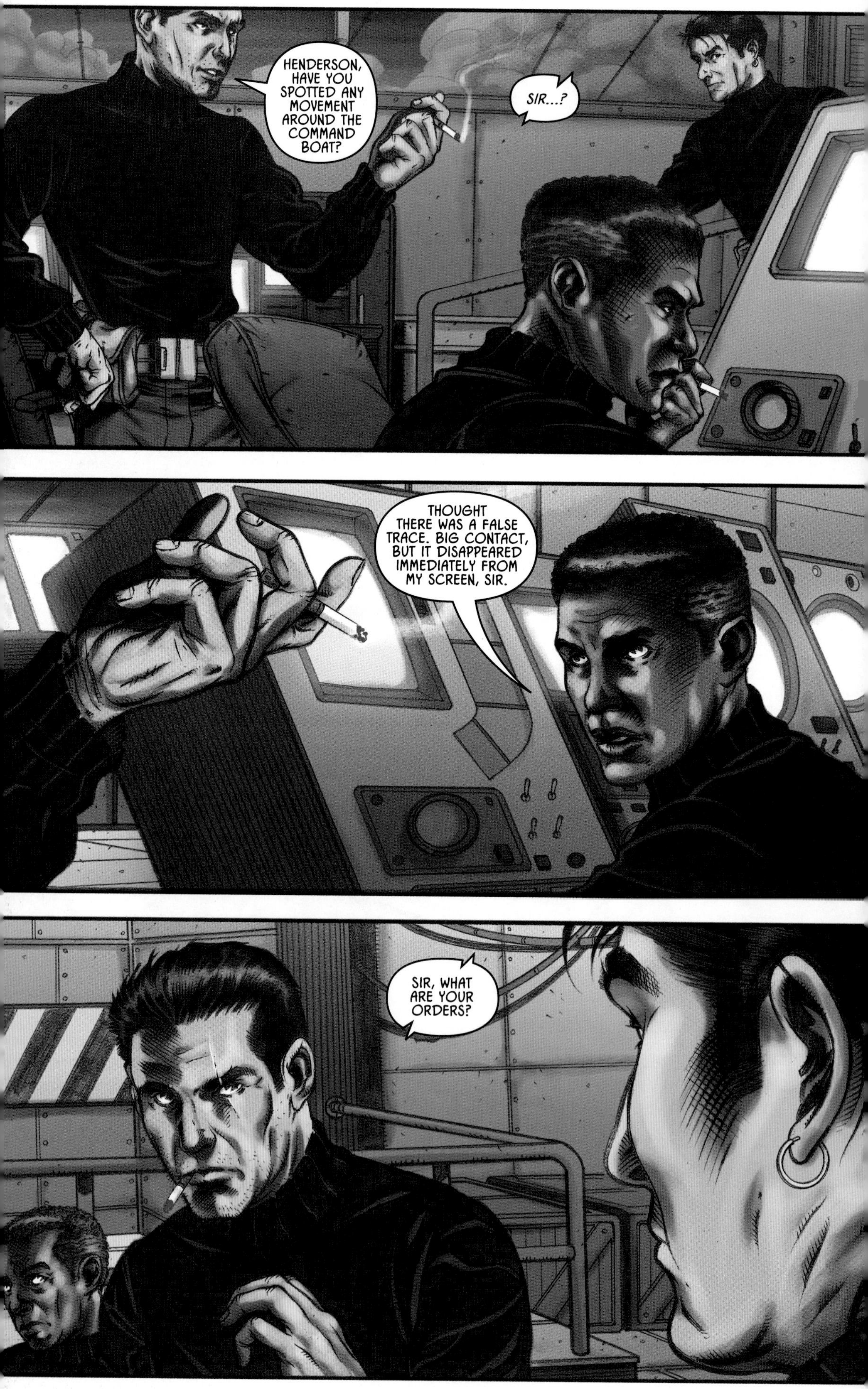
HENDERSON, HAVE YOU SPOTTED ANY MOVEMENT AROUND THE COMMAND BOAT?
SIR...?
THOUGHT THERE WAS A FALSE TRACE. BIG CONTACT, BUT IT DISAPPEARED IMMEDIATELY FROM MY SCREEN, SIR.
SIR, WHAT ARE YOUR ORDERS?

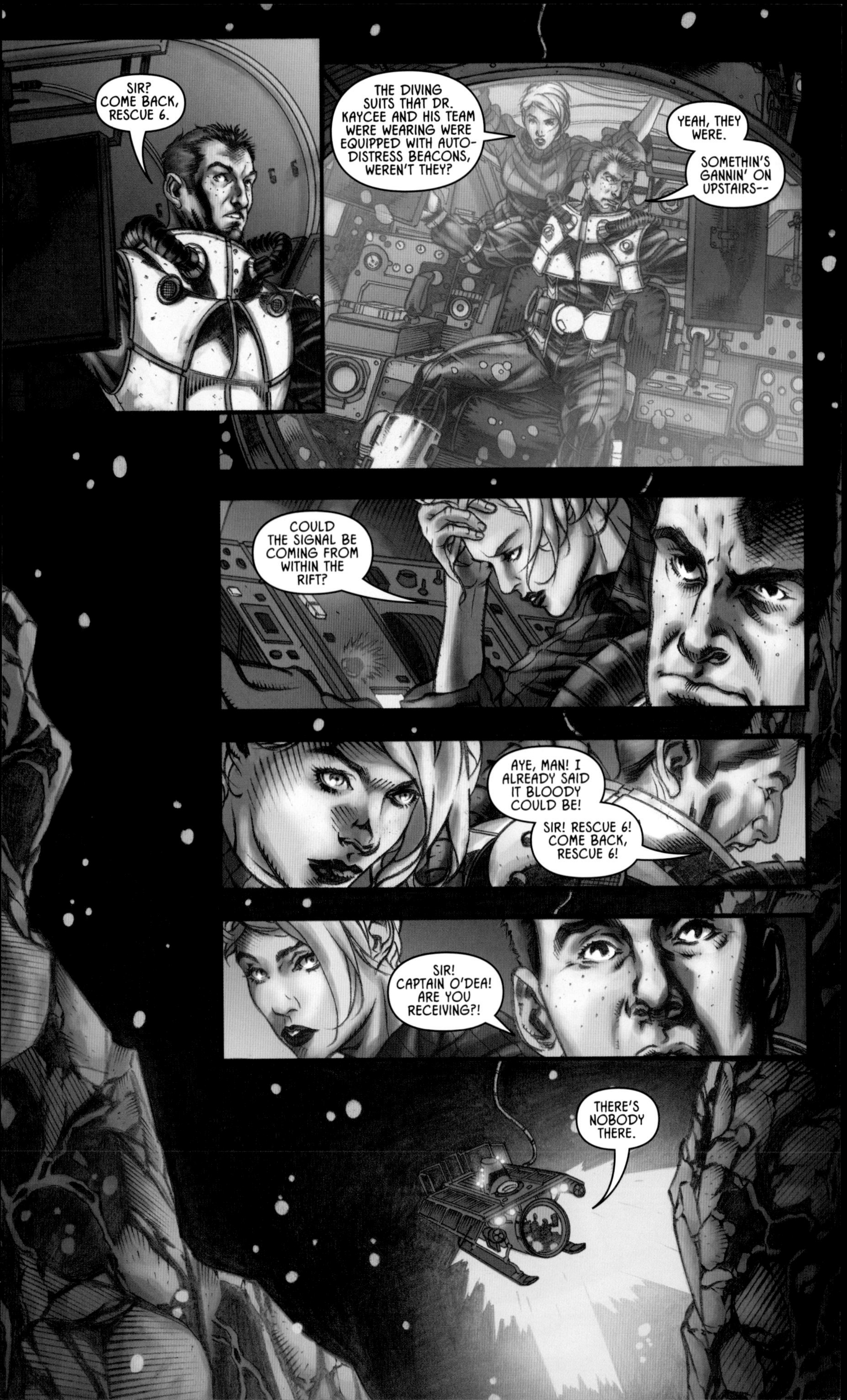
SIR? COME BACK, RESCUE 6.
THE DIVING SUITS THAT DR. KAYCEE AND HIS TEAM WERE WEARING WERE EQUIPPED WITH AUTO-DISTRESS BEACONS, WEREN'T THEY?
YEAH, THEY WERE.
SOMETHIN'S GANNIN' ON UPSTAIRS--
COULD THE SIGNAL BE COMING FROM WITHIN THE RIFT?
AYE, MAN! I ALREADY SAID IT BLOODY COULD BE!
SIR! RESCUE 6! COME BACK, RESCUE 6!
SIR! CAPTAIN O'DEA! ARE YOU RECEIVING?!
THERE'S NOBODY THERE.

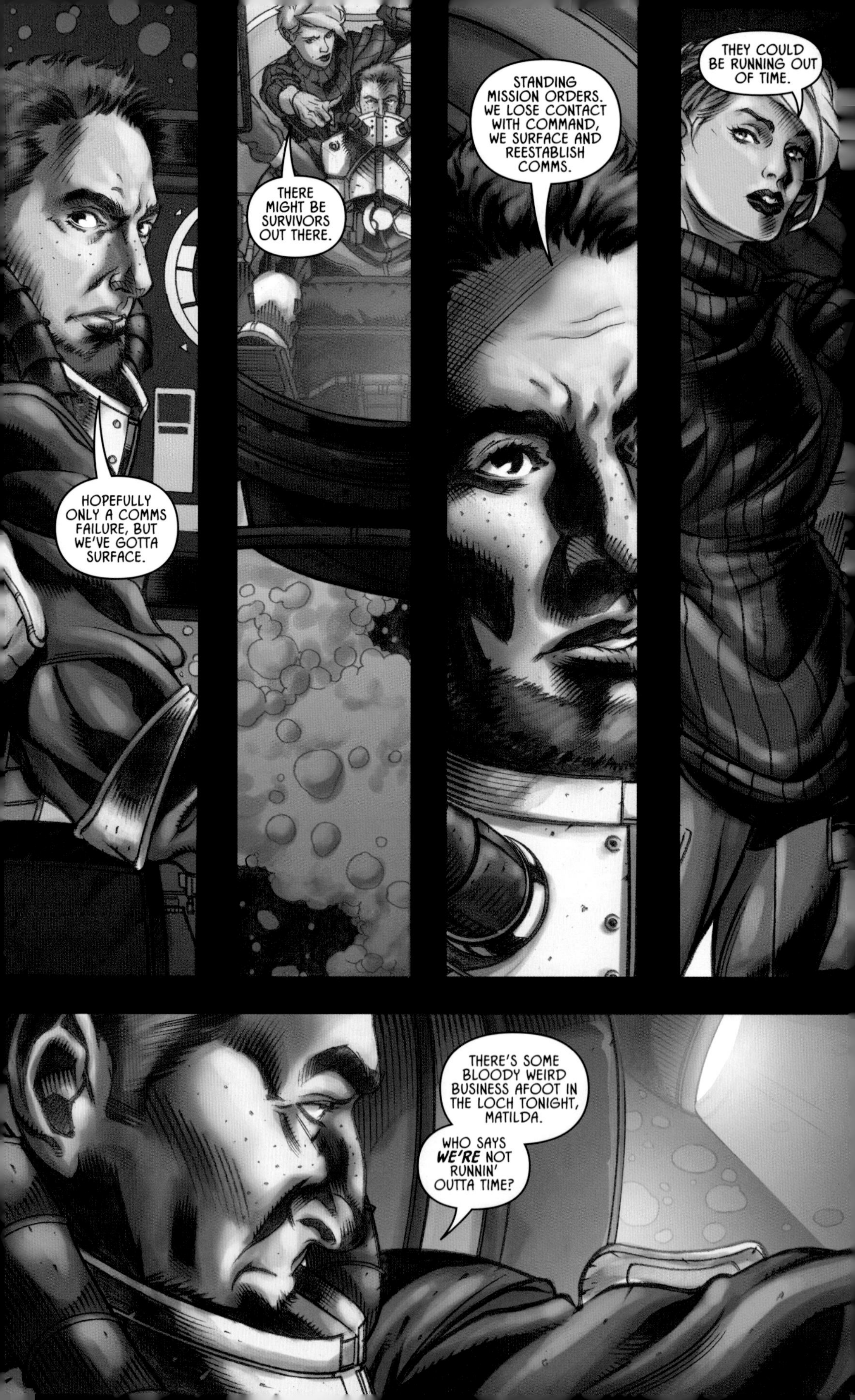
HOPEFULLY ONLY A COMMS FAILURE, BUT WE'VE GOTTA SURFACE.
THERE MIGHT BE SURVIVORS OUT THERE.
STANDING MISSION ORDERS. WE LOSE CONTACT WITH COMMAND, WE SURFACE AND REESTABLISH COMMS.
THEY COULD BE RUNNING OUT OF TIME.
THERE'S SOME BLOODY WEIRD BUSINESS AFOOT IN THE LOCH TONIGHT, MATILDA.
WHO SAYS ***WE'RE*** NOT RUNNIN' OUTTA TIME?

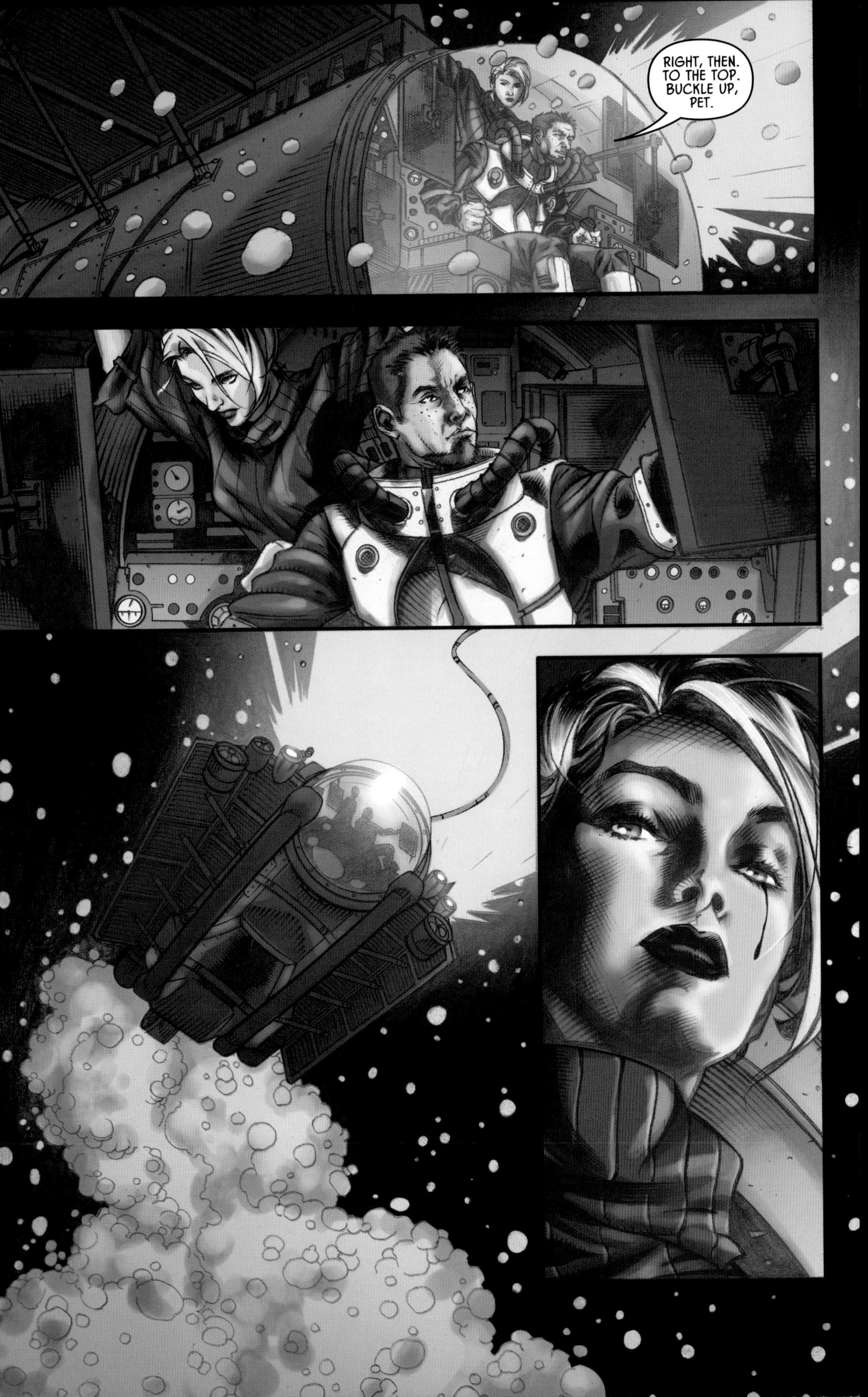
RIGHT, THEN. TO THE TOP. BUCKLE UP, PET.

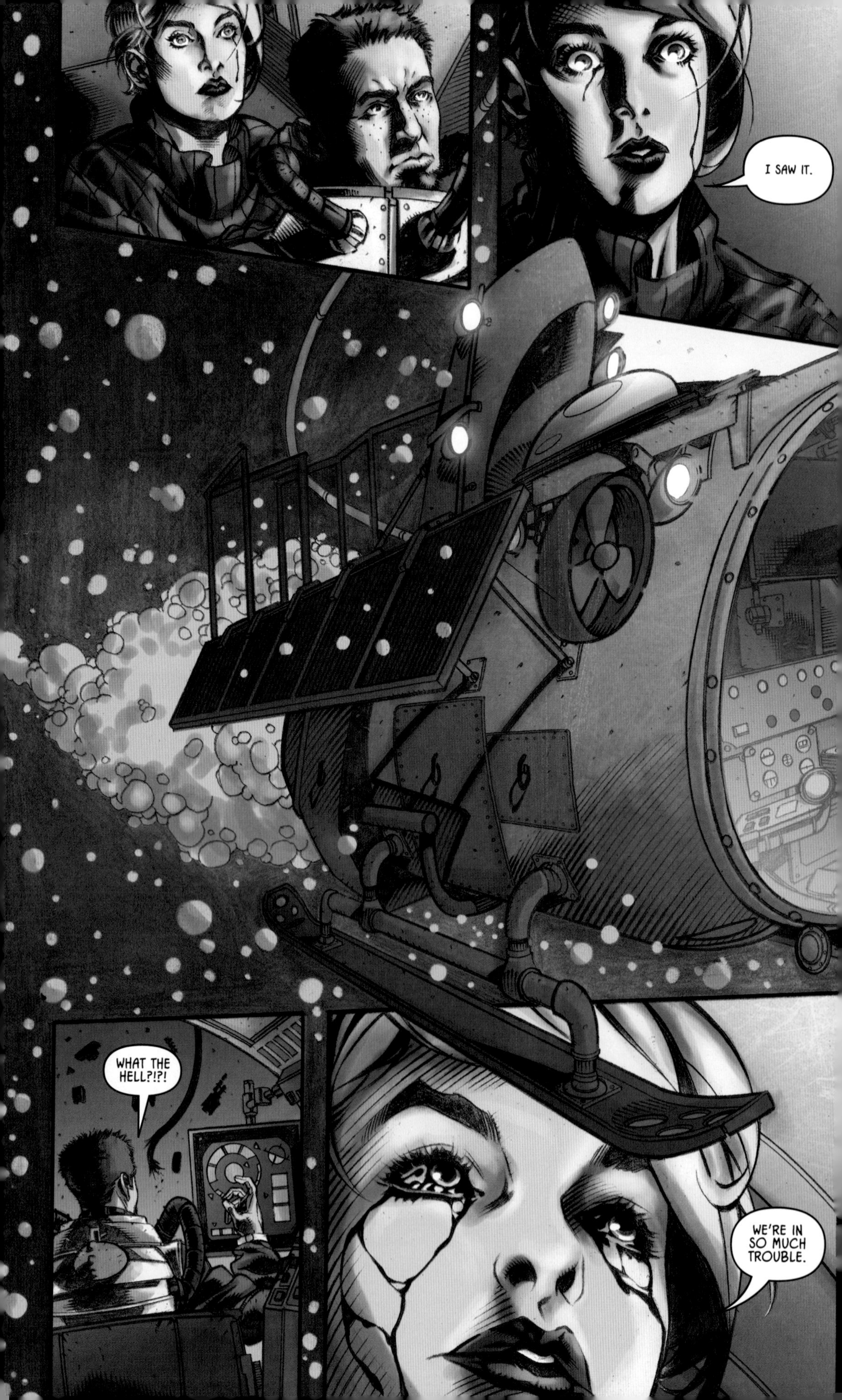
I SAW IT.
WHAT THE HELL?!?!
WE'RE IN SO MUCH TROUBLE.

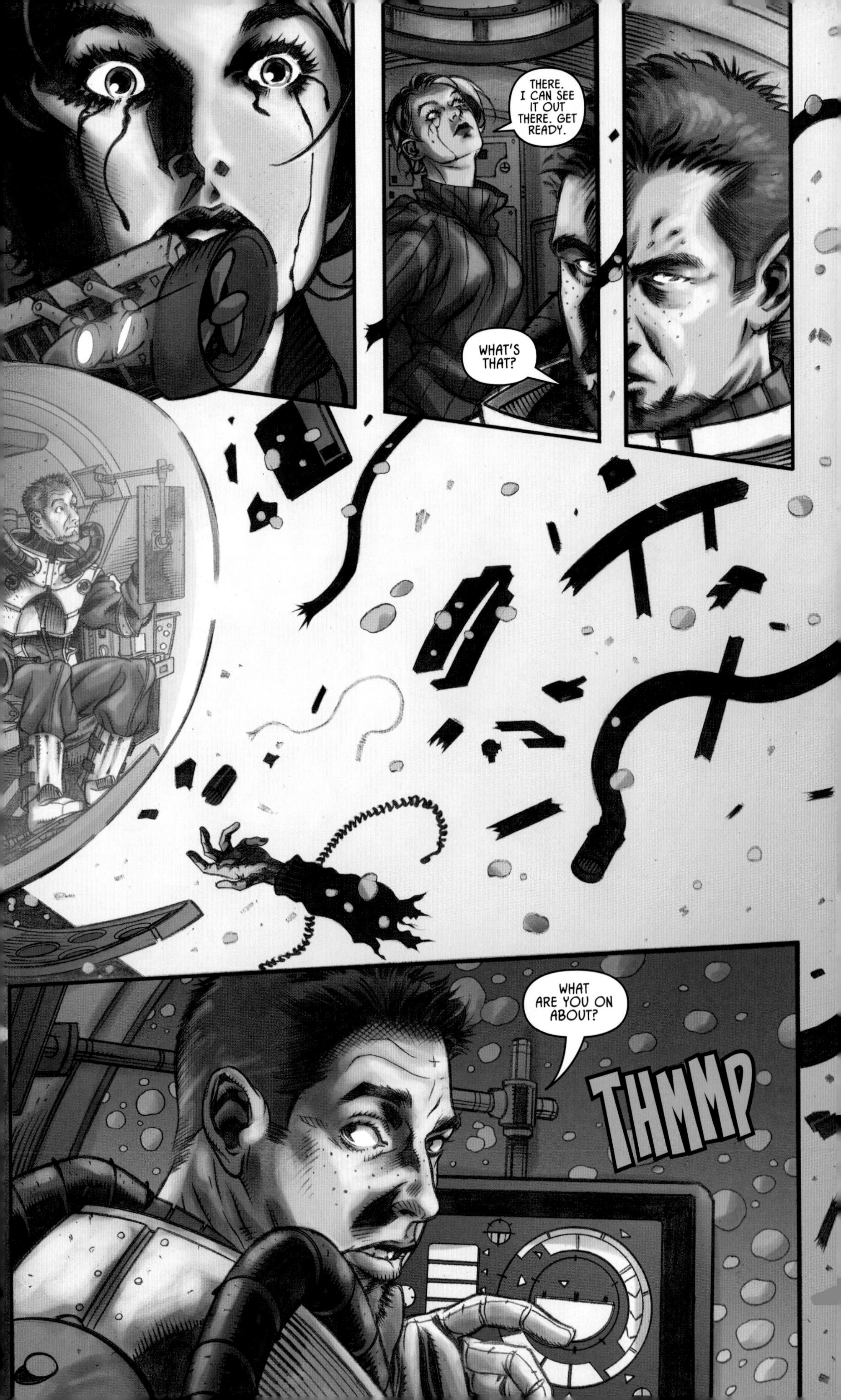
THERE. I CAN SEE IT OUT THERE. GET READY.
WHAT'S THAT?
WHAT ARE YOU ON ABOUT?
THMMP

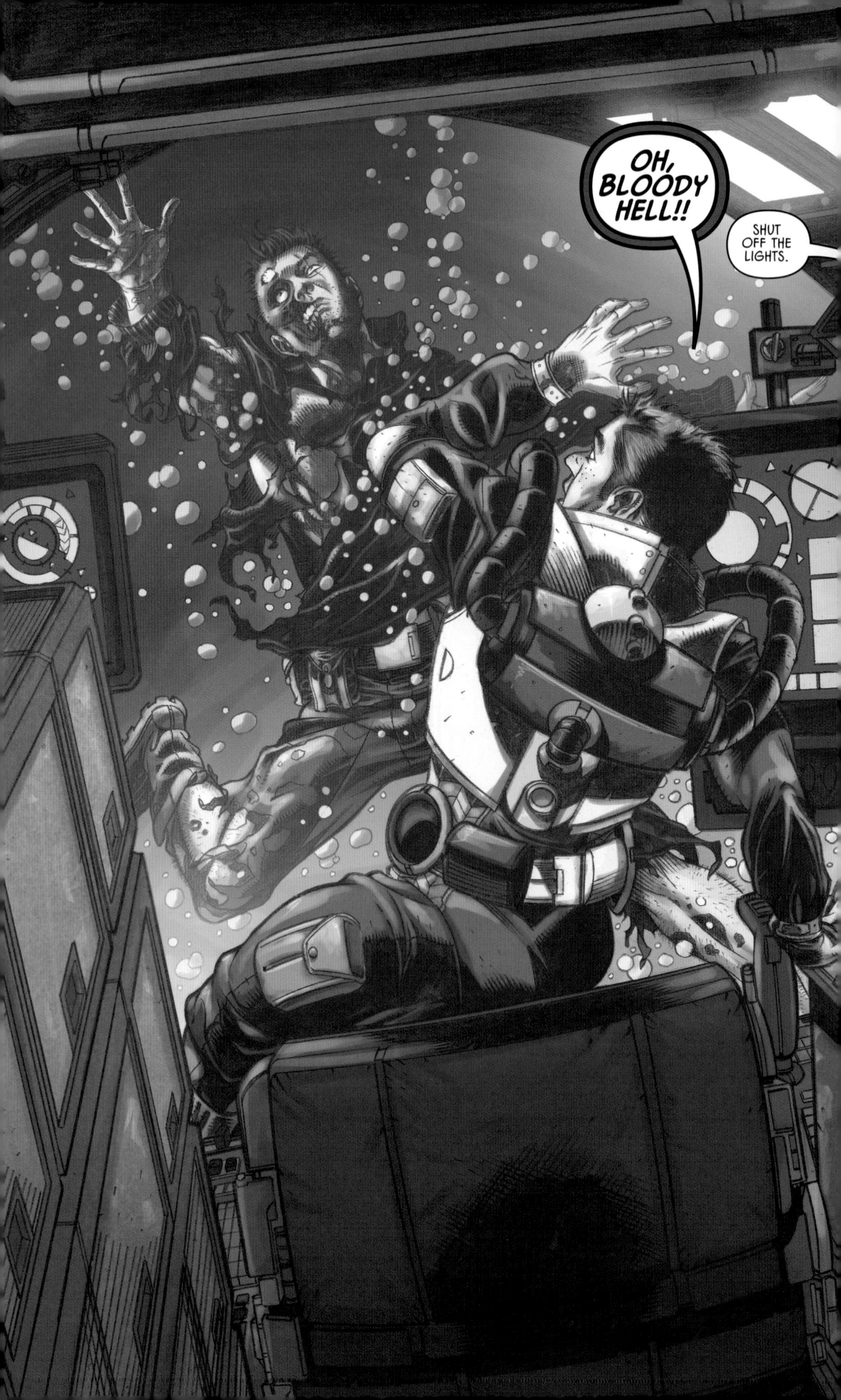
OH, BLOODY HELL!!
SHUT OFF THE LIGHTS.

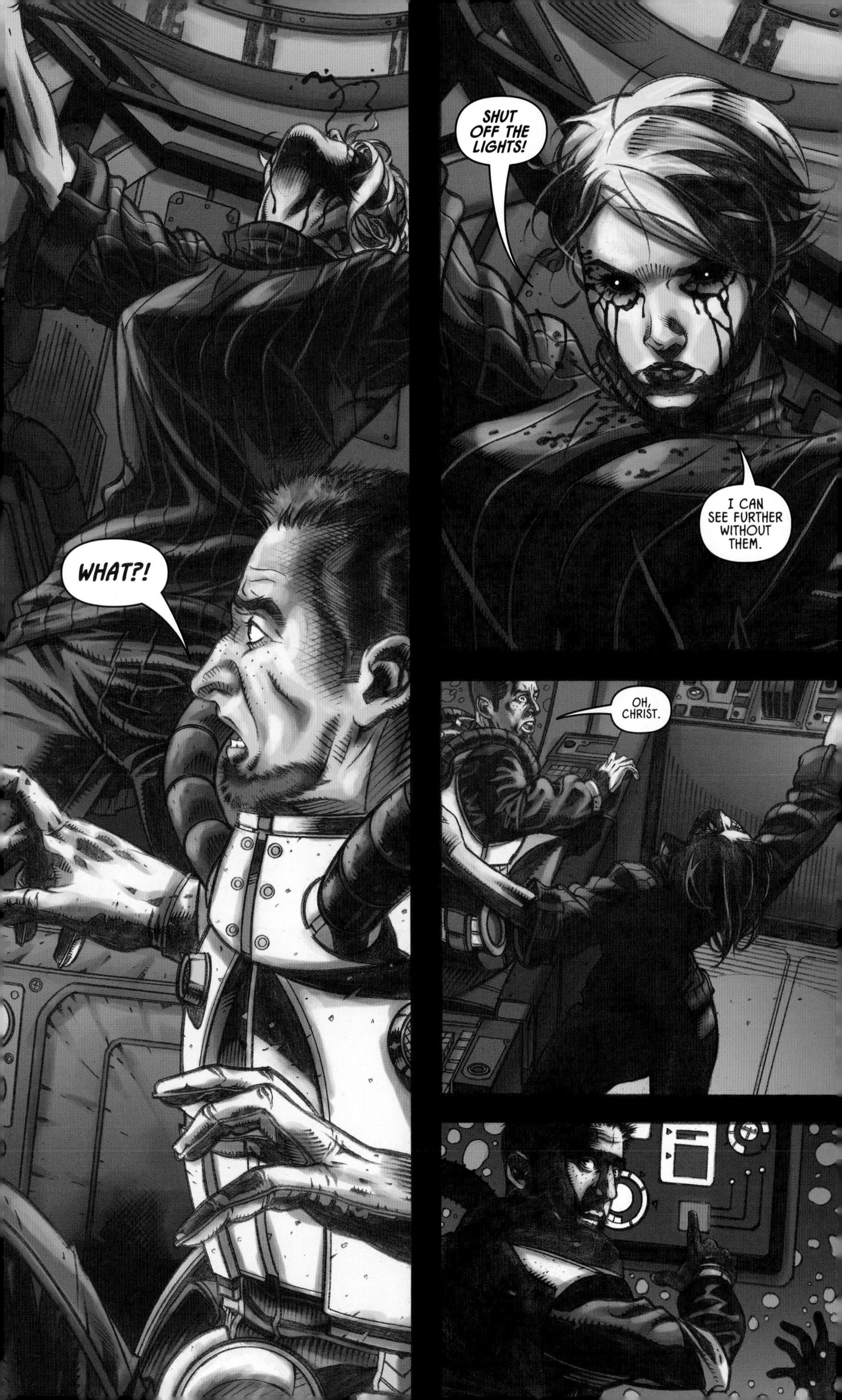
SHUT OFF THE LIGHTS!
WHAT?!
I CAN SEE FURTHER WITHOUT THEM.
OH, CHRIST.

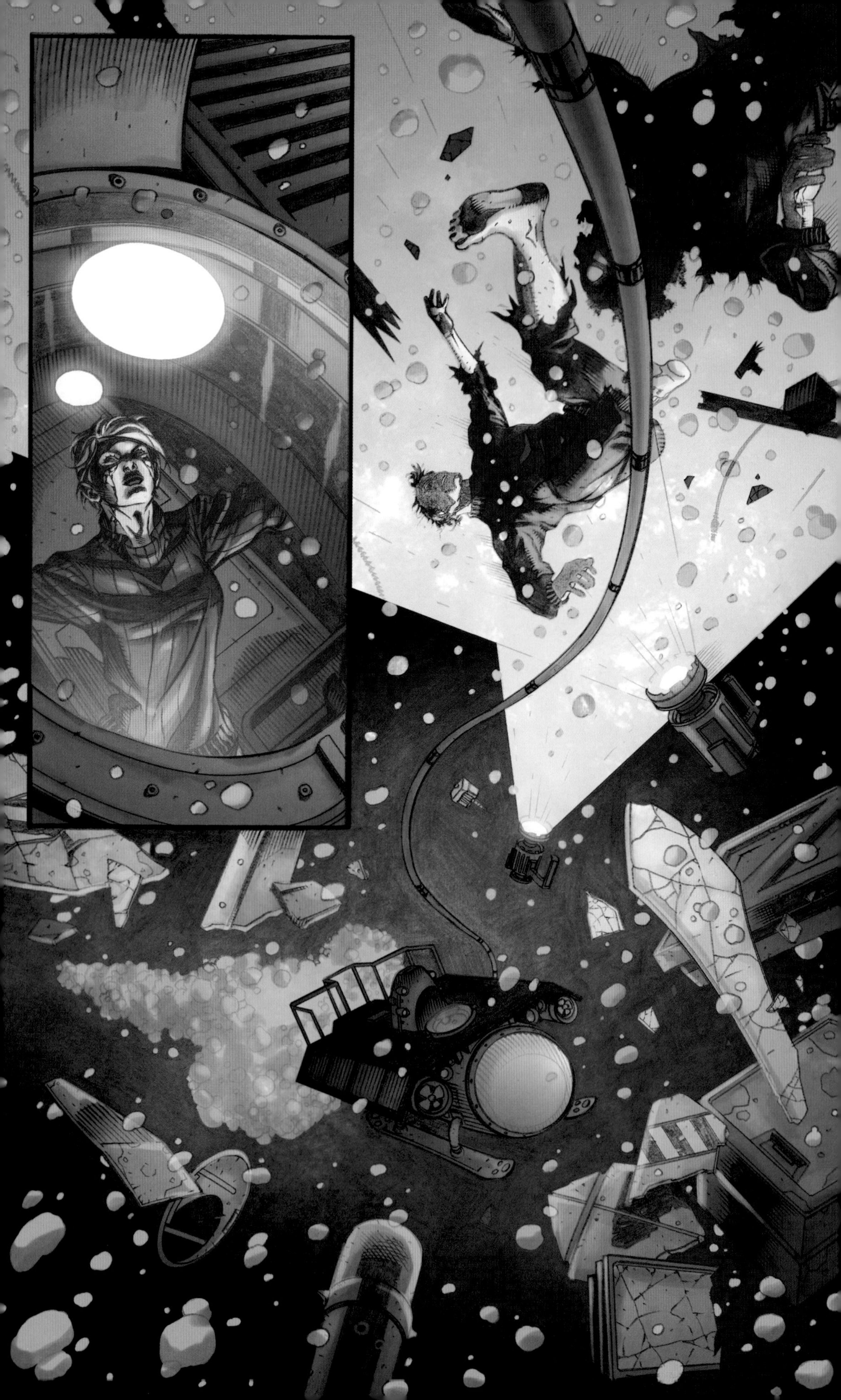

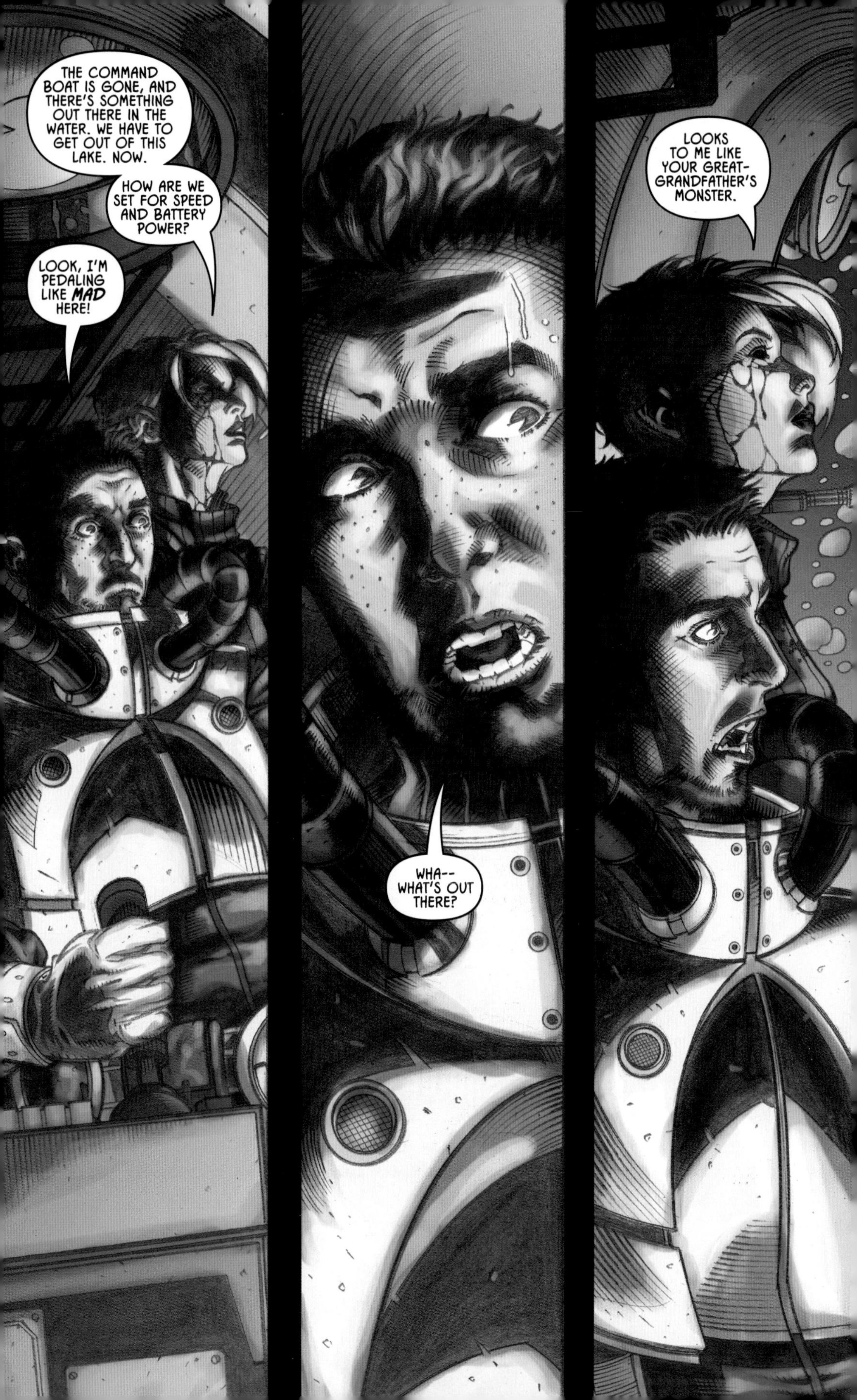
THE COMMAND BOAT IS GONE, AND THERE'S SOMETHING OUT THERE IN THE WATER. WE HAVE TO GET OUT OF THIS LAKE. NOW.
HOW ARE WE SET FOR SPEED AND BATTERY POWER?
LOOK, I'M PEDALING LIKE MAD HERE!
WHA-- WHAT'S OUT THERE?
LOOKS TO ME LIKE YOUR GREAT-GRANDFATHER'S MONSTER.

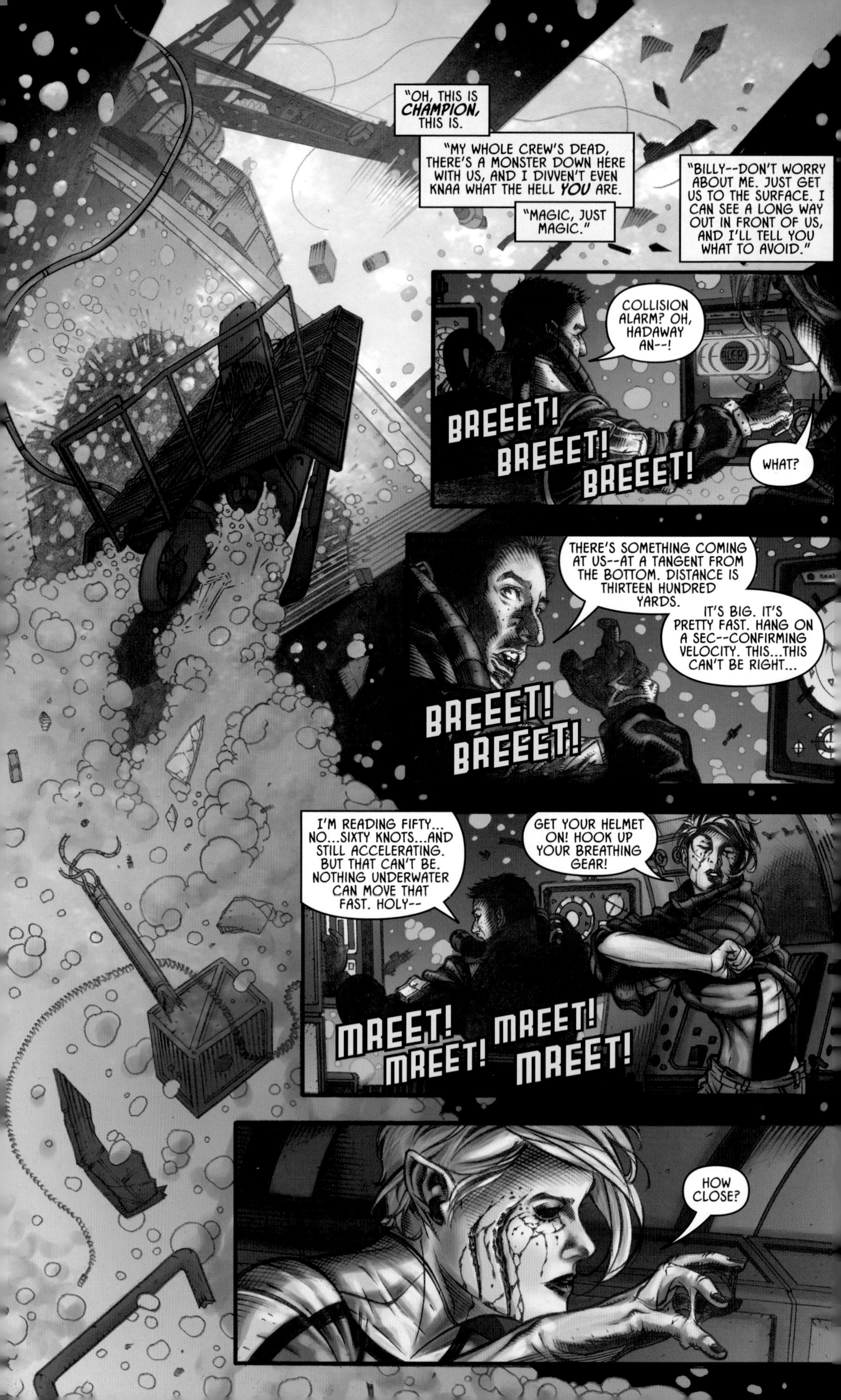
"OH, THIS IS CHAMPION, THIS IS.
"MY WHOLE CREW'S DEAD, THERE'S A MONSTER DOWN HERE WITH US, AND I DIVVEN'T EVEN KNAA WHAT THE HELL YOU ARE.
"MAGIC, JUST MAGIC."
"BILLY--DON'T WORRY ABOUT ME. JUST GET US TO THE SURFACE. I CAN SEE A LONG WAY OUT IN FRONT OF US, AND I'LL TELL YOU WHAT TO AVOID."
COLLISION ALARM? OH, HADAWAY AN--!
BREEET! BREEET! BREEET!
WHAT?
THERE'S SOMETHING COMING AT US--AT A TANGENT FROM THE BOTTOM. DISTANCE IS THIRTEEN HUNDRED YARDS.
IT'S BIG. IT'S PRETTY FAST. HANG ON A SEC--CONFIRMING VELOCITY. THIS...THIS CAN'T BE RIGHT...
BREEET! BREEET!
I'M READING FIFTY... NO...SIXTY KNOTS...AND STILL ACCELERATING. BUT THAT CAN'T BE. NOTHING UNDERWATER CAN MOVE THAT FAST. HOLY--
GET YOUR HELMET ON! HOOK UP YOUR BREATHING GEAR!
MREET! MREET! MREET! MREET!
HOW CLOSE?

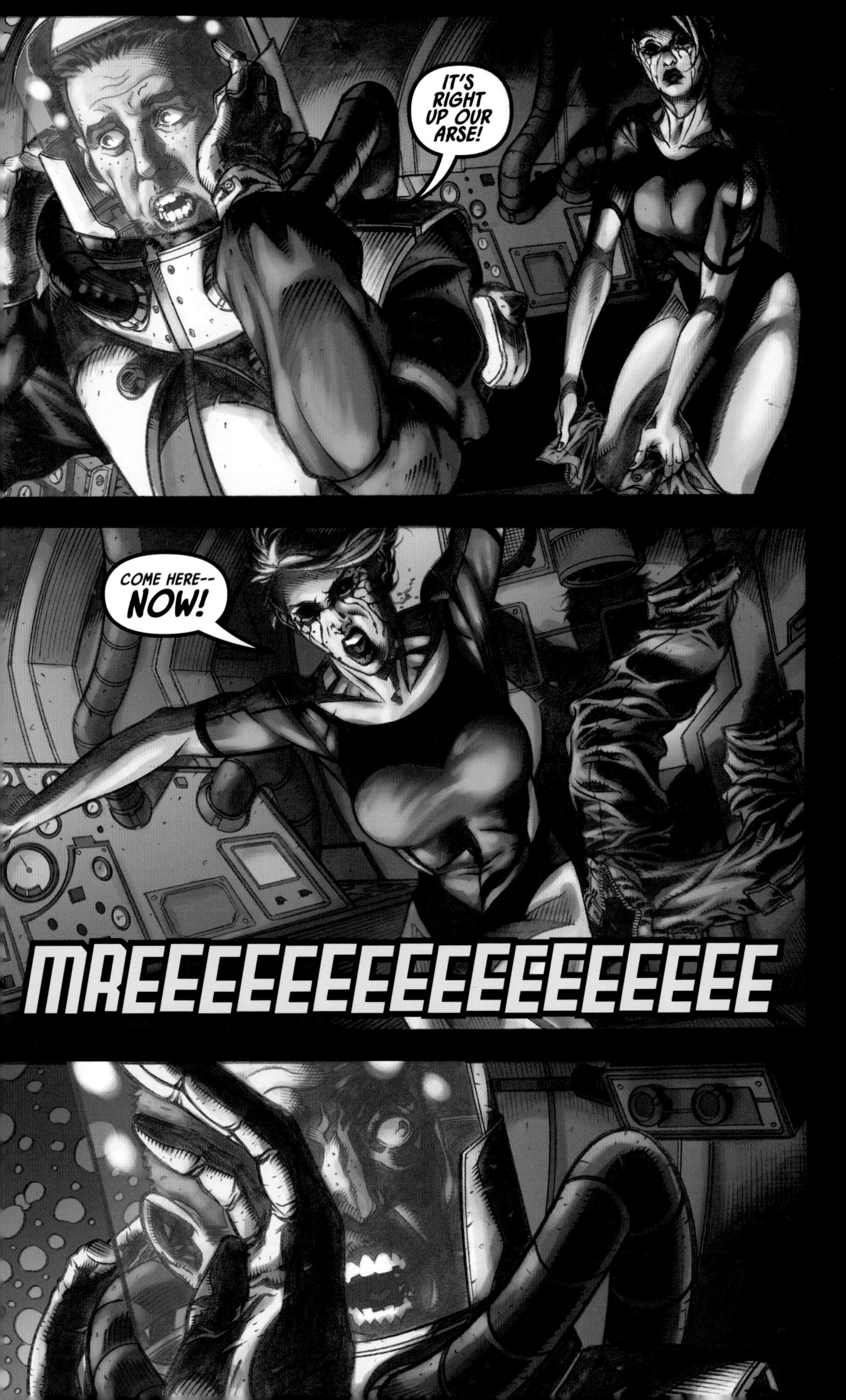
IT'S RIGHT UP OUR ARSE!
COME HERE-- NOW!
MREEEEEEEEEEEEEEEEEE

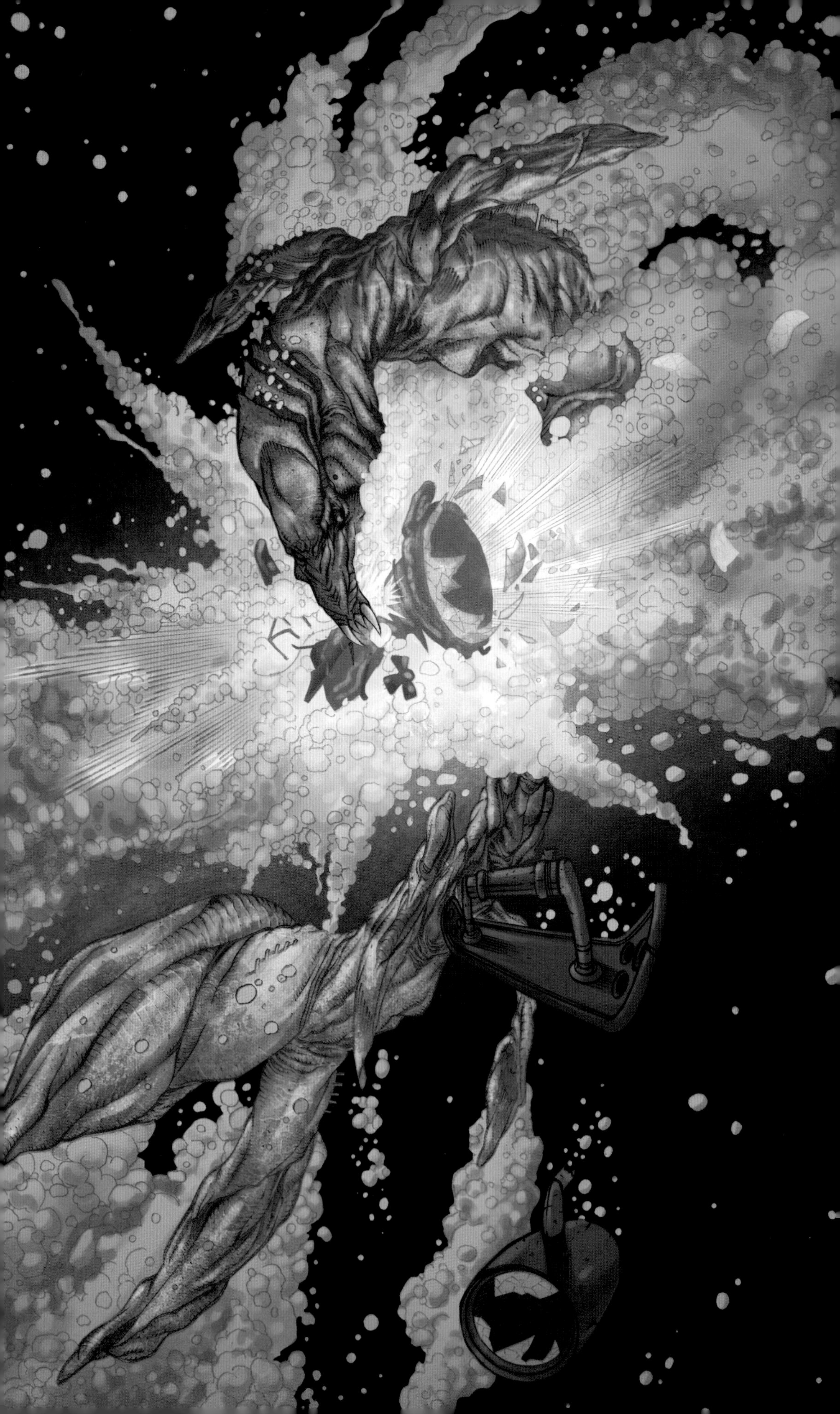

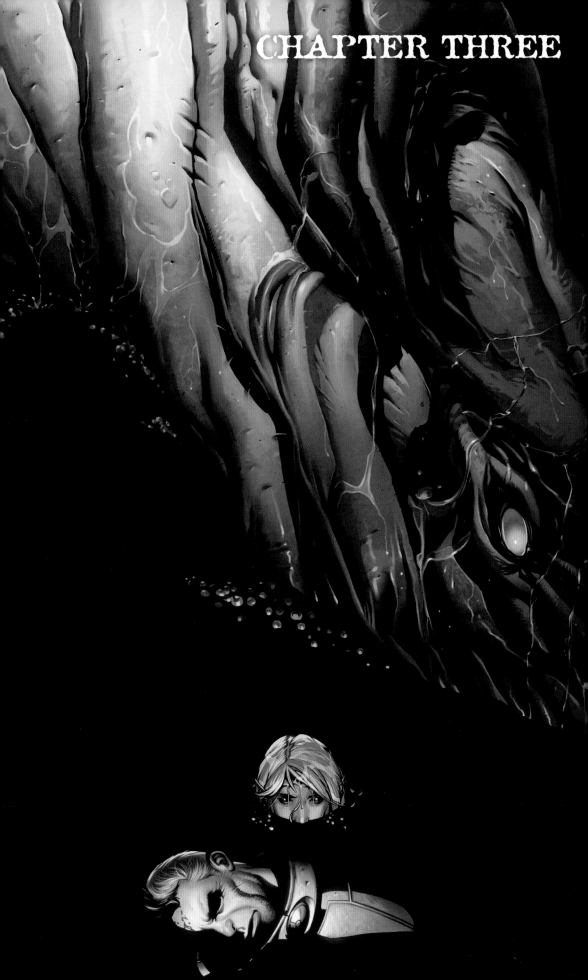

CHAPTER THREE

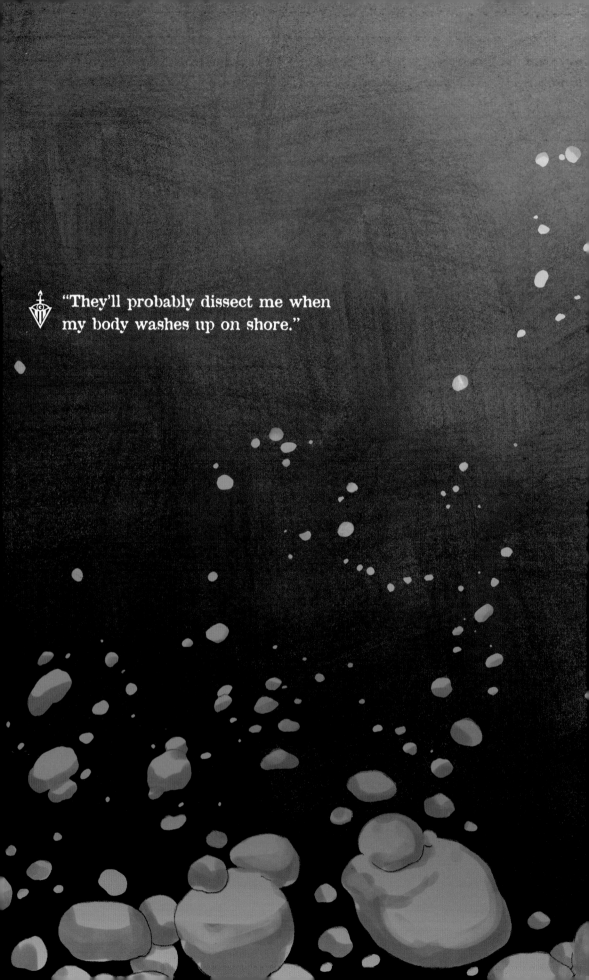

"They'll probably dissect me when my body washes up on shore."

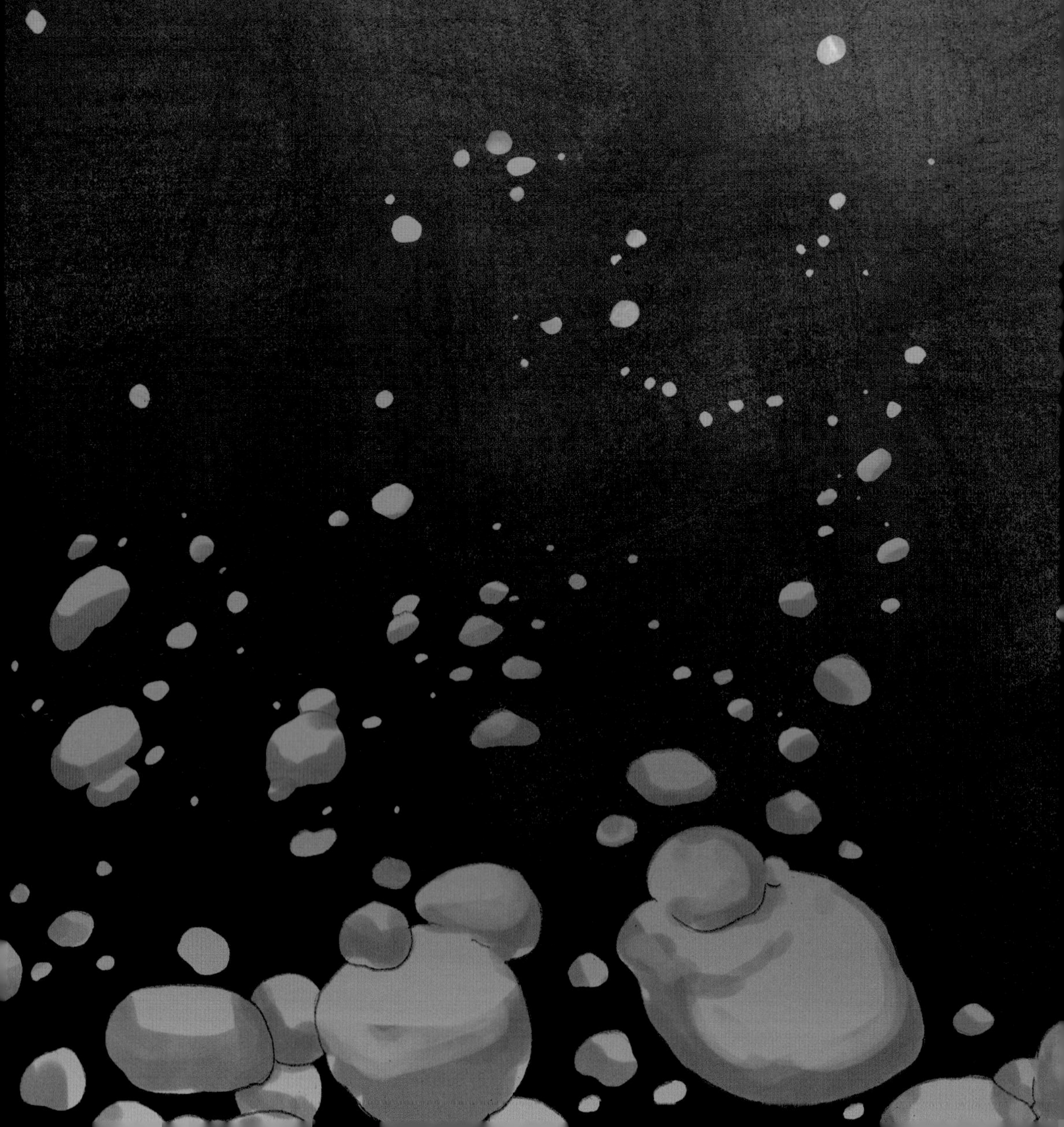

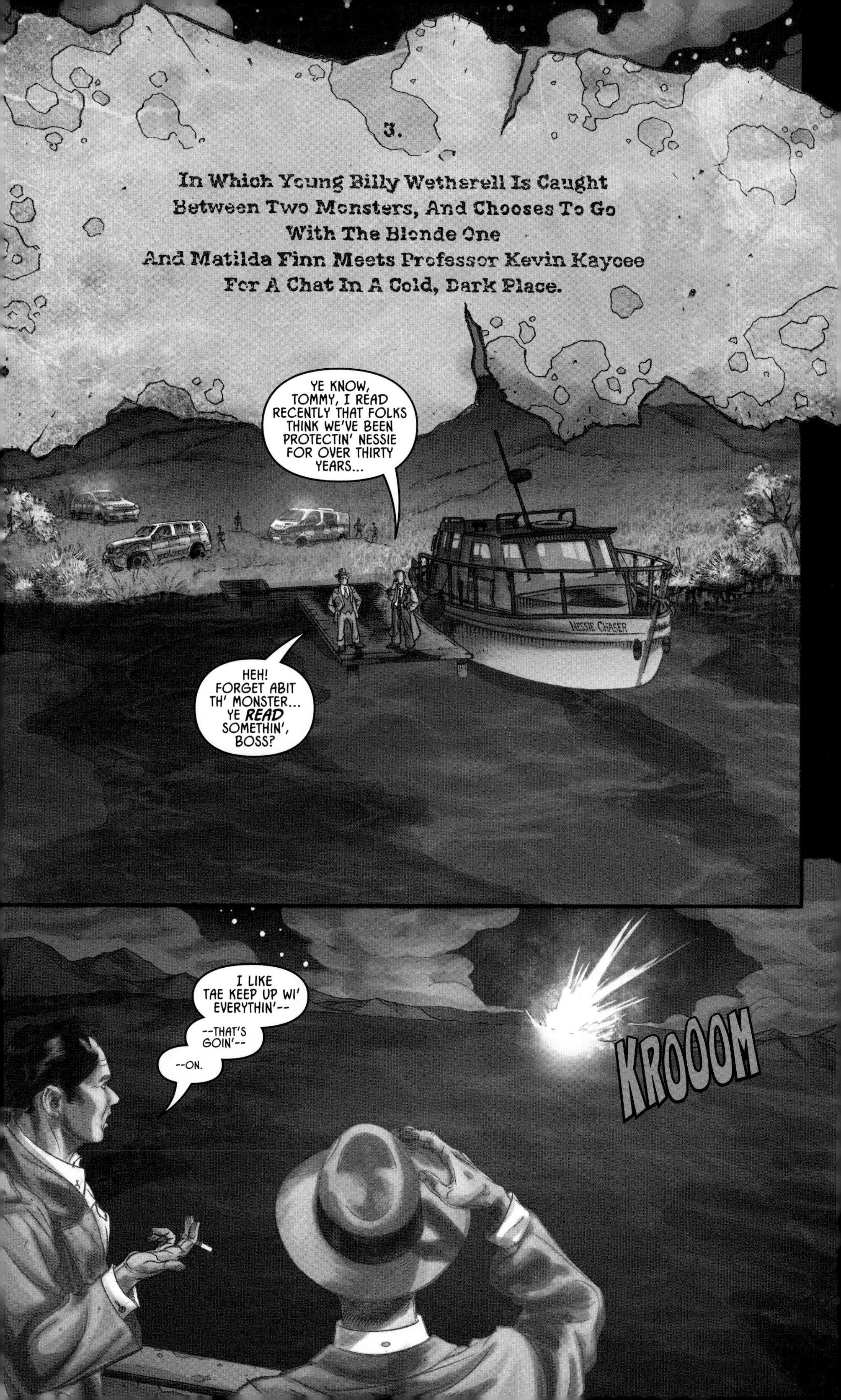

3.
In Which Young Billy Wetherell Is Caught Between Two Monsters, And Chooses To Go With The Blonde One And Matilda Finn Meets Professor Kevin Kaycee For A Chat In A Cold, Dark Place.
YE KNOW, TOMMY, I READ RECENTLY THAT FOLKS THINK WE'VE BEEN PROTECTIN' NESSIE FOR OVER THIRTY YEARS...
HEH! FORGET ABIT TH' MONSTER... YE *READ* SOMETHIN', BOSS?
NESSIE CHASER
I LIKE TAE KEEP UP WI' EVERYTHIN'--
--THAT'S GOIN'--
--ON.
KROOOM

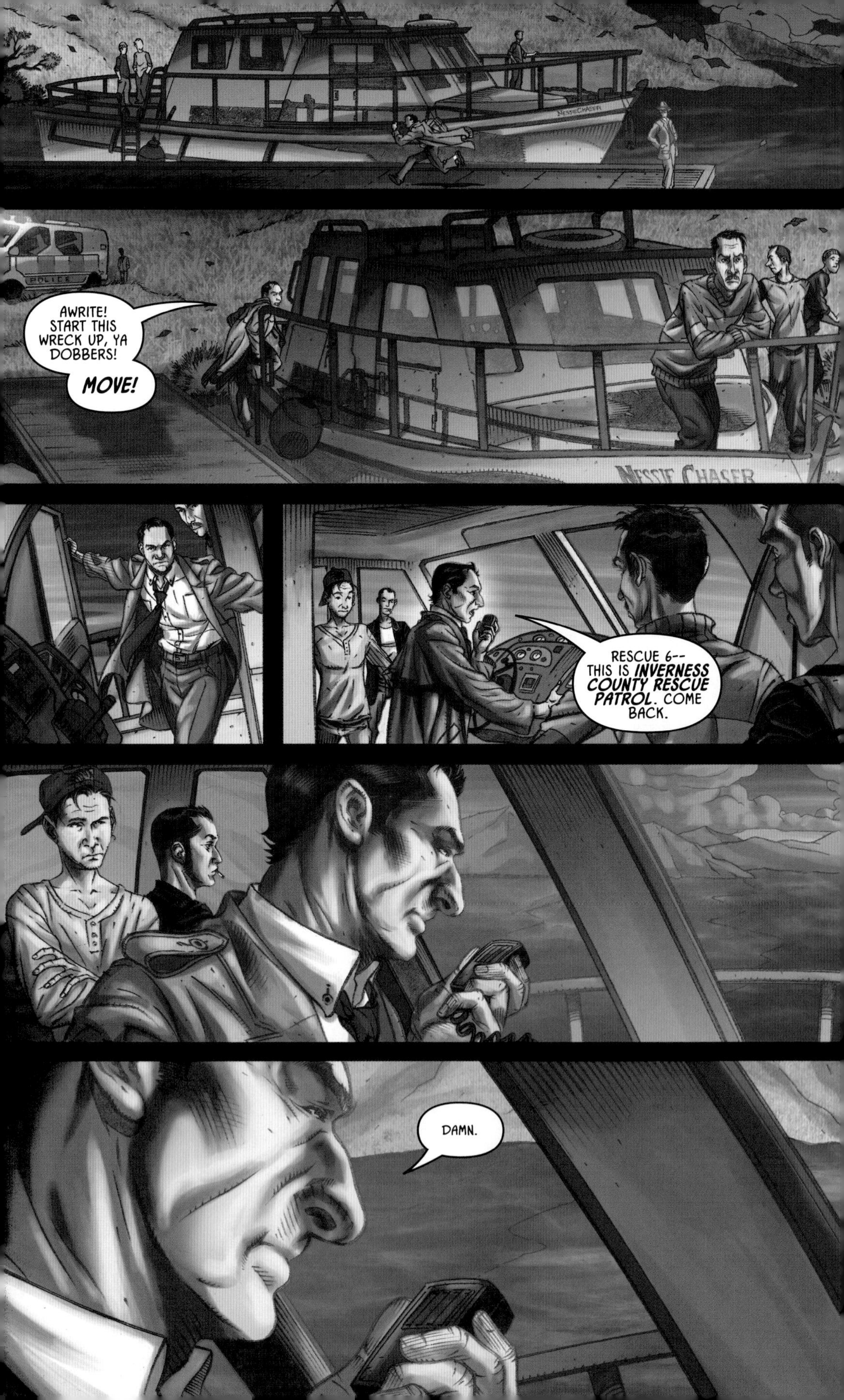
NESSIE CHASER
AWRITE! START THIS WRECK UP, YA DOBBERS!
MOVE!
NESSIE CHASER
RESCUE 6-- THIS IS INVERNESS COUNTY RESCUE PATROL. COME BACK.
DAMN.

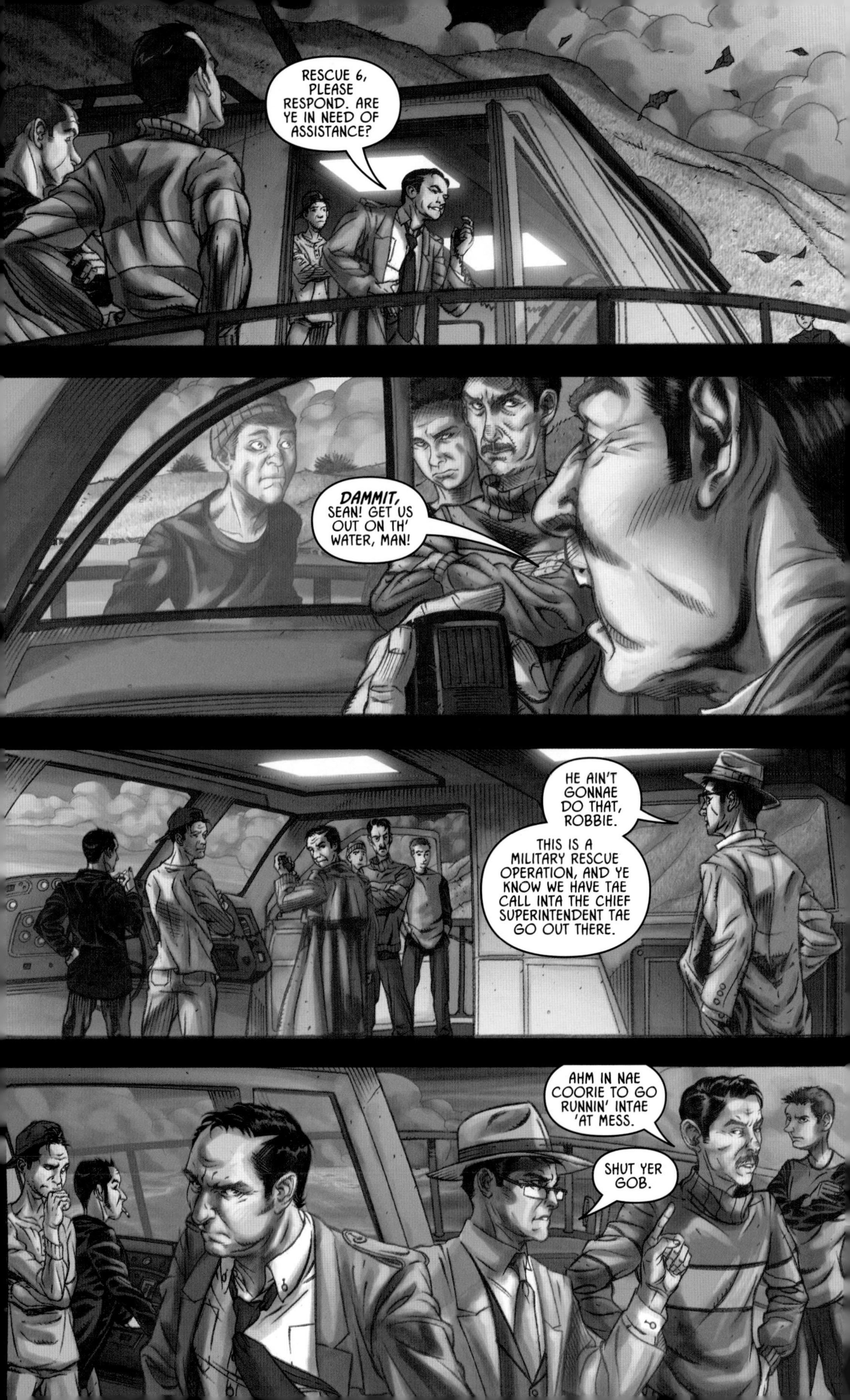
RESCUE 6, PLEASE RESPOND. ARE YE IN NEED OF ASSISTANCE?
DAMMIT, SEAN! GET US OUT ON TH' WATER, MAN!
HE AIN'T GONNAE DO THAT, ROBBIE.
THIS IS A MILITARY RESCUE OPERATION, AND YE KNOW WE HAVE TAE CALL INTA THE CHIEF SUPERINTENDENT TAE GO OUT THERE.
AHM IN NAE COORIE TO GO RUNNIN' INTAE 'AT MESS.
SHUT YER GOB.

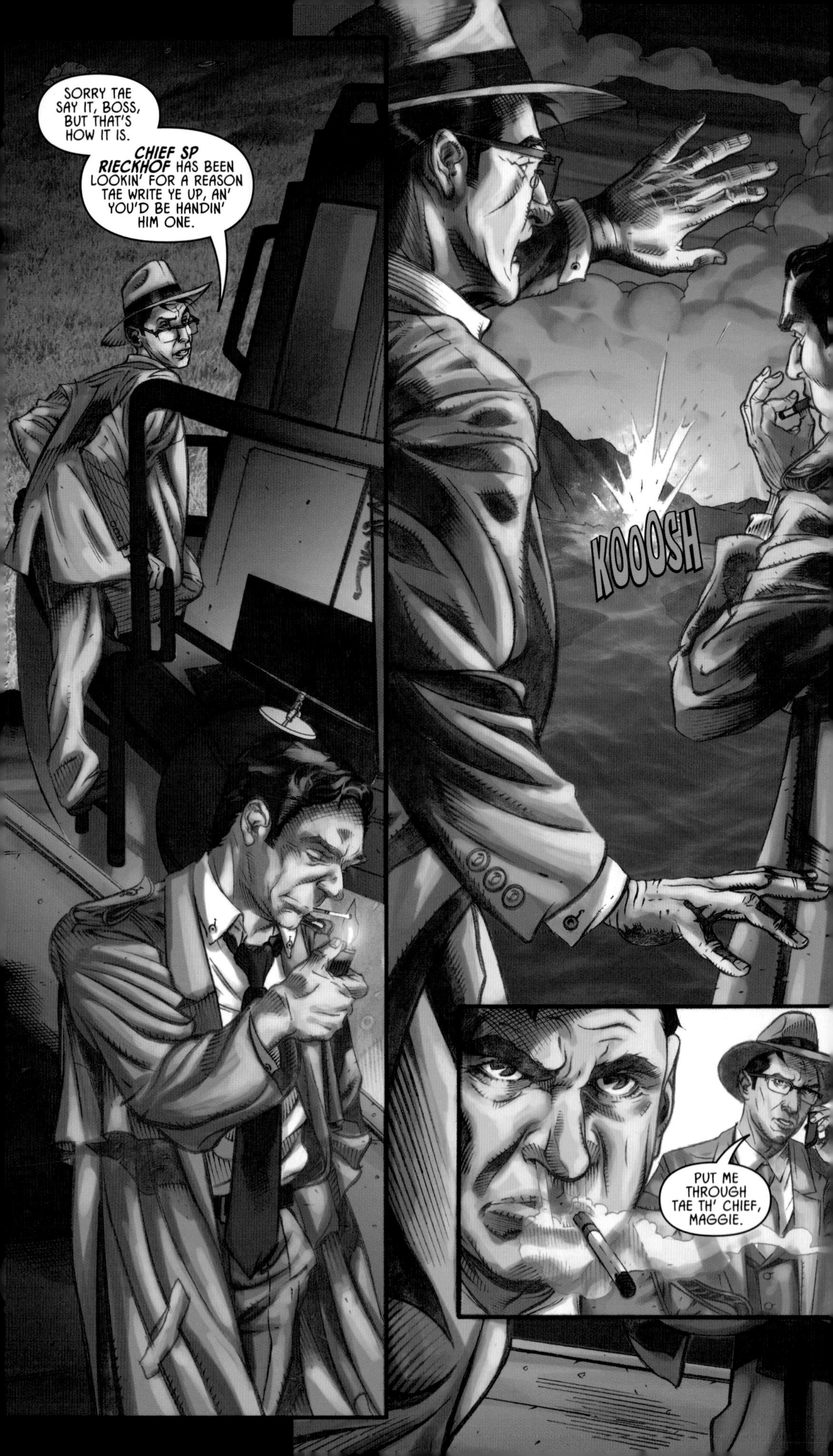
SORRY TAE SAY IT, BOSS, BUT THAT'S HOW IT IS.
CHIEF SP RIECKHOF HAS BEEN LOOKIN' FOR A REASON TAE WRITE YE UP, AN' YOU'D BE HANDIN' HIM ONE.
KOOOSH
PUT ME THROUGH TAE TH' CHIEF, MAGGIE.

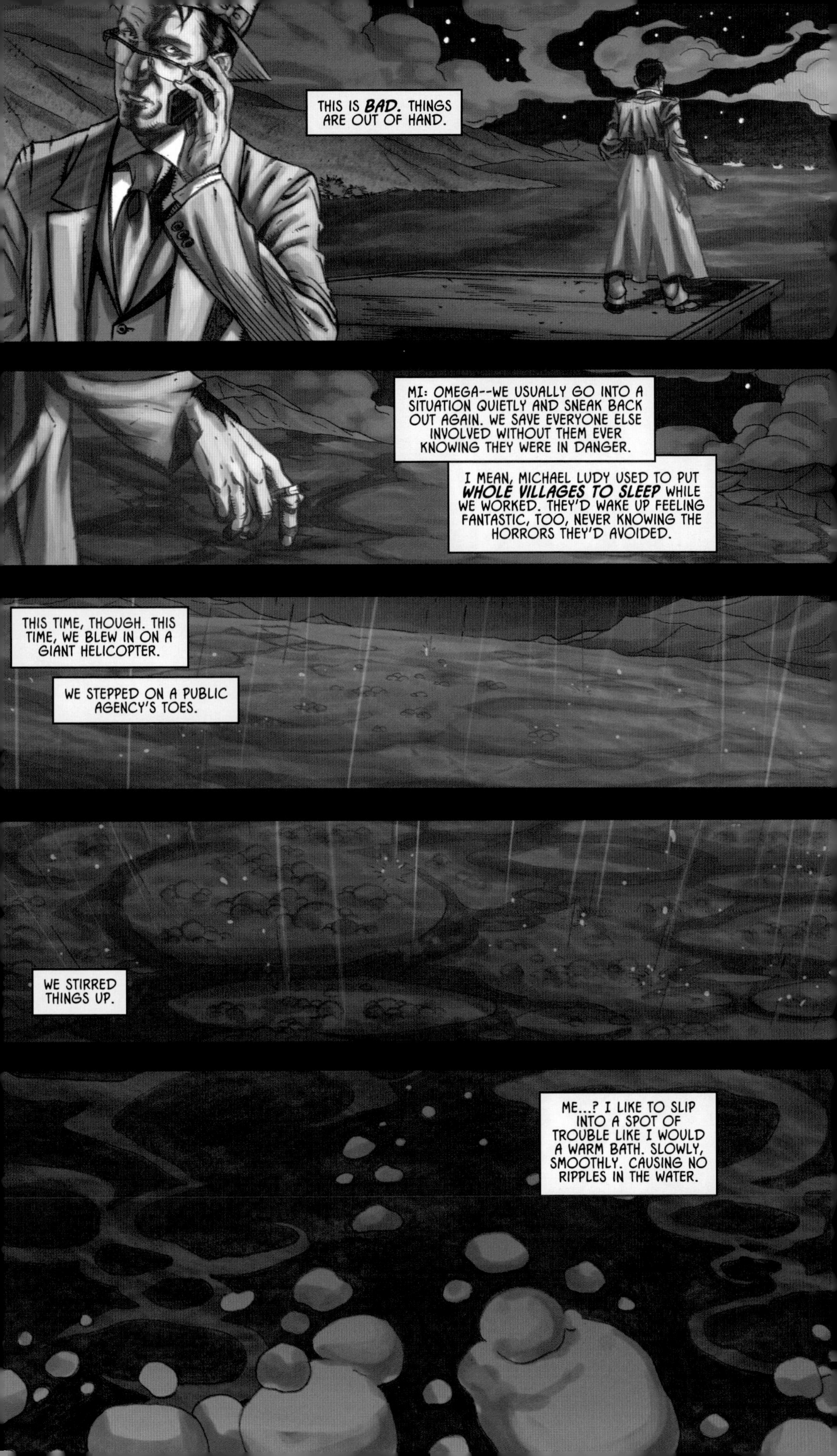
THIS IS BAD. THINGS ARE OUT OF HAND.
MI: OMEGA--WE USUALLY GO INTO A SITUATION QUIETLY AND SNEAK BACK OUT AGAIN. WE SAVE EVERYONE ELSE INVOLVED WITHOUT THEM EVER KNOWING THEY WERE IN DANGER.
I MEAN, MICHAEL LUDY USED TO PUT WHOLE VILLAGES TO SLEEP WHILE WE WORKED. THEY'D WAKE UP FEELING FANTASTIC, TOO, NEVER KNOWING THE HORRORS THEY'D AVOIDED.
THIS TIME, THOUGH. THIS TIME, WE BLEW IN ON A GIANT HELICOPTER.
WE STEPPED ON A PUBLIC AGENCY'S TOES.
WE STIRRED THINGS UP.
ME...? I LIKE TO SLIP INTO A SPOT OF TROUBLE LIKE I WOULD A WARM BATH. SLOWLY, SMOOTHLY. CAUSING NO RIPPLES IN THE WATER.

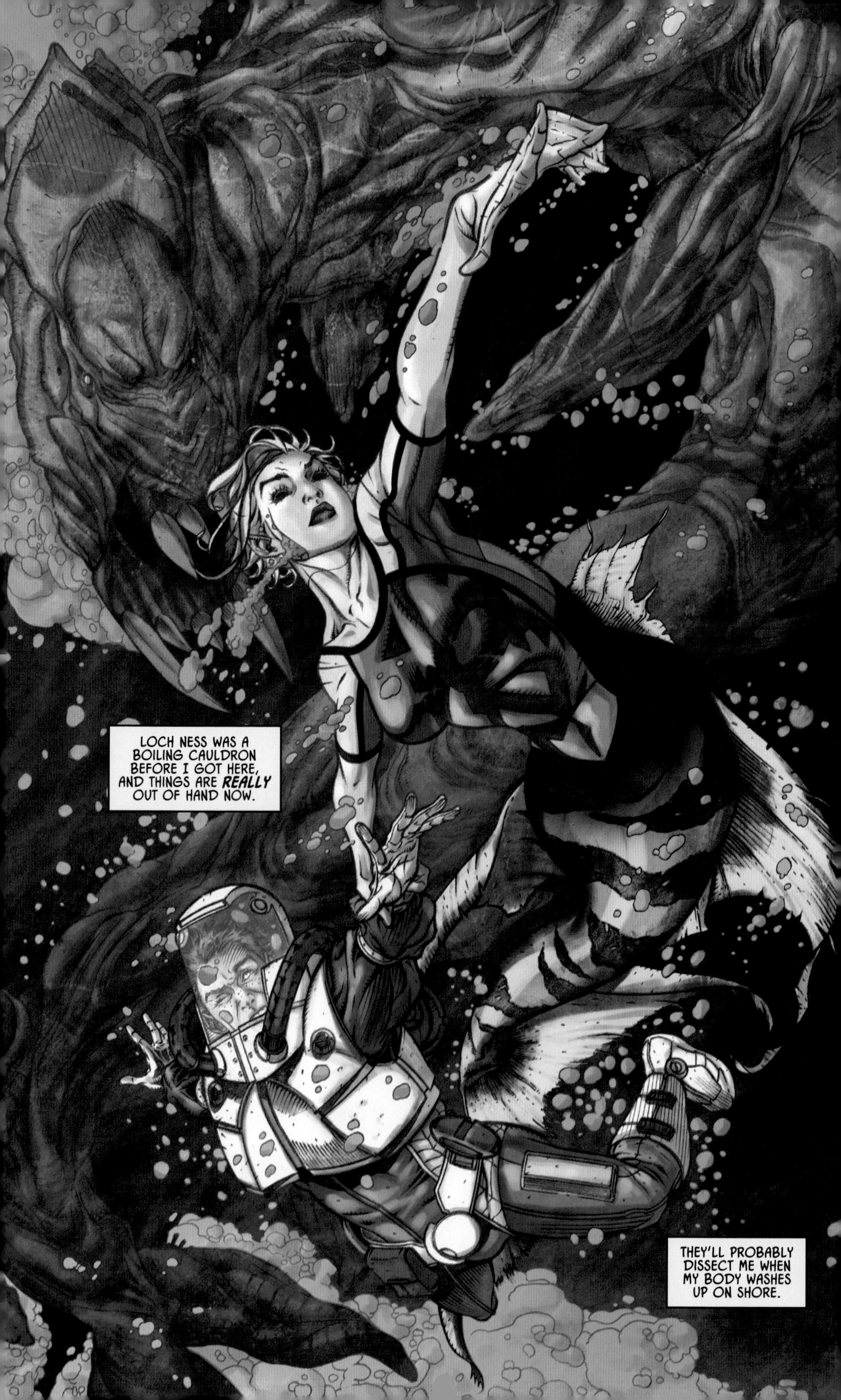
LOCH NESS WAS A BOILING CAULDRON BEFORE I GOT HERE, AND THINGS ARE *REALLY* OUT OF HAND NOW.
THEY'LL PROBABLY DISSECT ME WHEN MY BODY WASHES UP ON SHORE.

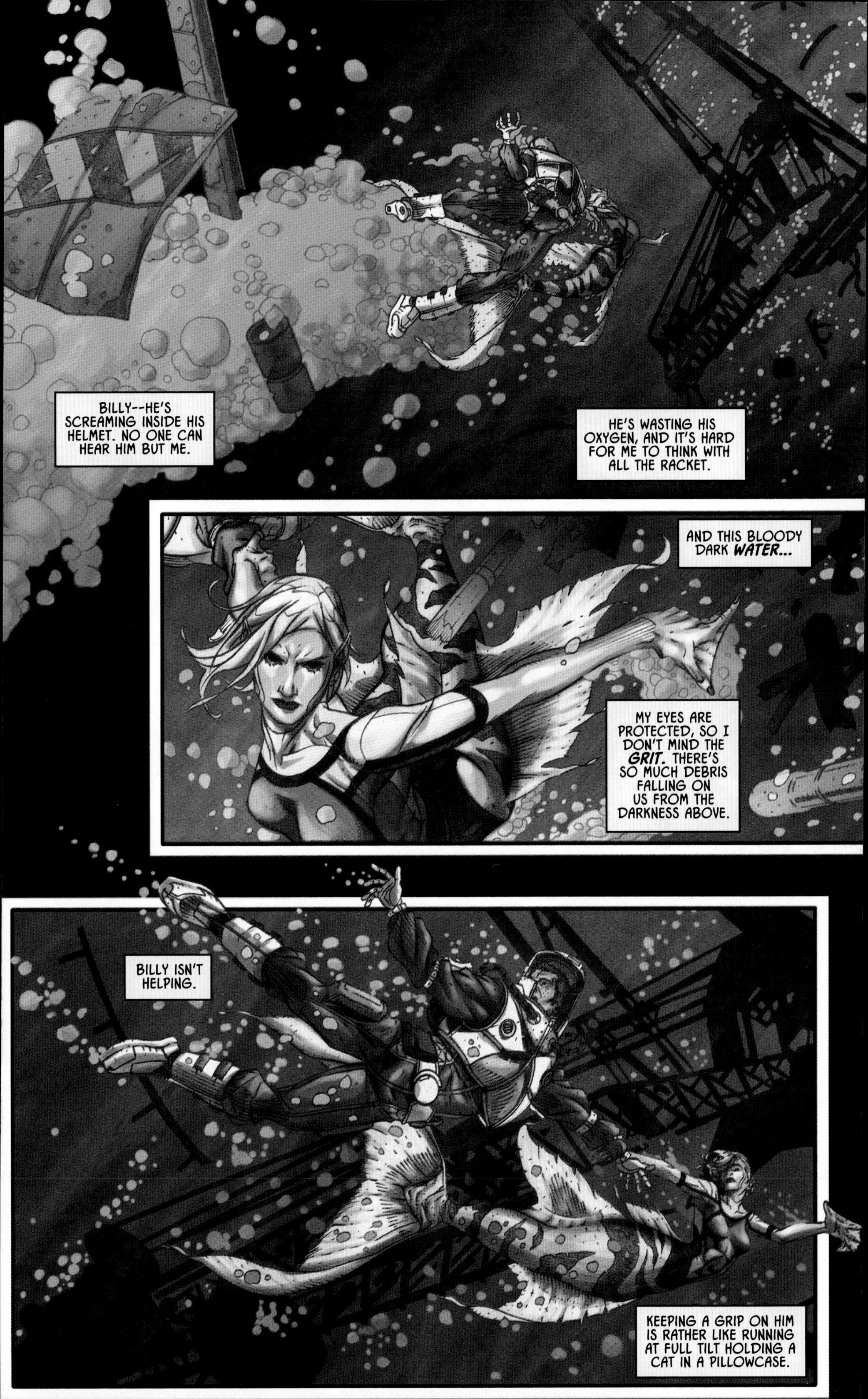
BILLY--HE'S SCREAMING INSIDE HIS HELMET. NO ONE CAN HEAR HIM BUT ME.
HE'S WASTING HIS OXYGEN, AND IT'S HARD FOR ME TO THINK WITH ALL THE RACKET.
AND THIS BLOODY DARK WATER...
MY EYES ARE PROTECTED, SO I DON'T MIND THE GRIT. THERE'S SO MUCH DEBRIS FALLING ON US FROM THE DARKNESS ABOVE.
BILLY ISN'T HELPING.
KEEPING A GRIP ON HIM IS RATHER LIKE RUNNING AT FULL TILT HOLDING A CAT IN A PILLOWCASE.

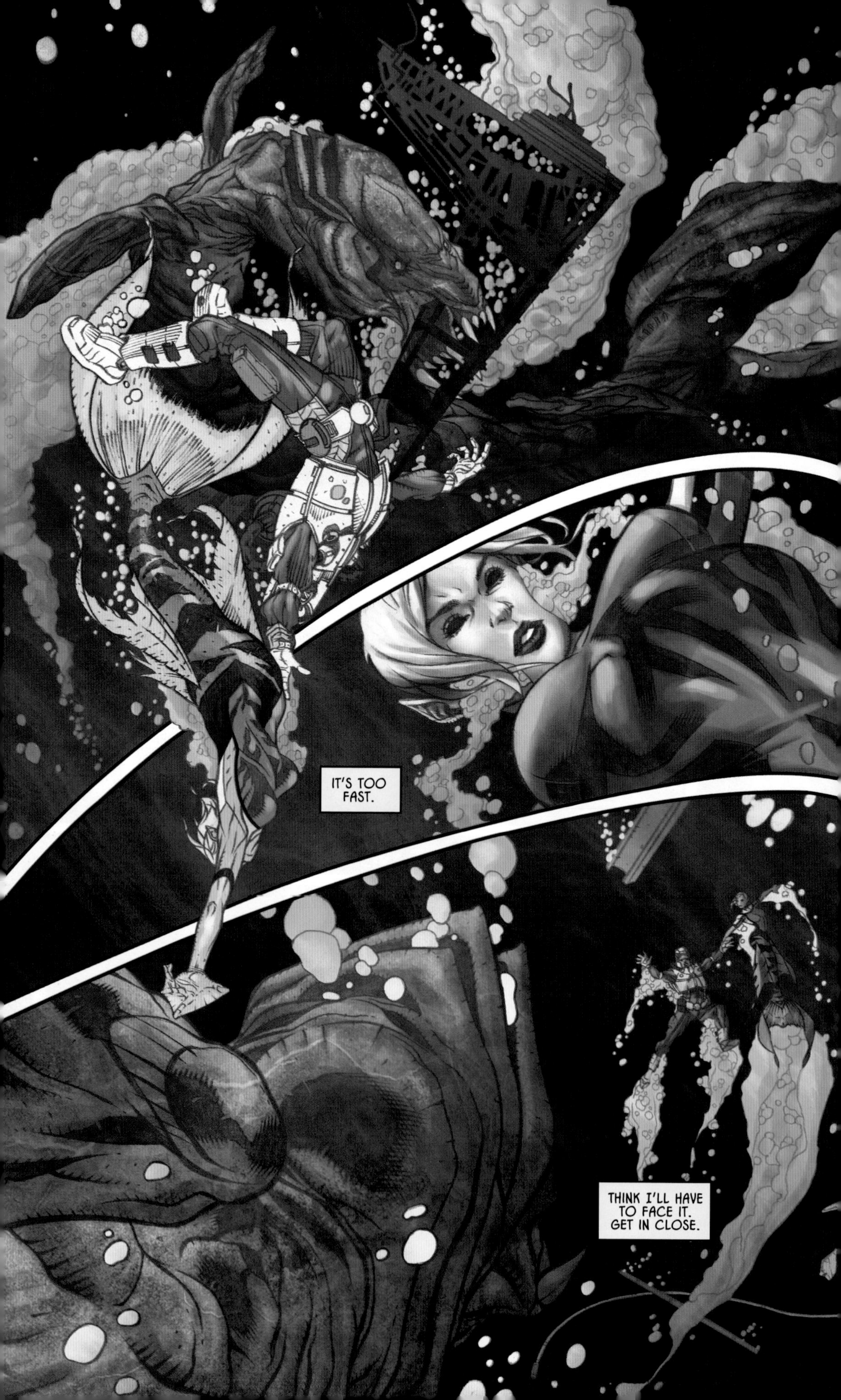
IT'S TOO
FAST.
THINK I'LL HAVE
TO FACE IT.
GET IN CLOSE.

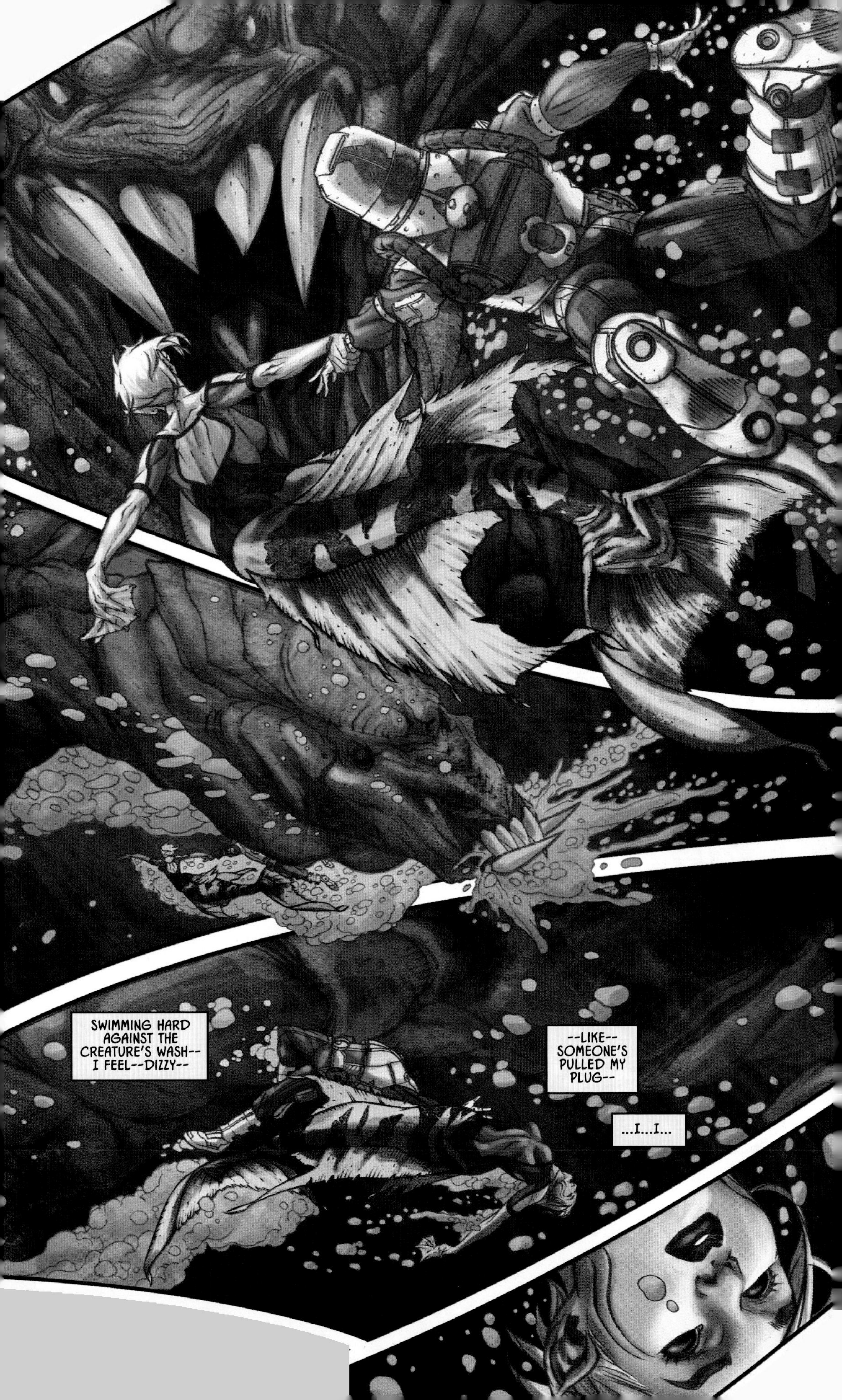
SWIMMING HARD AGAINST THE CREATURE'S WASH--I FEEL--DIZZY--
--LIKE--SOMEONE'S PULLED MY PLUG--
...I...I...

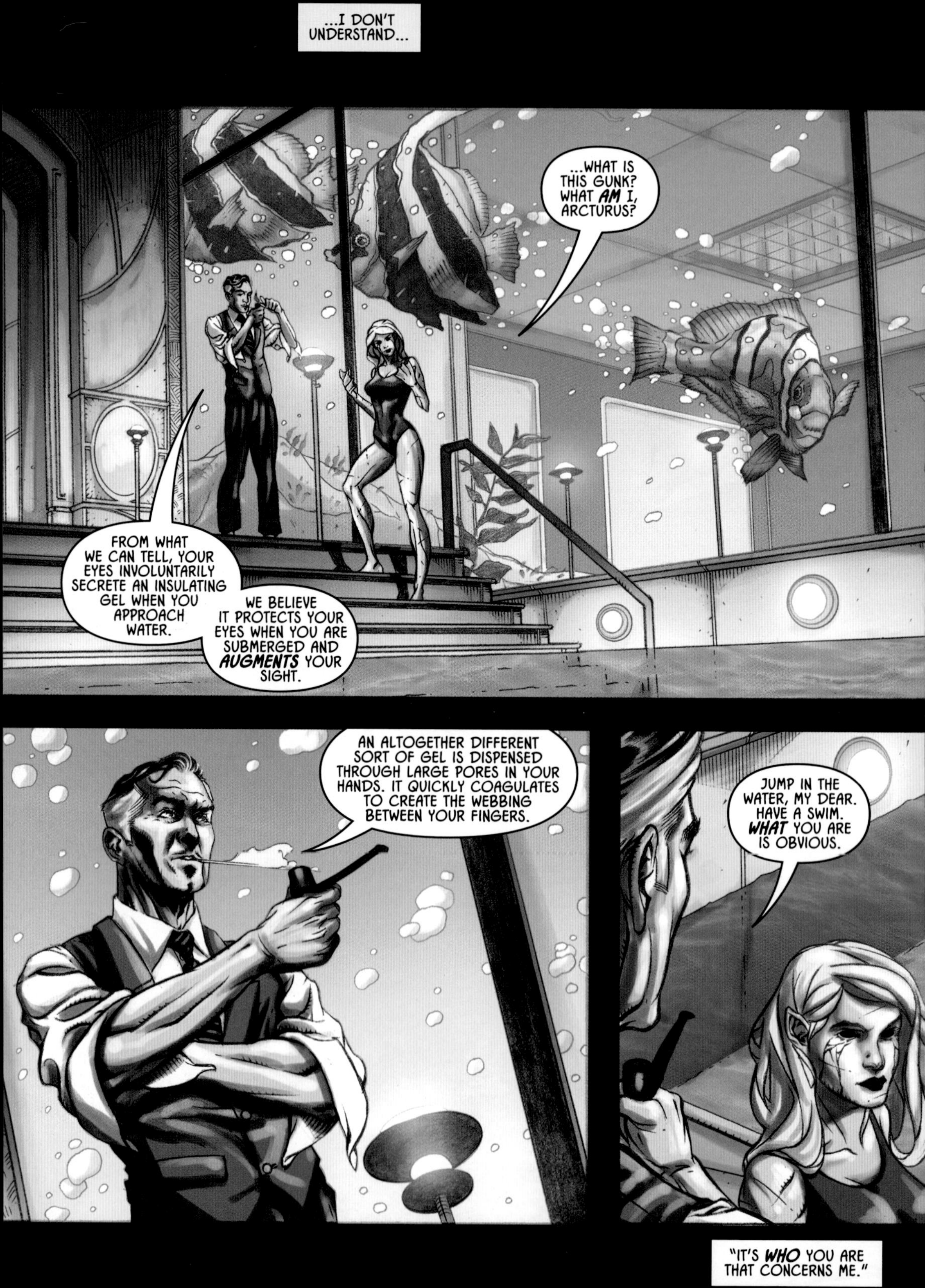

...I DON'T UNDERSTAND...
...WHAT IS THIS GUNK? WHAT AM I, ARCTURUS?
FROM WHAT WE CAN TELL, YOUR EYES INVOLUNTARILY SECRETE AN INSULATING GEL WHEN YOU APPROACH WATER.
WE BELIEVE IT PROTECTS YOUR EYES WHEN YOU ARE SUBMERGED AND AUGMENTS YOUR SIGHT.
AN ALTOGETHER DIFFERENT SORT OF GEL IS DISPENSED THROUGH LARGE PORES IN YOUR HANDS. IT QUICKLY COAGULATES TO CREATE THE WEBBING BETWEEN YOUR FINGERS.
JUMP IN THE WATER, MY DEAR. HAVE A SWIM. WHAT YOU ARE IS OBVIOUS.
"IT'S WHO YOU ARE THAT CONCERNS ME."

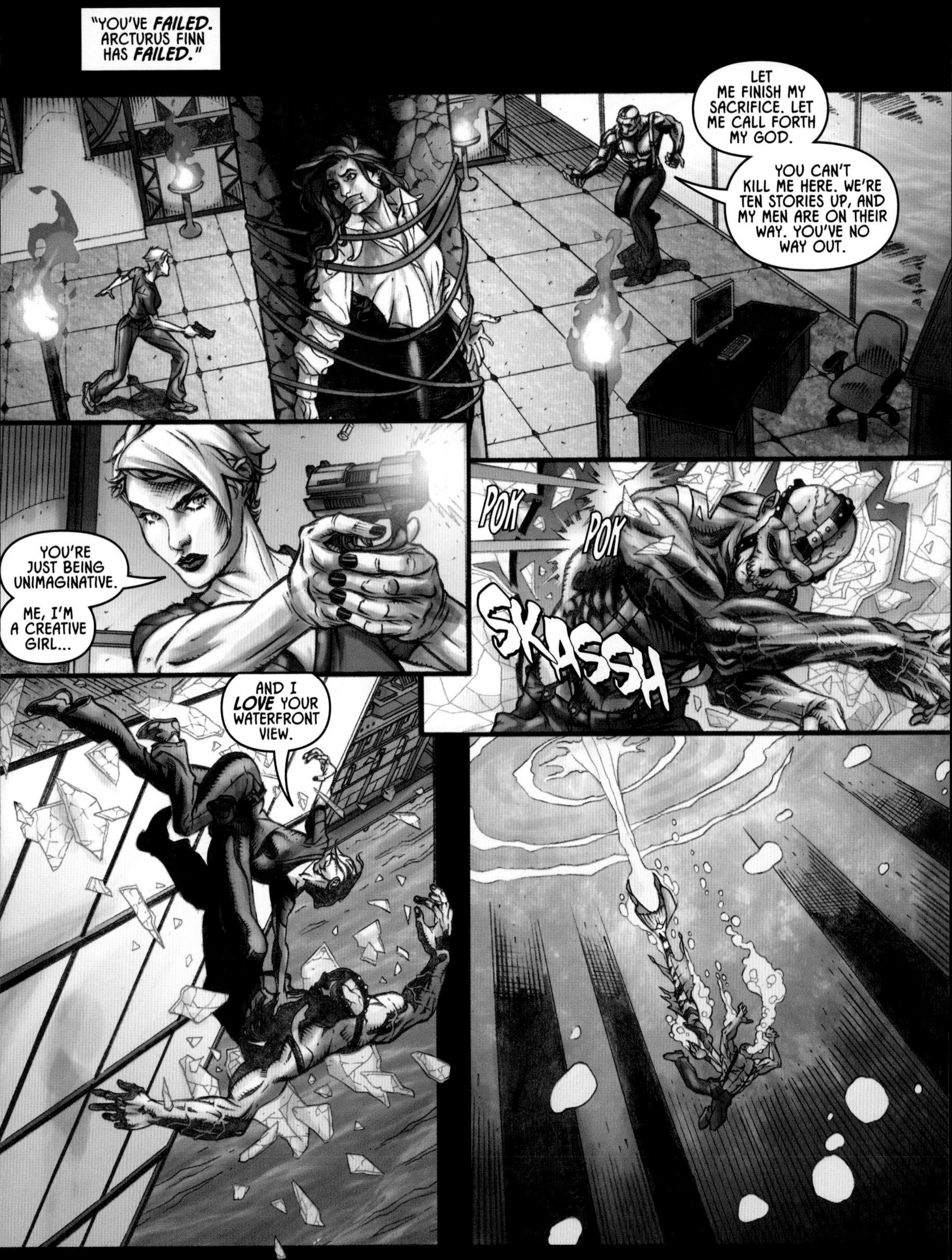
"YOU'VE FAILED. ARCTURUS FINN HAS FAILED."
LET ME FINISH MY SACRIFICE. LET ME CALL FORTH MY GOD.
YOU CAN'T KILL ME HERE. WE'RE TEN STORIES UP, AND MY MEN ARE ON THEIR WAY. YOU'VE NO WAY OUT.
YOU'RE JUST BEING UNIMAGINATIVE.
ME, I'M A CREATIVE GIRL...
POK
POK
SKASSH
AND I LOVE YOUR WATERFRONT VIEW.

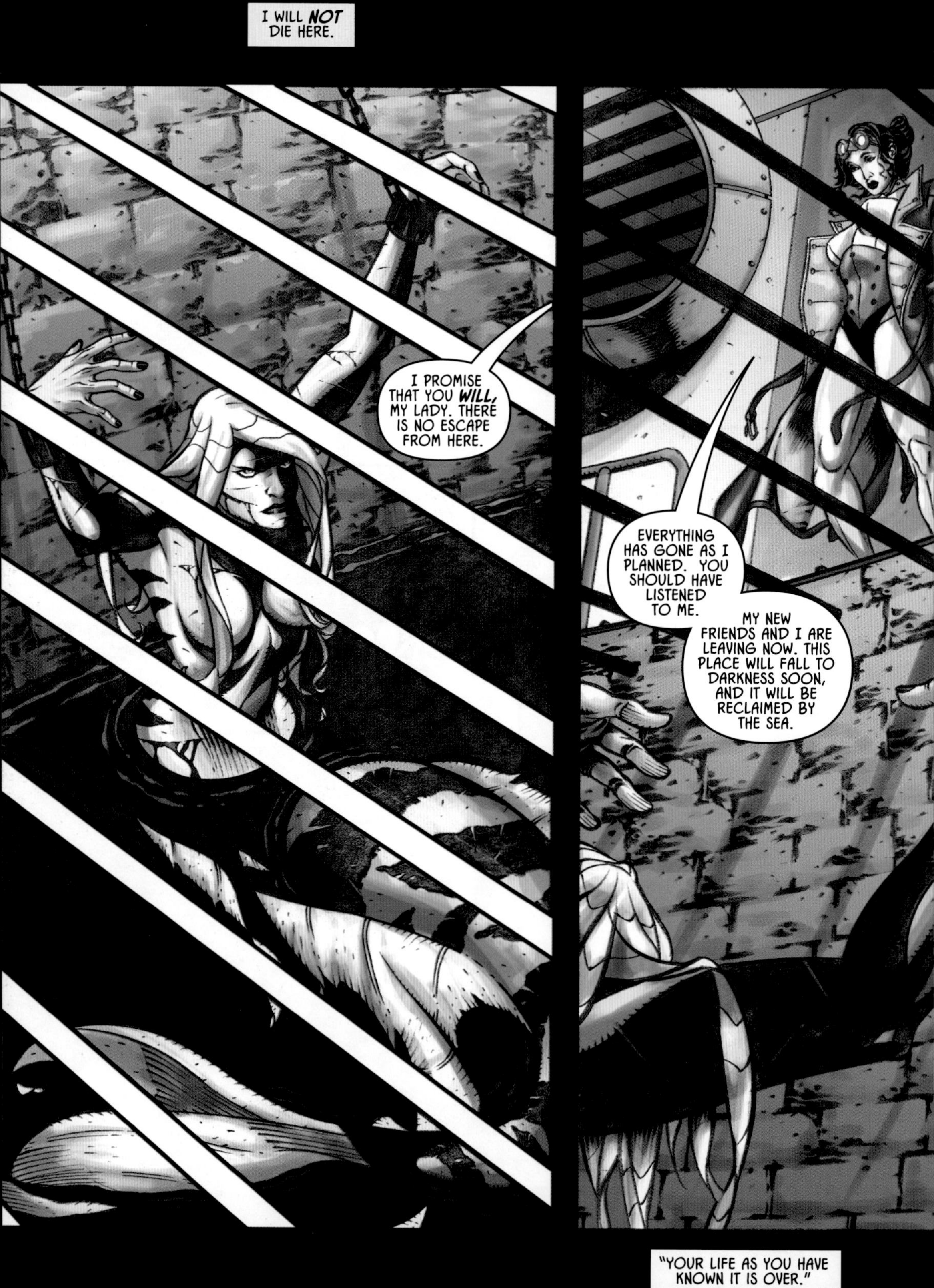
I WILL NOT DIE HERE.
I PROMISE THAT YOU WILL, MY LADY. THERE IS NO ESCAPE FROM HERE.
EVERYTHING HAS GONE AS I PLANNED. YOU SHOULD HAVE LISTENED TO ME.
MY NEW FRIENDS AND I ARE LEAVING NOW. THIS PLACE WILL FALL TO DARKNESS SOON, AND IT WILL BE RECLAIMED BY THE SEA.
"YOUR LIFE AS YOU HAVE KNOWN IT IS OVER."

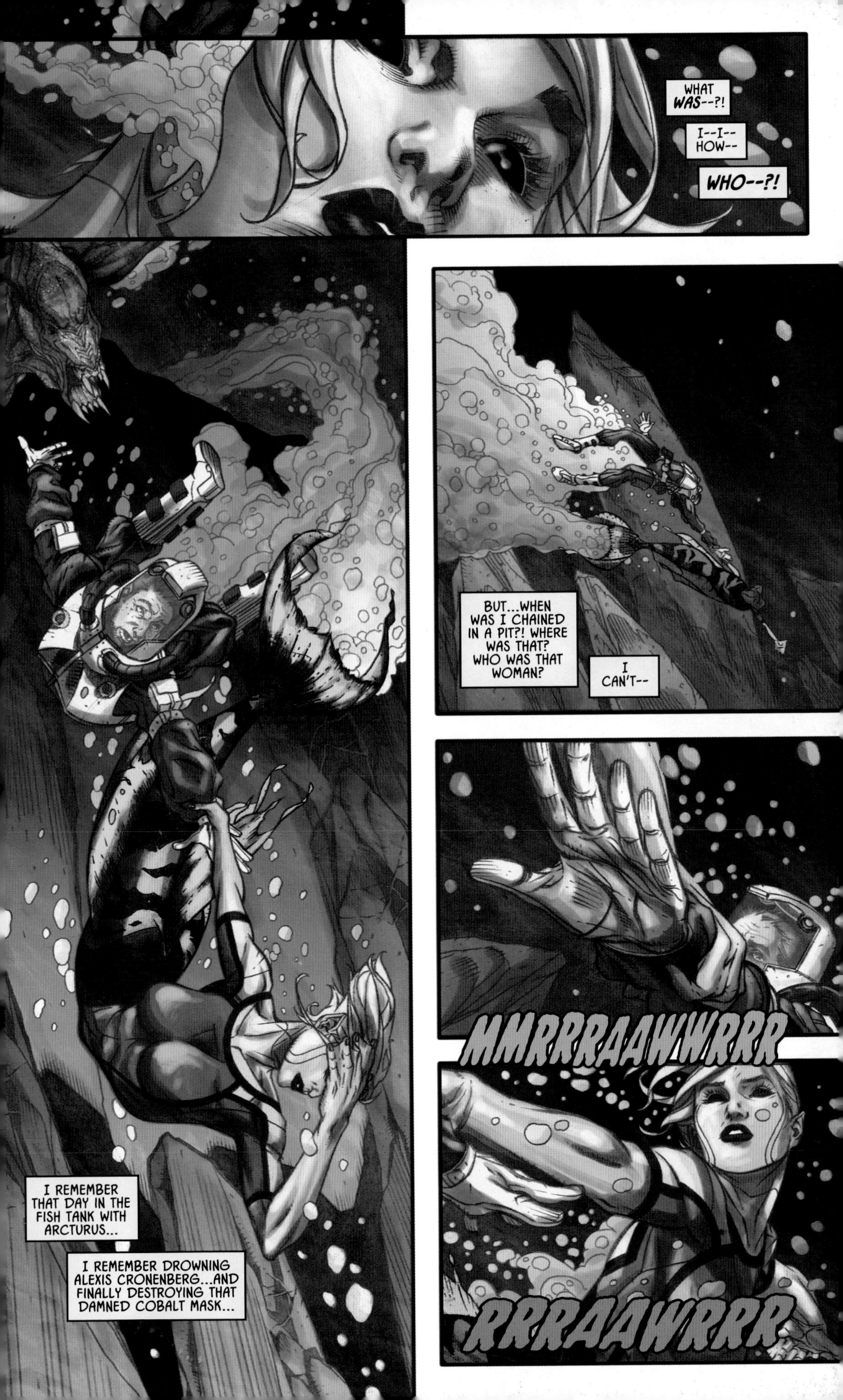

WHAT WAS--?!
I--I-- HOW--
WHO--?!
I REMEMBER THAT DAY IN THE FISH TANK WITH ARCTURUS...
I REMEMBER DROWNING ALEXIS CRONENBERG...AND FINALLY DESTROYING THAT DAMNED COBALT MASK...
BUT...WHEN WAS I CHAINED IN A PIT?! WHERE WAS THAT? WHO WAS THAT WOMAN?
I CAN'T--
MMRRRAAWWRRR
RRRAAWRRR

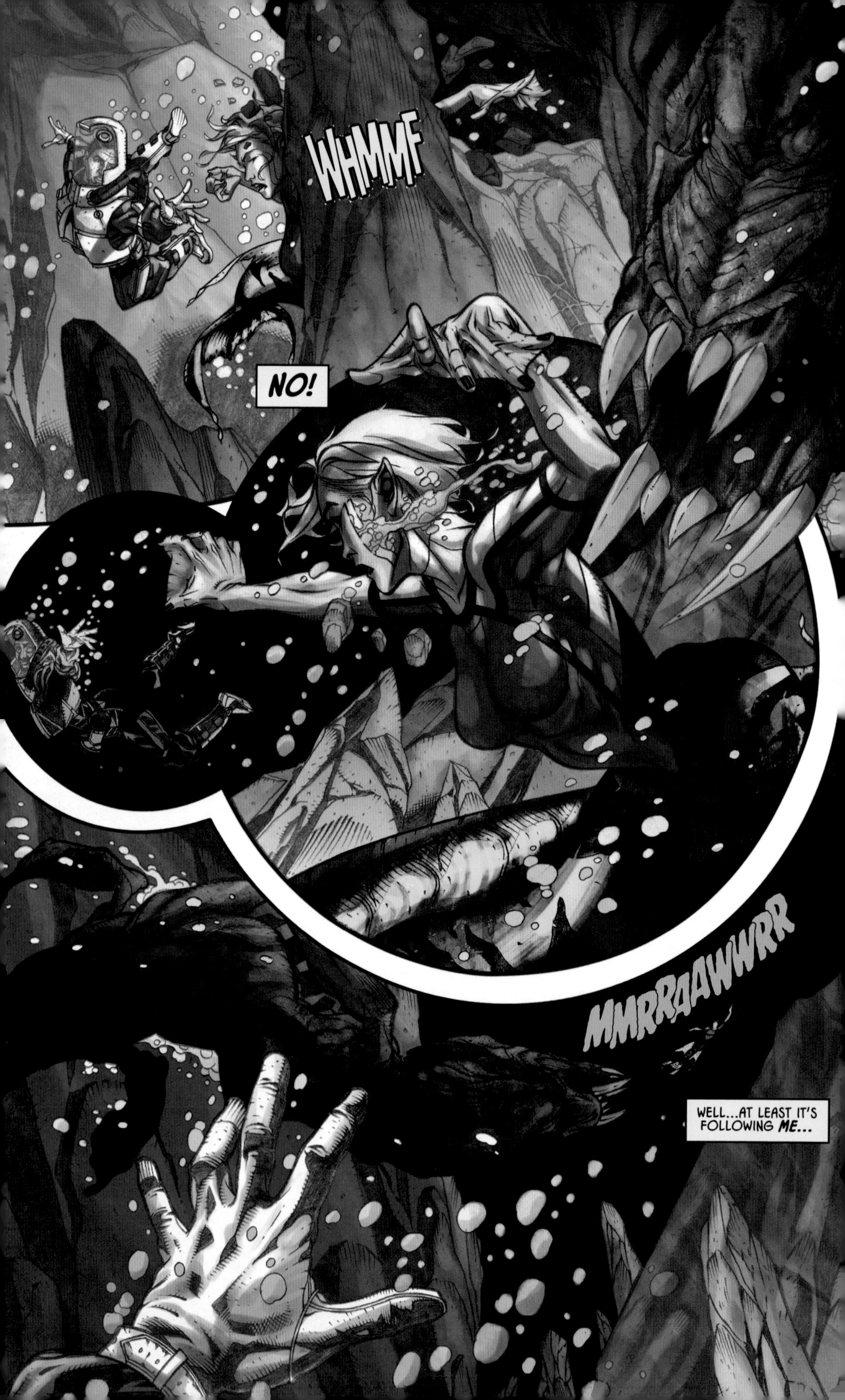
WHMMF
NO!
MMRRAAWWRR
WELL...AT LEAST IT'S FOLLOWING ME...

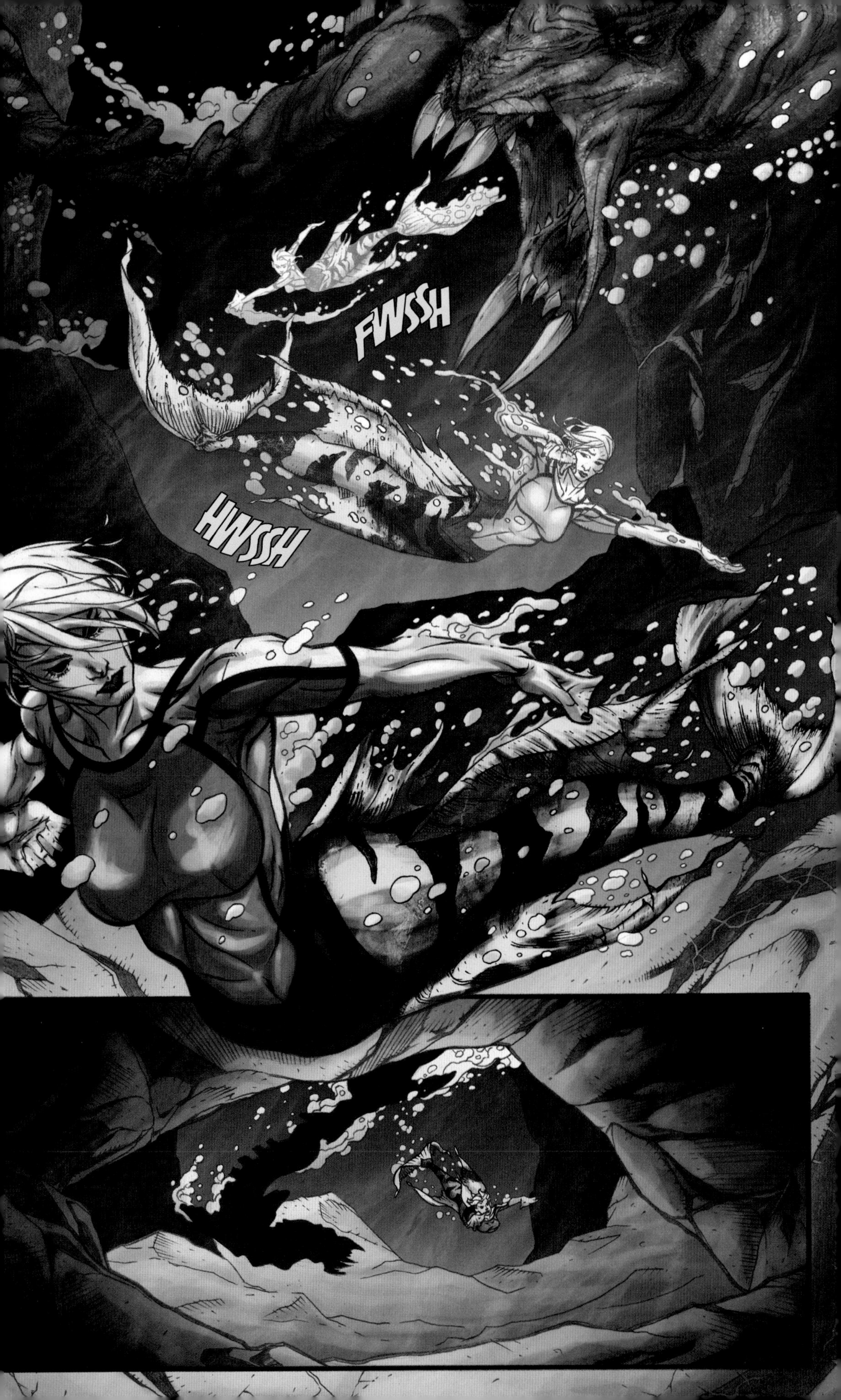
FWSSH
HWSSH

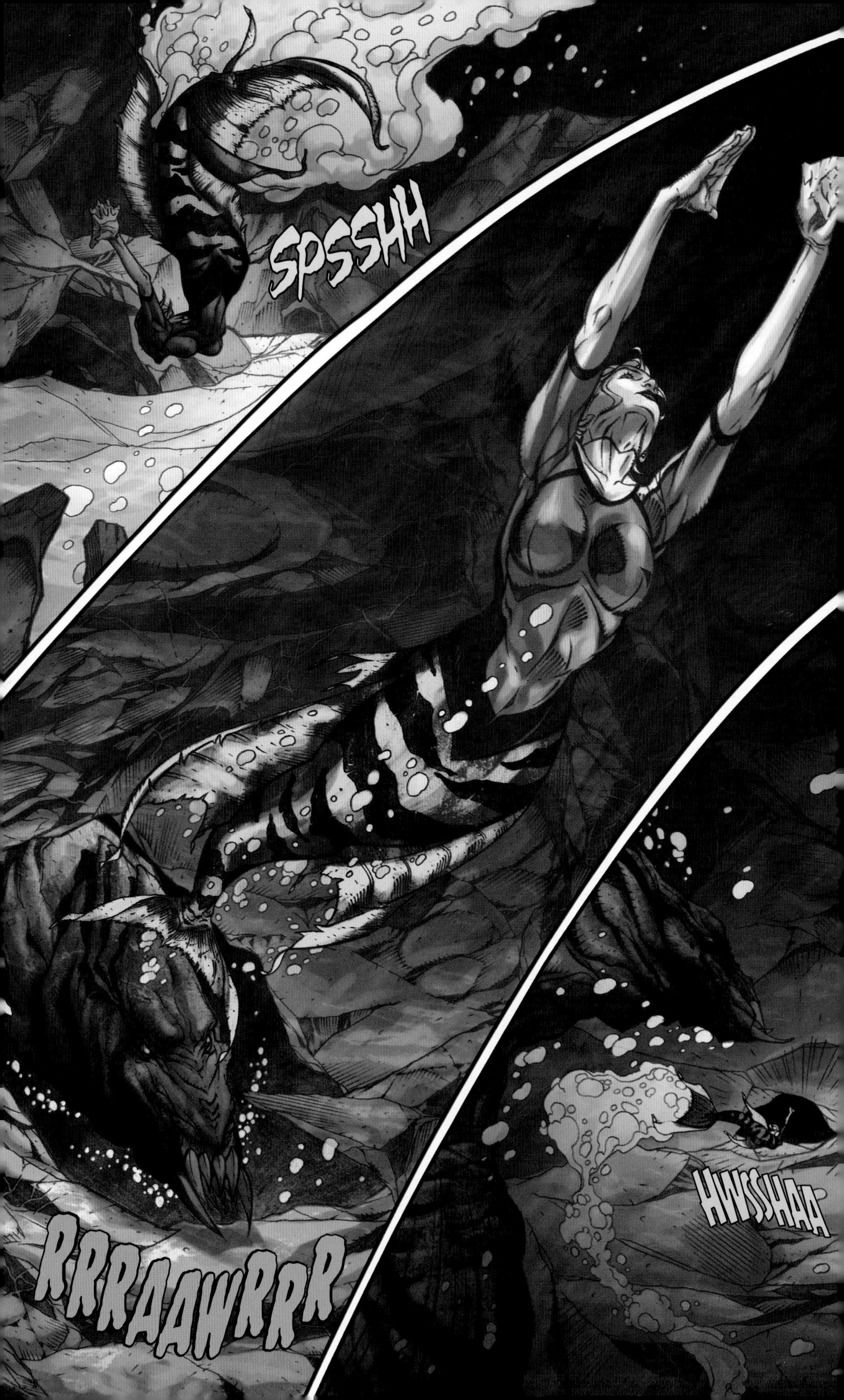
SPSSHH
RRRAAAWRRR
HWSSHAA

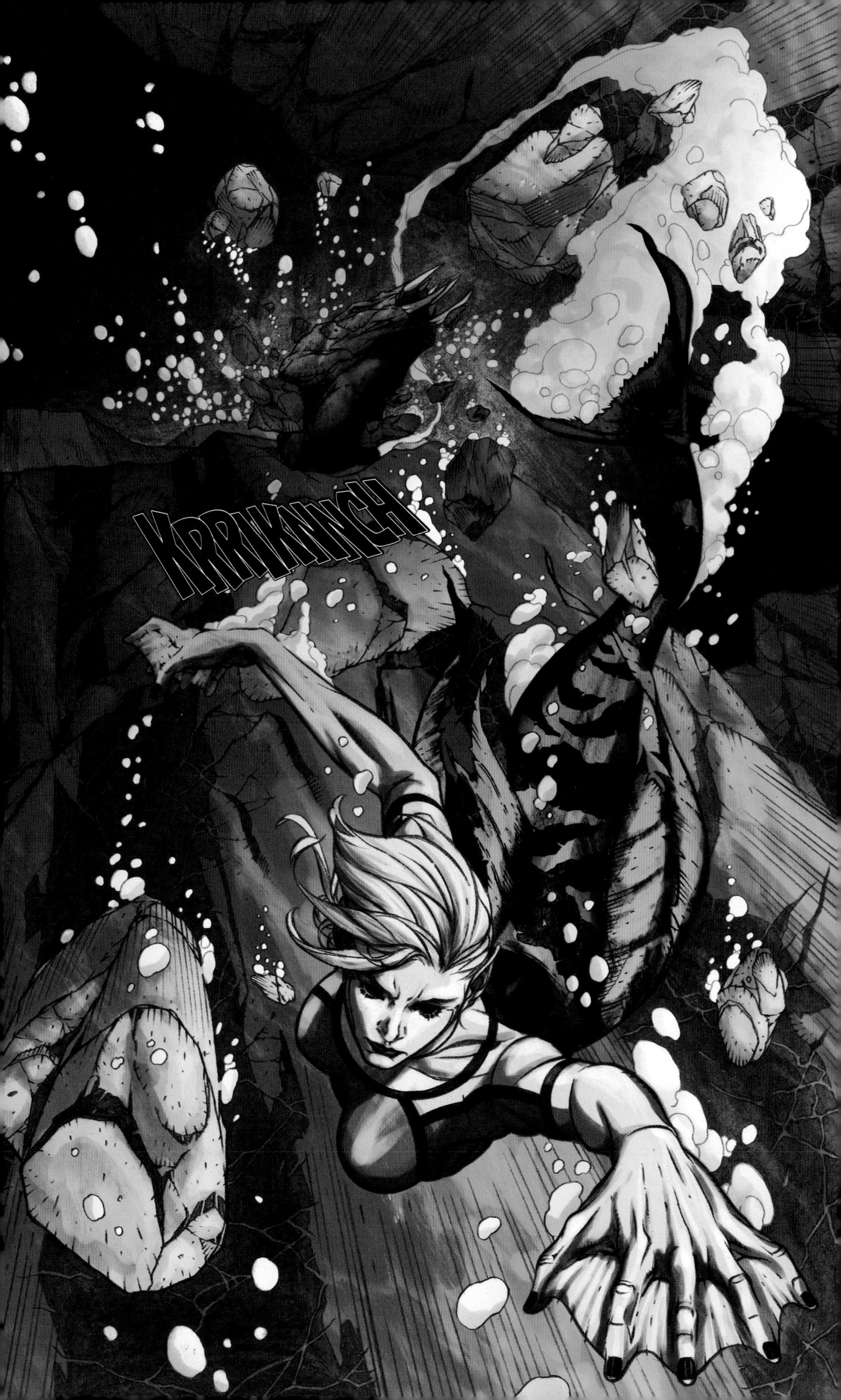
KRRKNNCH

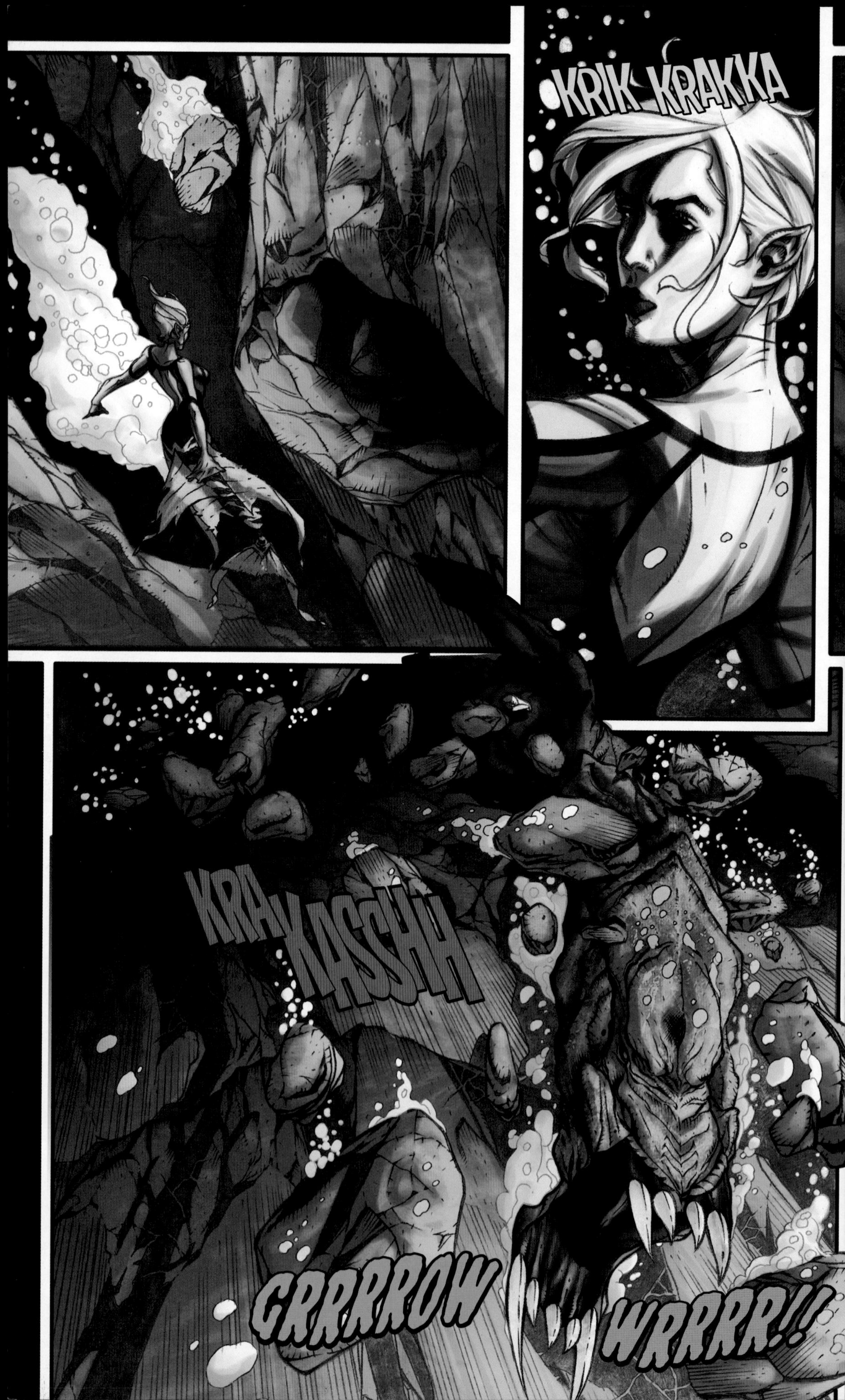
KRIK KRAKKA
KRAKASHH
GRRRROW
WRRRR!!

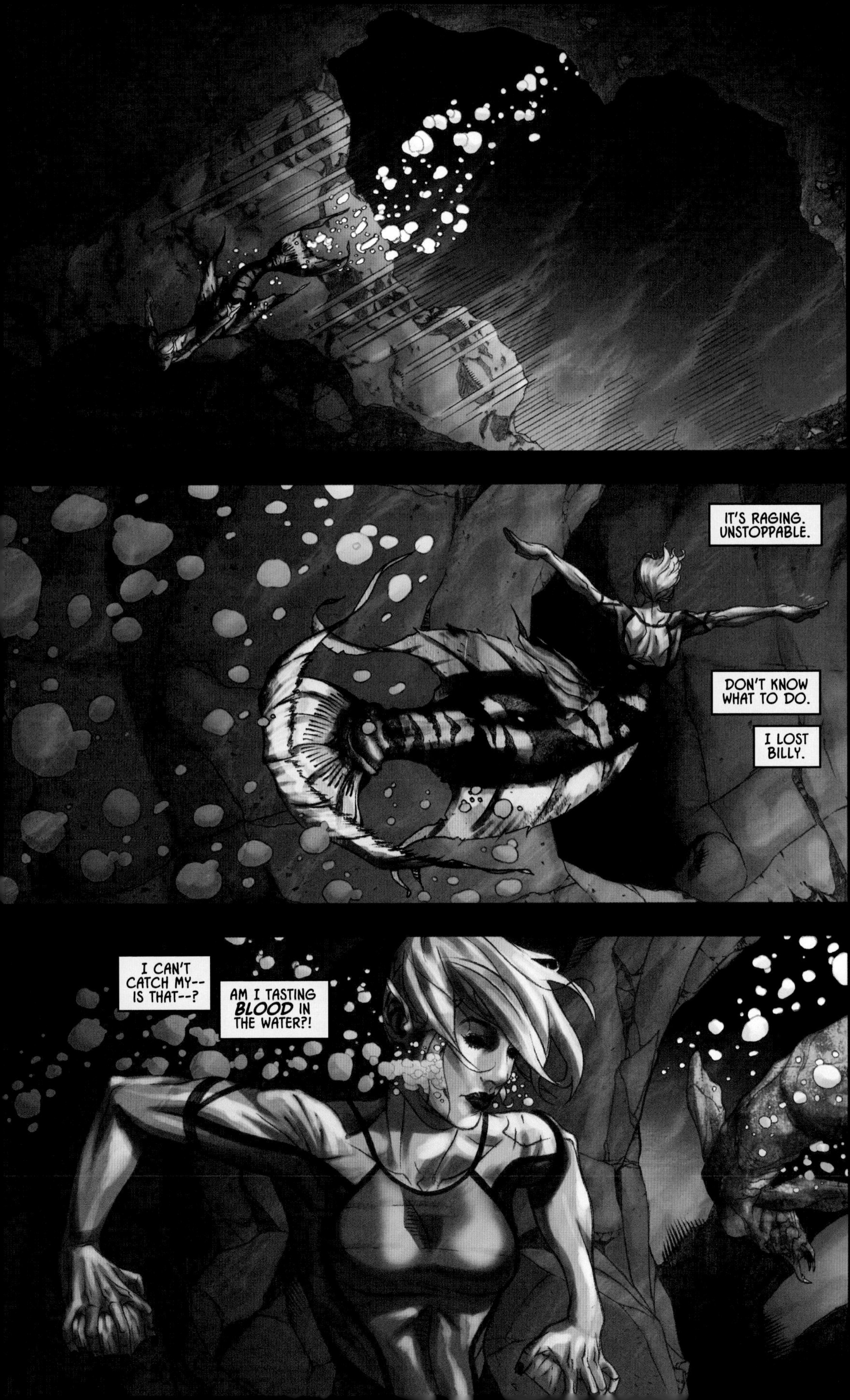
IT'S RAGING. UNSTOPPABLE.
DON'T KNOW WHAT TO DO.
I LOST BILLY.
I CAN'T CATCH MY-- IS THAT--?
AM I TASTING BLOOD IN THE WATER?!

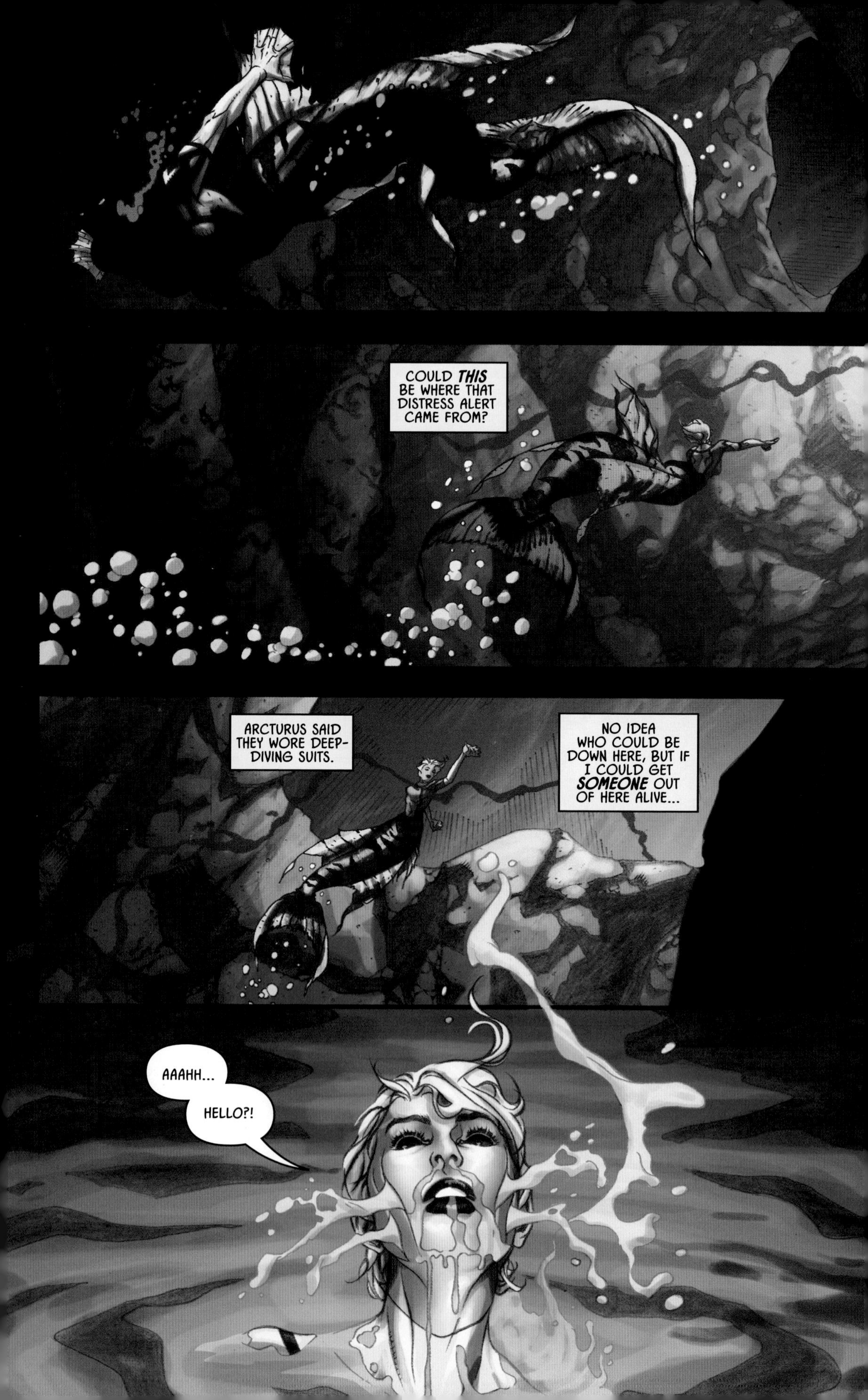

COULD THIS BE WHERE THAT DISTRESS ALERT CAME FROM?
ARCTURUS SAID THEY WORE DEEP-DIVING SUITS.
NO IDEA WHO COULD BE DOWN HERE, BUT IF I COULD GET SOMEONE OUT OF HERE ALIVE...
AAAHH...
HELLO?!

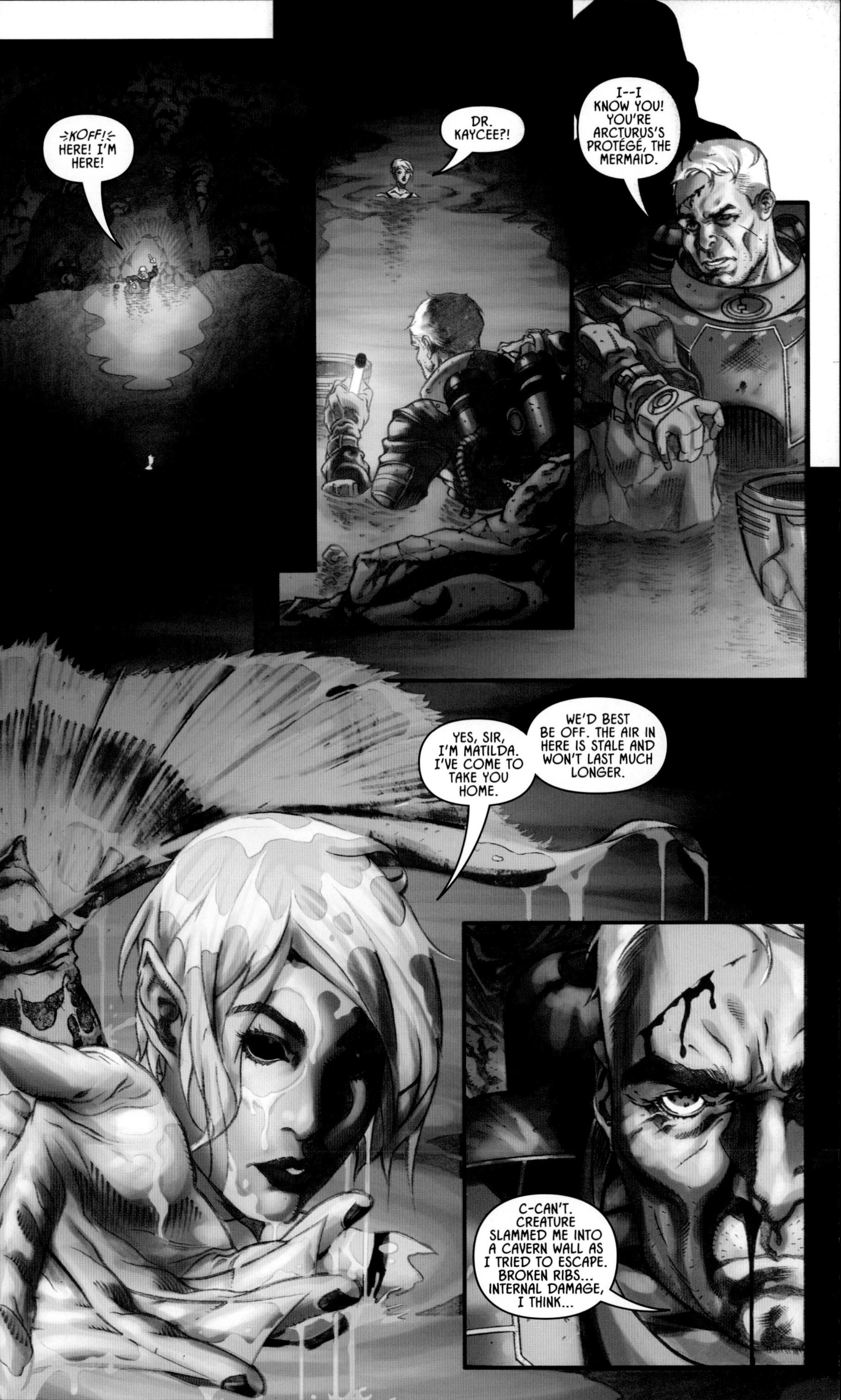

KOFF! HERE! I'M HERE!
DR. KAYCEE?!
I--I KNOW YOU! YOU'RE ARCTURUS'S PROTÉGÉ, THE MERMAID.
YES, SIR, I'M MATILDA. I'VE COME TO TAKE YOU HOME.
WE'D BEST BE OFF. THE AIR IN HERE IS STALE AND WON'T LAST MUCH LONGER.
C-CAN'T. CREATURE SLAMMED ME INTO A CAVERN WALL AS I TRIED TO ESCAPE. BROKEN RIBS... INTERNAL DAMAGE, I THINK...

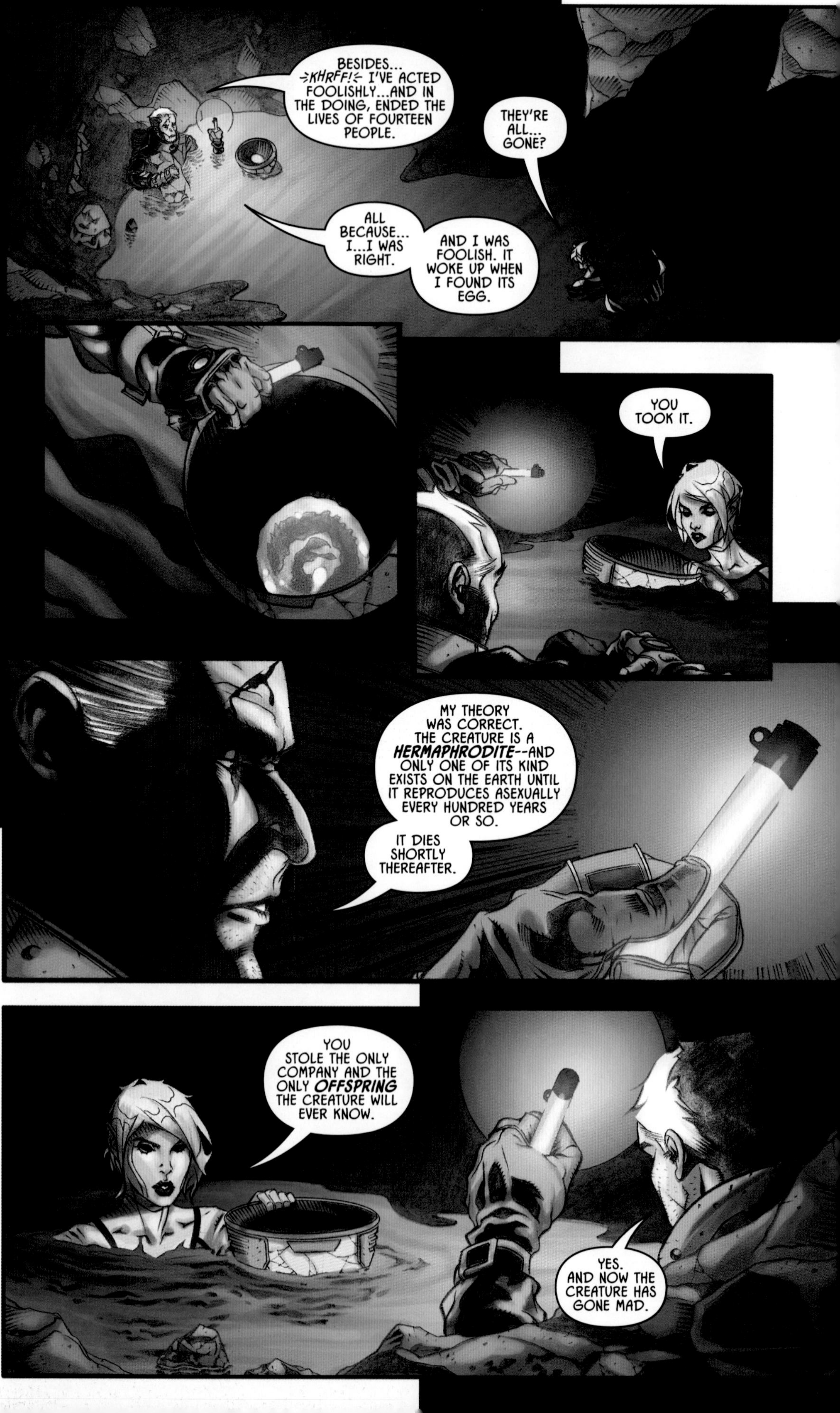

BESIDES... ⇒KHRFF!⇐ I'VE ACTED FOOLISHLY...AND IN THE DOING, ENDED THE LIVES OF FOURTEEN PEOPLE.
THEY'RE ALL... GONE?
ALL BECAUSE... I...I WAS RIGHT.
AND I WAS FOOLISH. IT WOKE UP WHEN I FOUND ITS EGG.
YOU TOOK IT.
MY THEORY WAS CORRECT. THE CREATURE IS A ***HERMAPHRODITE***--AND ONLY ONE OF ITS KIND EXISTS ON THE EARTH UNTIL IT REPRODUCES ASEXUALLY EVERY HUNDRED YEARS OR SO.
IT DIES SHORTLY THEREAFTER.
YOU STOLE THE ONLY COMPANY AND THE ONLY ***OFFSPRING*** THE CREATURE WILL EVER KNOW.
YES. AND NOW THE CREATURE HAS GONE MAD.

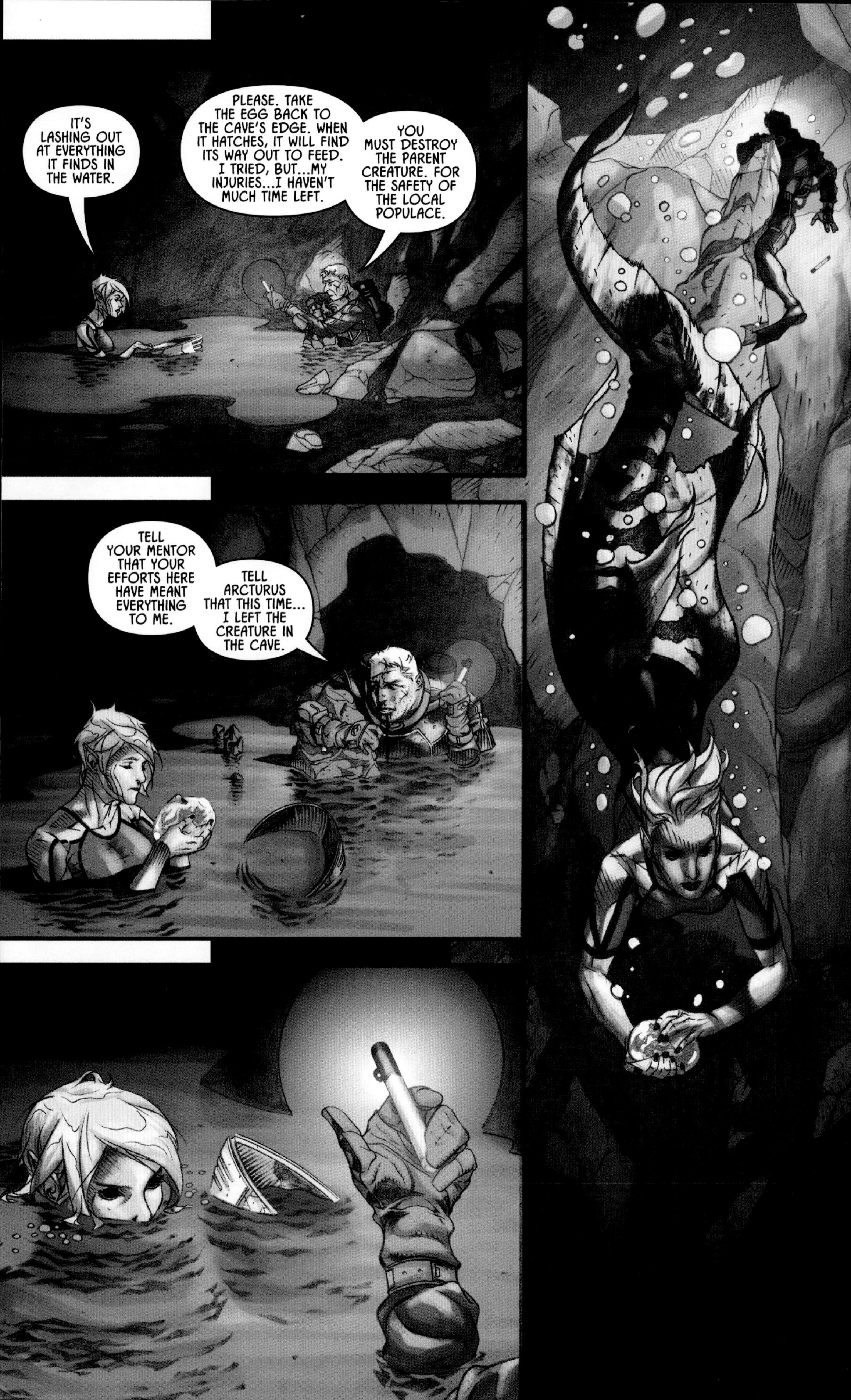
IT'S LASHING OUT AT EVERYTHING IT FINDS IN THE WATER.
PLEASE. TAKE THE EGG BACK TO THE CAVE'S EDGE. WHEN IT HATCHES, IT WILL FIND ITS WAY OUT TO FEED. I TRIED, BUT...MY INJURIES...I HAVEN'T MUCH TIME LEFT.
YOU MUST DESTROY THE PARENT CREATURE. FOR THE SAFETY OF THE LOCAL POPULACE.
TELL YOUR MENTOR THAT YOUR EFFORTS HERE HAVE MEANT EVERYTHING TO ME.
TELL ARCTURUS THAT THIS TIME... I LEFT THE CREATURE IN THE CAVE.

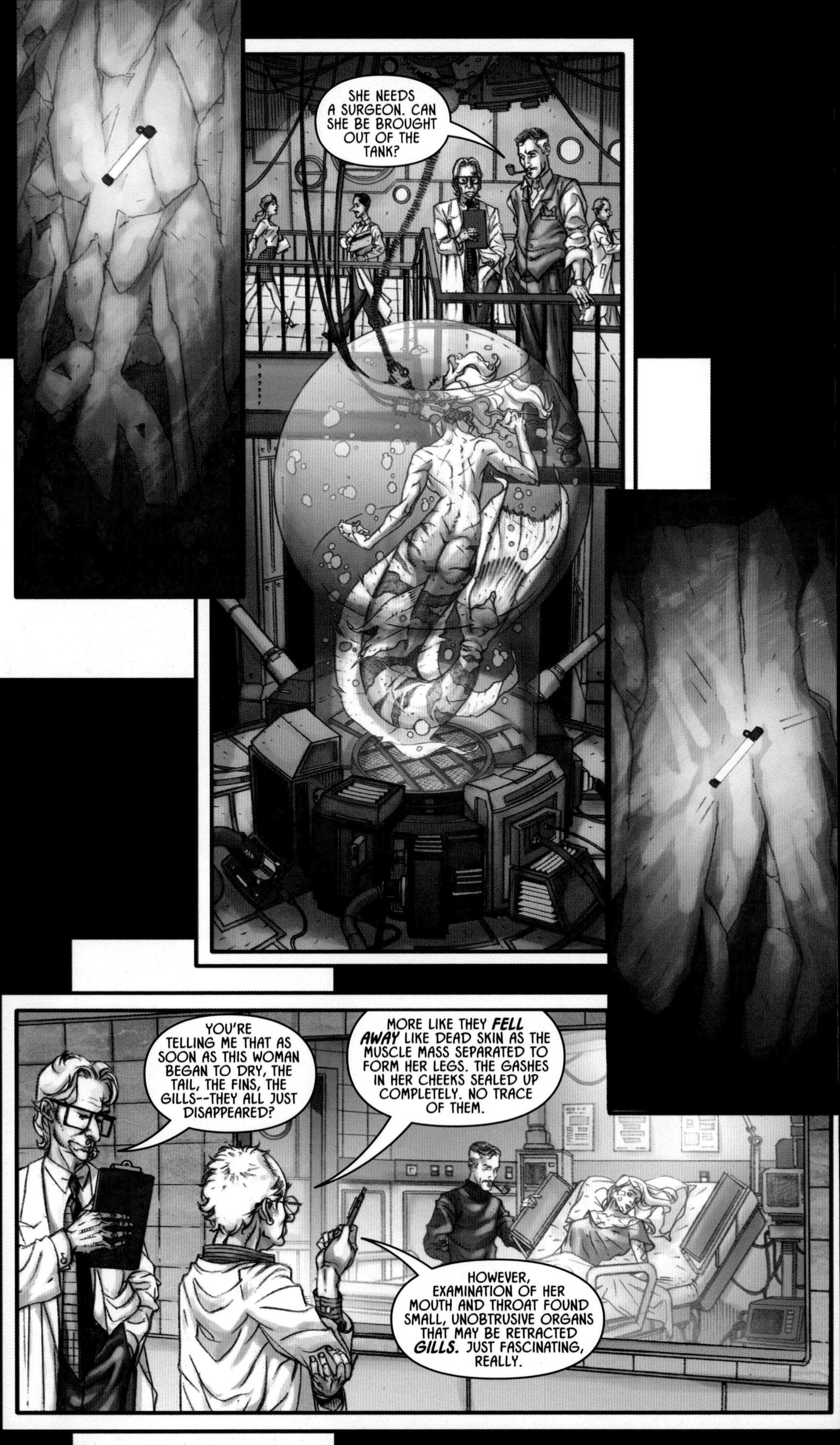

SHE NEEDS A SURGEON. CAN SHE BE BROUGHT OUT OF THE TANK?
YOU'RE TELLING ME THAT AS SOON AS THIS WOMAN BEGAN TO DRY, THE TAIL, THE FINS, THE GILLS--THEY ALL JUST DISAPPEARED?
MORE LIKE THEY FELL AWAY LIKE DEAD SKIN AS THE MUSCLE MASS SEPARATED TO FORM HER LEGS. THE GASHES IN HER CHEEKS SEALED UP COMPLETELY. NO TRACE OF THEM.
HOWEVER, EXAMINATION OF HER MOUTH AND THROAT FOUND SMALL, UNOBTRUSIVE ORGANS THAT MAY BE RETRACTED GILLS. JUST FASCINATING, REALLY.

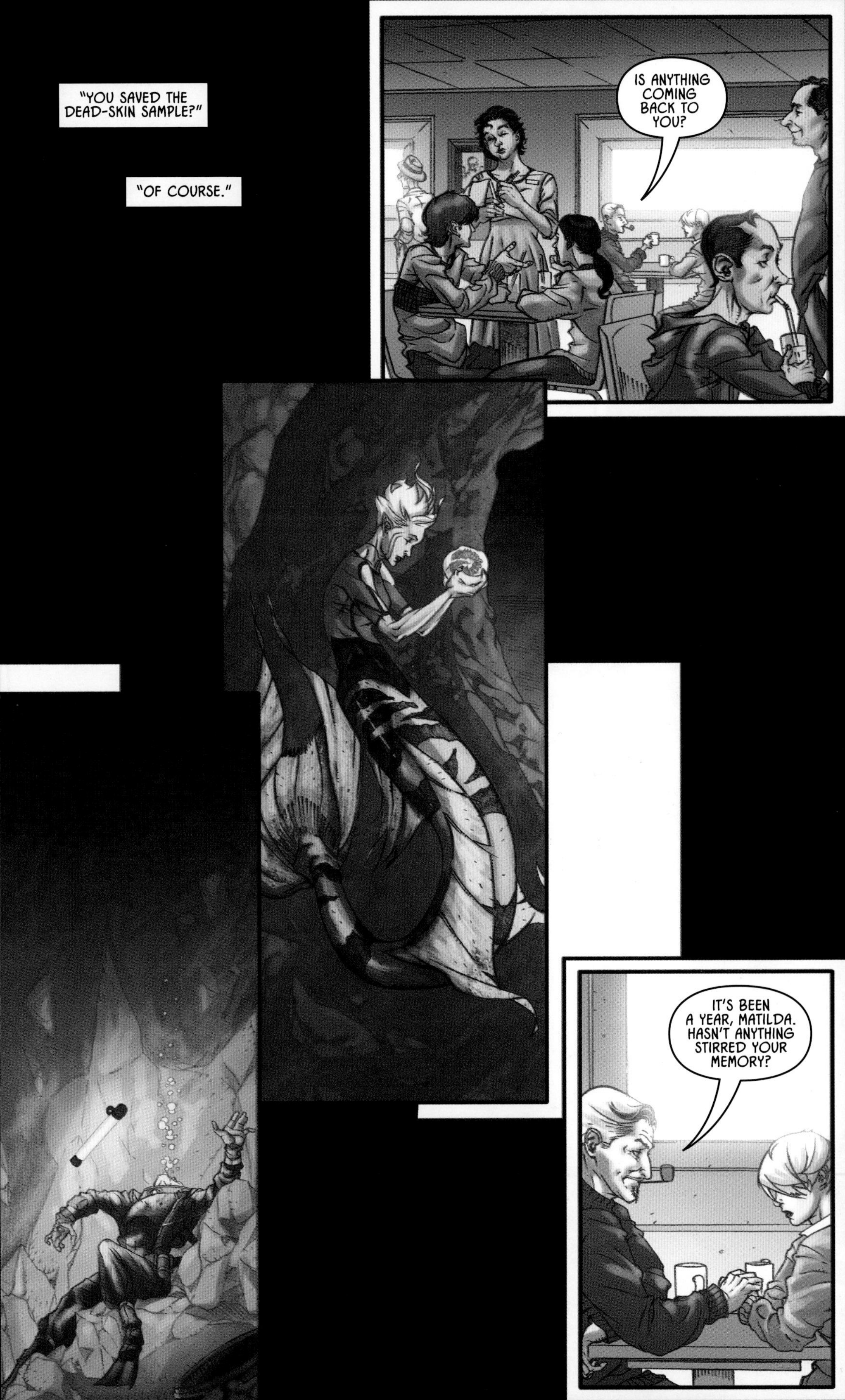
"YOU SAVED THE DEAD-SKIN SAMPLE?"
"OF COURSE."
IS ANYTHING COMING BACK TO YOU?
IT'S BEEN A YEAR, MATILDA. HASN'T ANYTHING STIRRED YOUR MEMORY?

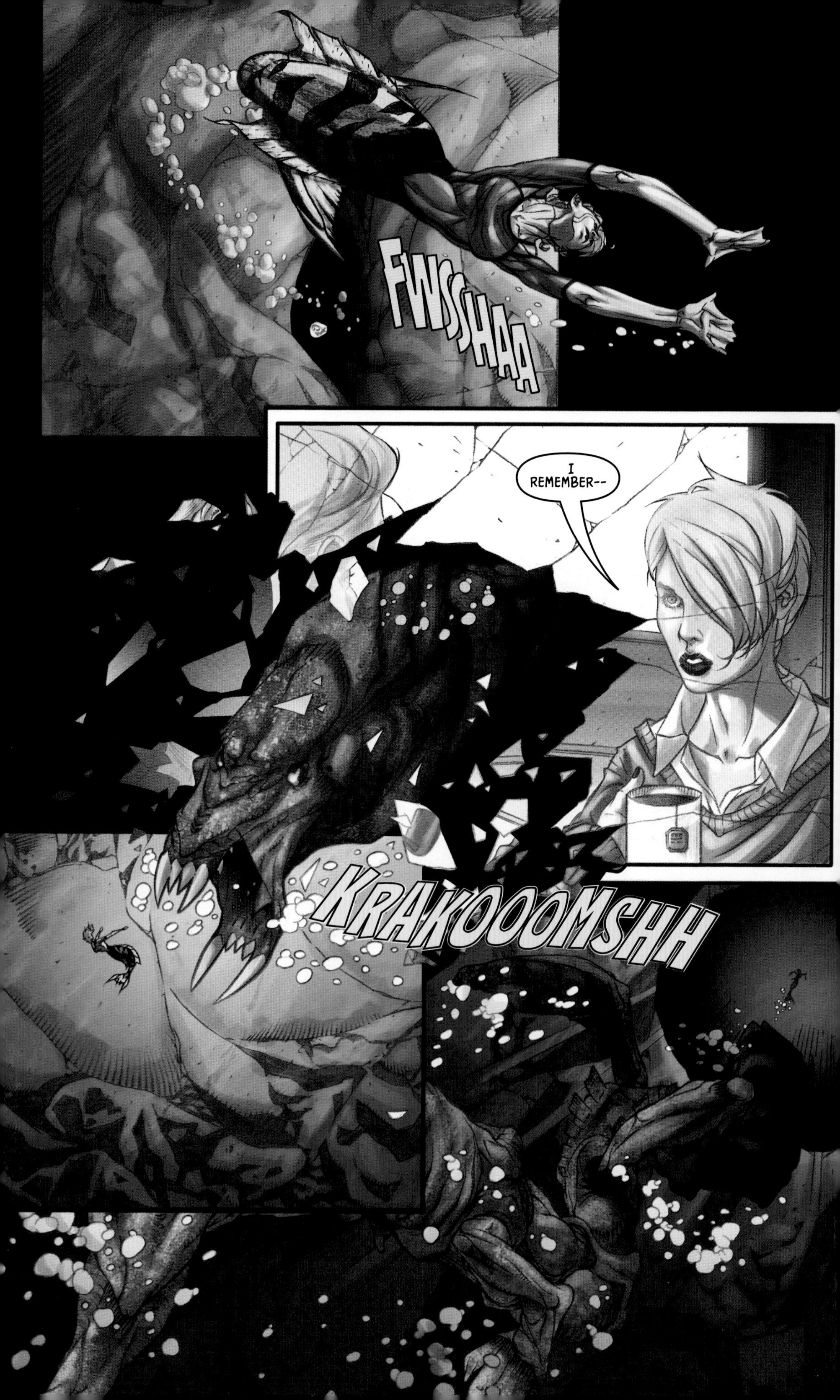
FWSSHAA
I REMEMBER--
KRAKOOOOMSHH

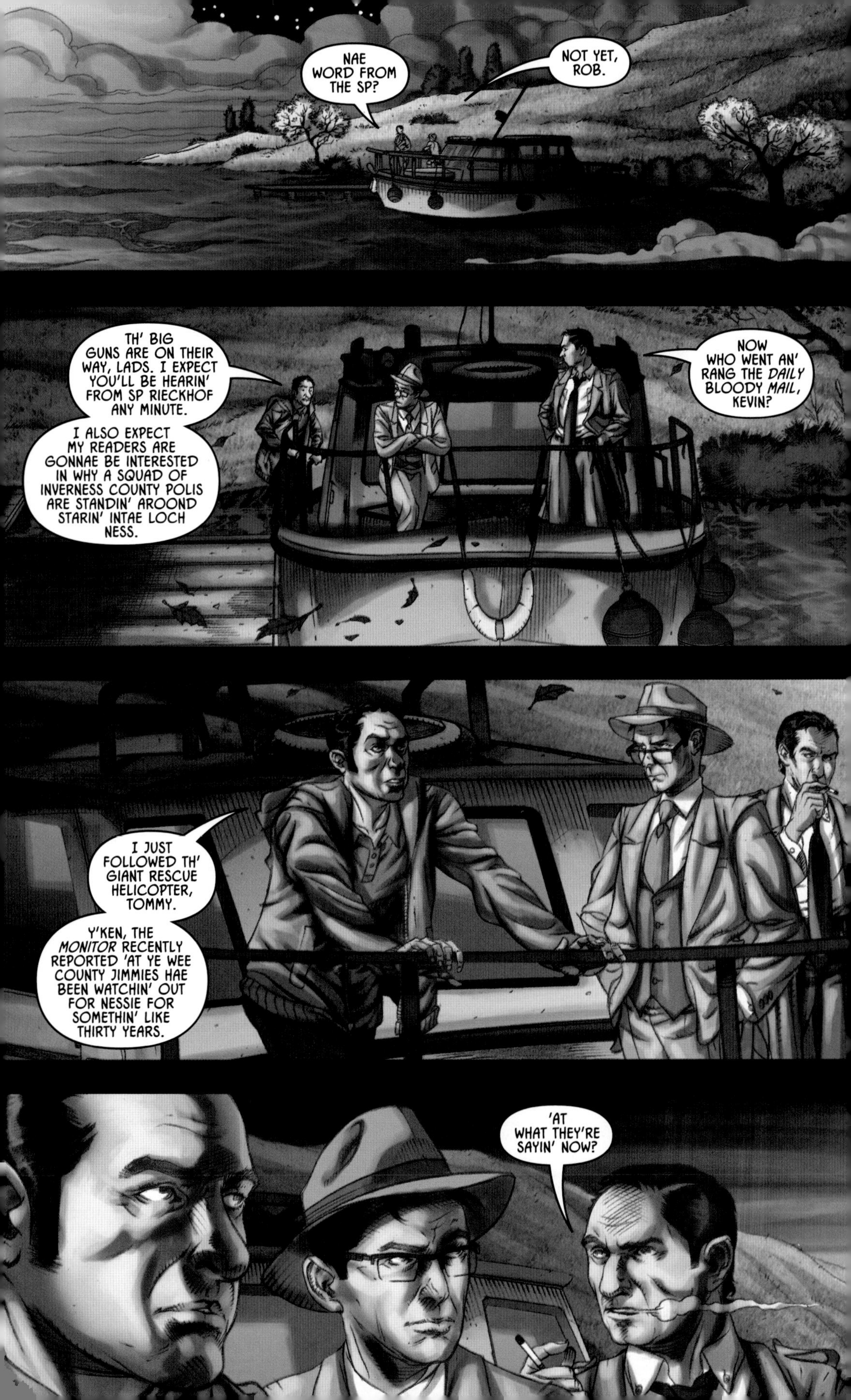
NAE WORD FROM THE SP?
NOT YET, ROB.
TH' BIG GUNS ARE ON THEIR WAY, LADS. I EXPECT YOU'LL BE HEARIN' FROM SP RIECKHOF ANY MINUTE.
I ALSO EXPECT MY READERS ARE GONNAE BE INTERESTED IN WHY A SQUAD OF INVERNESS COUNTY POLIS ARE STANDIN' AROOND STARIN' INTAE LOCH NESS.
NOW WHO WENT AN' RANG THE *DAILY* BLOODY *MAIL*, KEVIN?
I JUST FOLLOWED TH' GIANT RESCUE HELICOPTER, TOMMY.
Y'KEN, THE *MONITOR* RECENTLY REPORTED 'AT YE WEE COUNTY JIMMIES HAE BEEN WATCHIN' OUT FOR NESSIE FOR SOMETHIN' LIKE THIRTY YEARS.
'AT WHAT THEY'RE SAYIN' NOW?

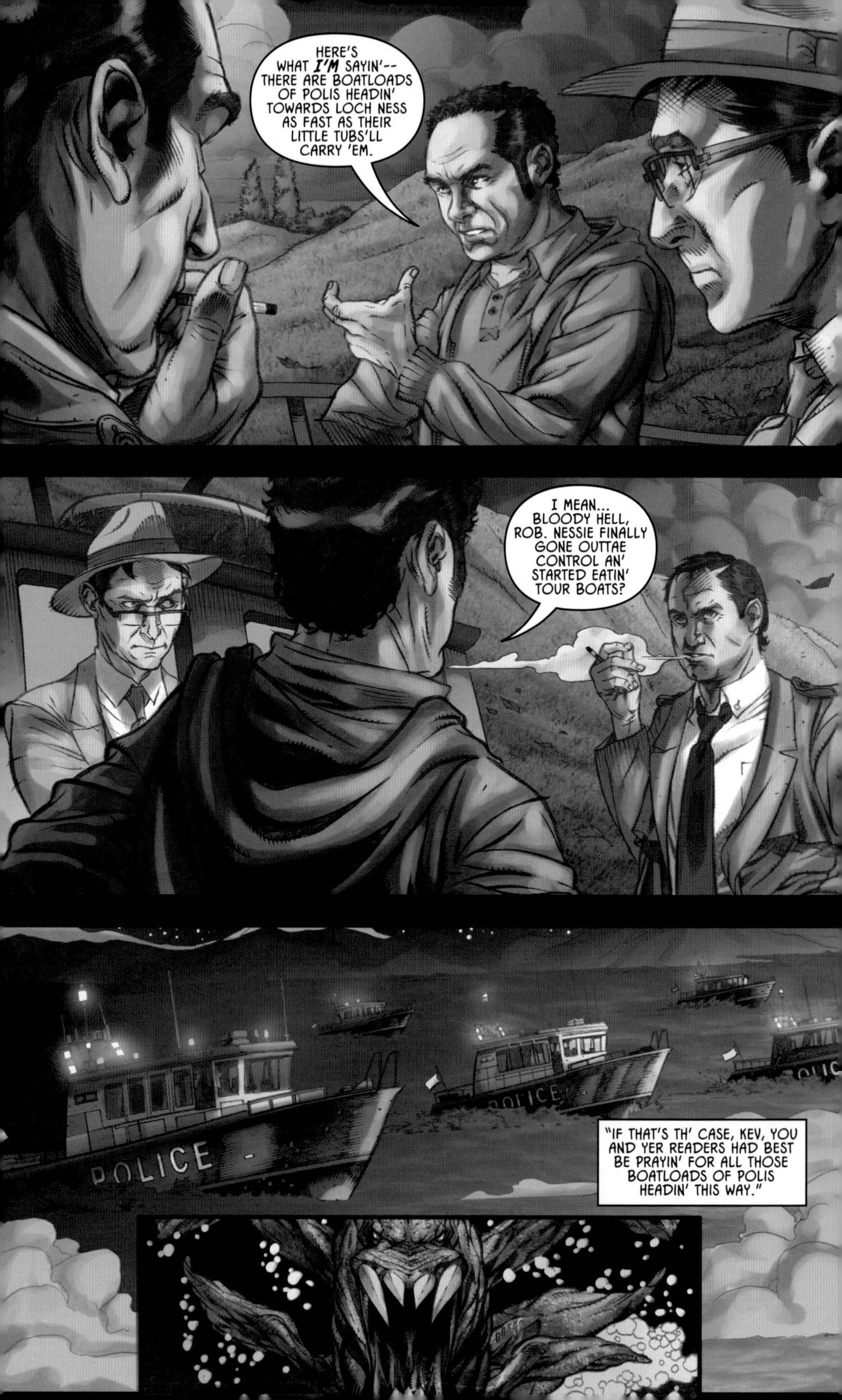
HERE'S WHAT I'M SAYIN'-- THERE ARE BOATLOADS OF POLIS HEADIN' TOWARDS LOCH NESS AS FAST AS THEIR LITTLE TUBS'LL CARRY 'EM.
I MEAN... BLOODY HELL, ROB. NESSIE FINALLY GONE OUTTAE CONTROL AN' STARTED EATIN' TOUR BOATS?
POLICE
POLICE
POLICE
"IF THAT'S TH' CASE, KEV, YOU AND YER READERS HAD BEST BE PRAYIN' FOR ALL THOSE BOATLOADS OF POLIS HEADIN' THIS WAY."

CHAPTER FOUR

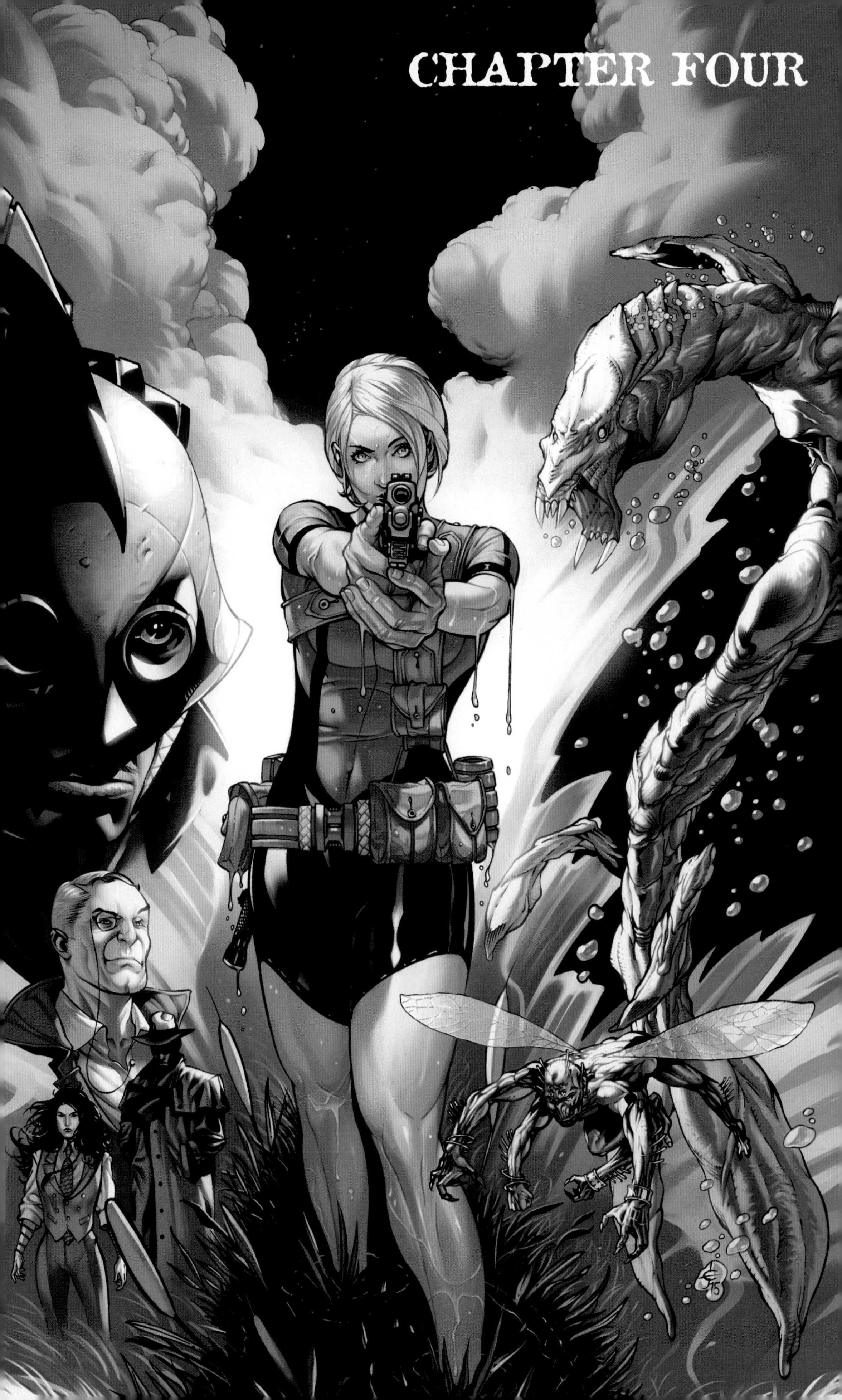

"One last meal, if only a small one . . . for a killer forced into action by circumstances outside its understanding."

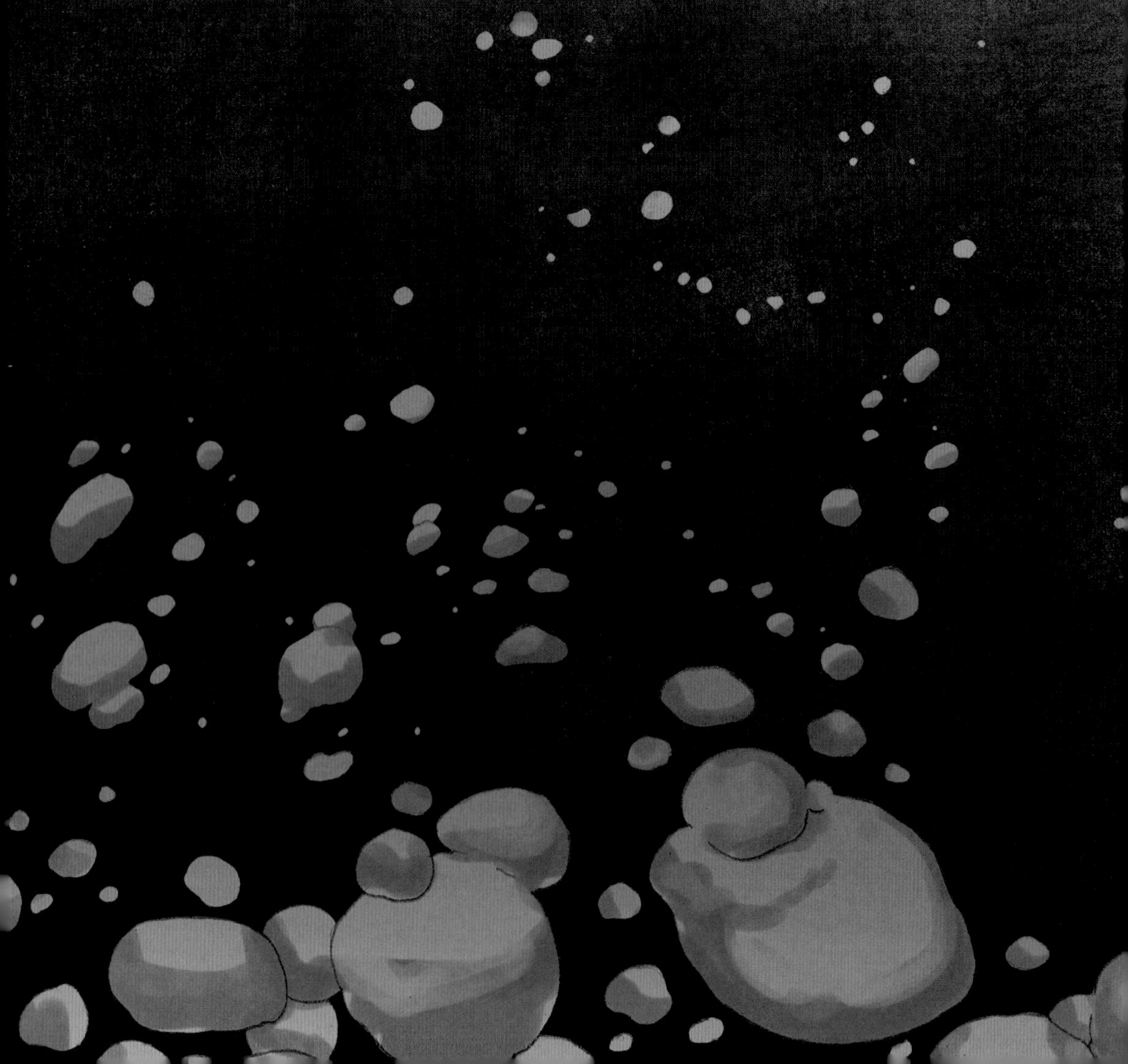

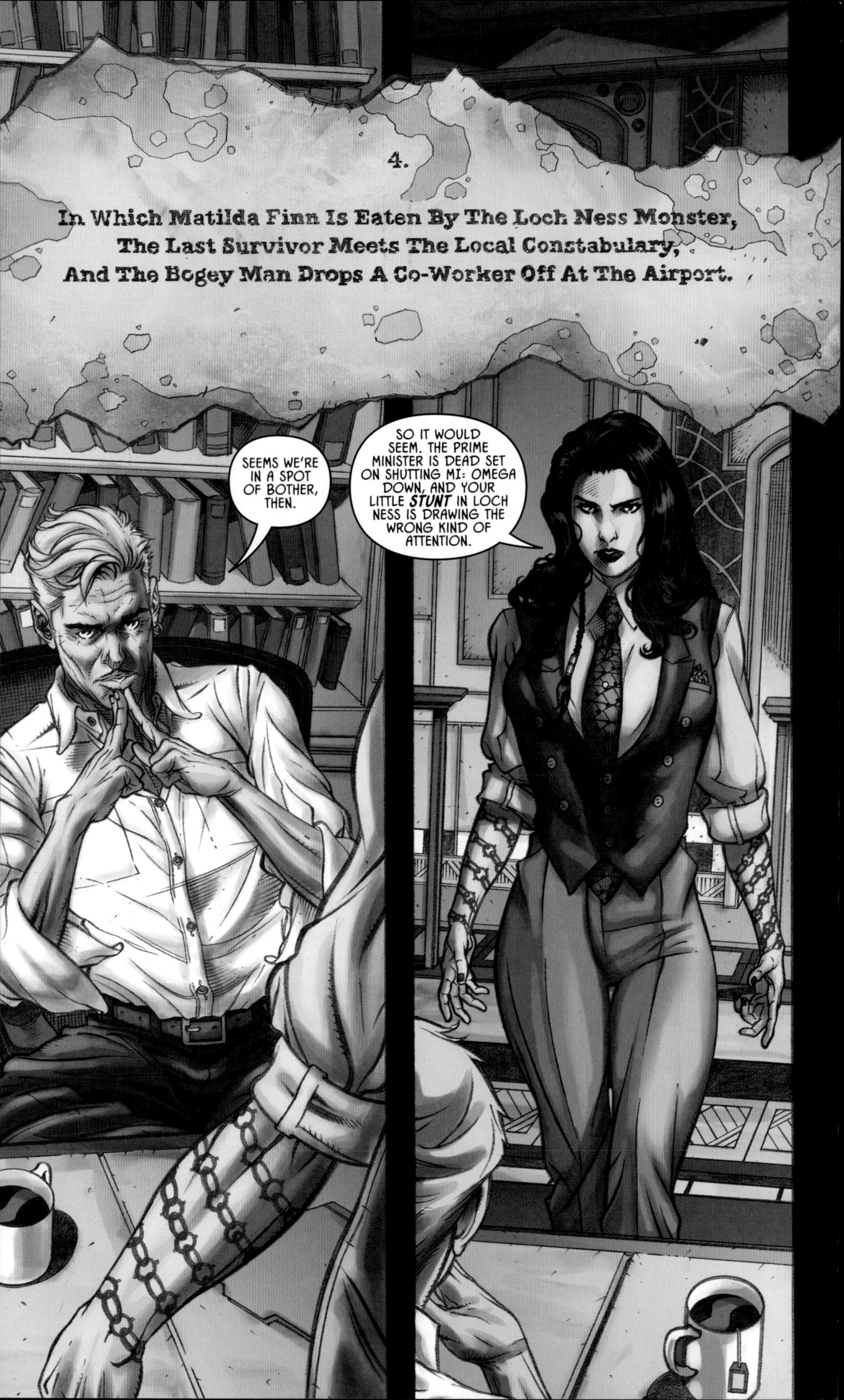
4.
In Which Matilda Finn Is Eaten By The Loch Ness Monster, The Last Survivor Meets The Local Constabulary, And The Bogey Man Drops A Co-Worker Off At The Airport.
SEEMS WE'RE IN A SPOT OF BOTHER, THEN.
SO IT WOULD SEEM. THE PRIME MINISTER IS DEAD SET ON SHUTTING MI: OMEGA DOWN, AND YOUR LITTLE STUNT IN LOCH NESS IS DRAWING THE WRONG KIND OF ATTENTION.

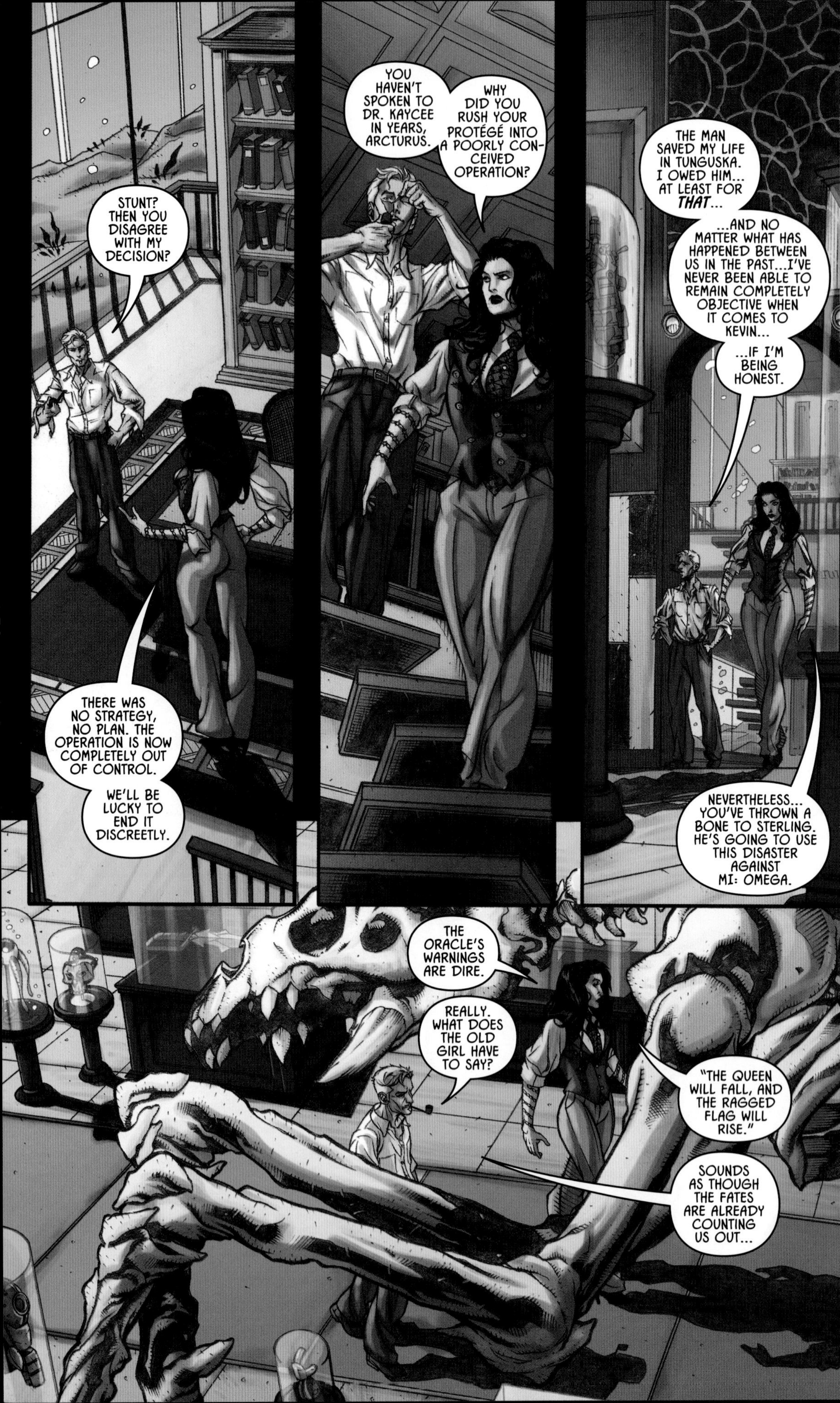
STUNT? THEN YOU DISAGREE WITH MY DECISION?
THERE WAS NO STRATEGY, NO PLAN. THE OPERATION IS NOW COMPLETELY OUT OF CONTROL.
WE'LL BE LUCKY TO END IT DISCREETLY.
YOU HAVEN'T SPOKEN TO DR. KAYCEE IN YEARS, ARCTURUS.
WHY DID YOU RUSH YOUR PROTÉGÉ INTO A POORLY CONCEIVED OPERATION?
THE MAN SAVED MY LIFE IN TUNGUSKA. I OWED HIM... AT LEAST FOR *THAT*...
...AND NO MATTER WHAT HAS HAPPENED BETWEEN US IN THE PAST...I'VE NEVER BEEN ABLE TO REMAIN COMPLETELY OBJECTIVE WHEN IT COMES TO KEVIN...
...IF I'M BEING HONEST.
NEVERTHELESS... YOU'VE THROWN A BONE TO STERLING. HE'S GOING TO USE THIS DISASTER AGAINST MI: OMEGA.
THE ORACLE'S WARNINGS ARE DIRE.
REALLY. WHAT DOES THE OLD GIRL HAVE TO SAY?
"THE QUEEN WILL FALL, AND THE RAGGED FLAG WILL RISE."
SOUNDS AS THOUGH THE FATES ARE ALREADY COUNTING US OUT...

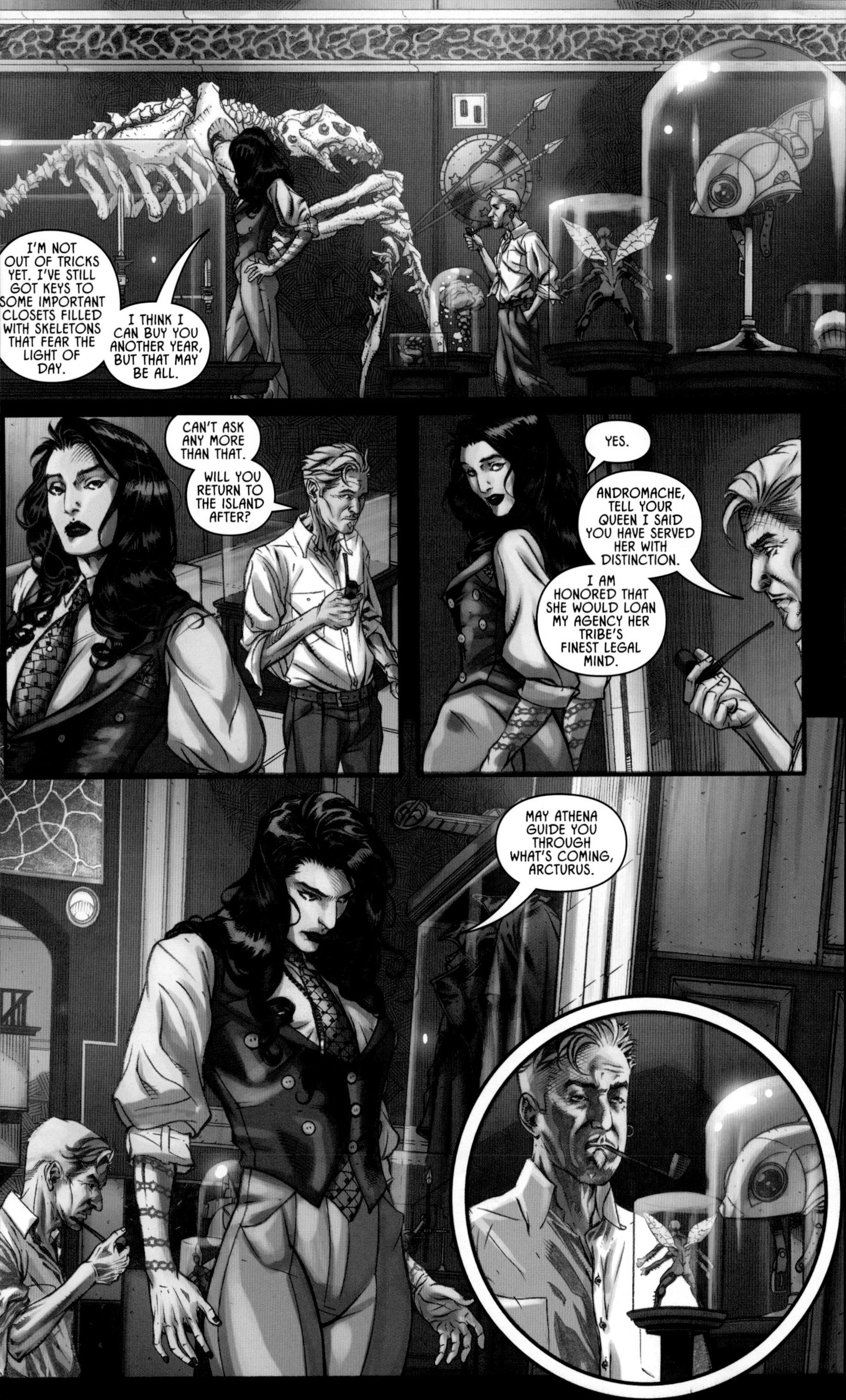

I'M NOT OUT OF TRICKS YET. I'VE STILL GOT KEYS TO SOME IMPORTANT CLOSETS FILLED WITH SKELETONS THAT FEAR THE LIGHT OF DAY.
I THINK I CAN BUY YOU ANOTHER YEAR, BUT THAT MAY BE ALL.
CAN'T ASK ANY MORE THAN THAT.
WILL YOU RETURN TO THE ISLAND AFTER?
YES.
ANDROMACHE, TELL YOUR QUEEN I SAID YOU HAVE SERVED HER WITH DISTINCTION.
I AM HONORED THAT SHE WOULD LOAN MY AGENCY HER TRIBE'S FINEST LEGAL MIND.
MAY ATHENA GUIDE YOU THROUGH WHAT'S COMING, ARCTURUS.

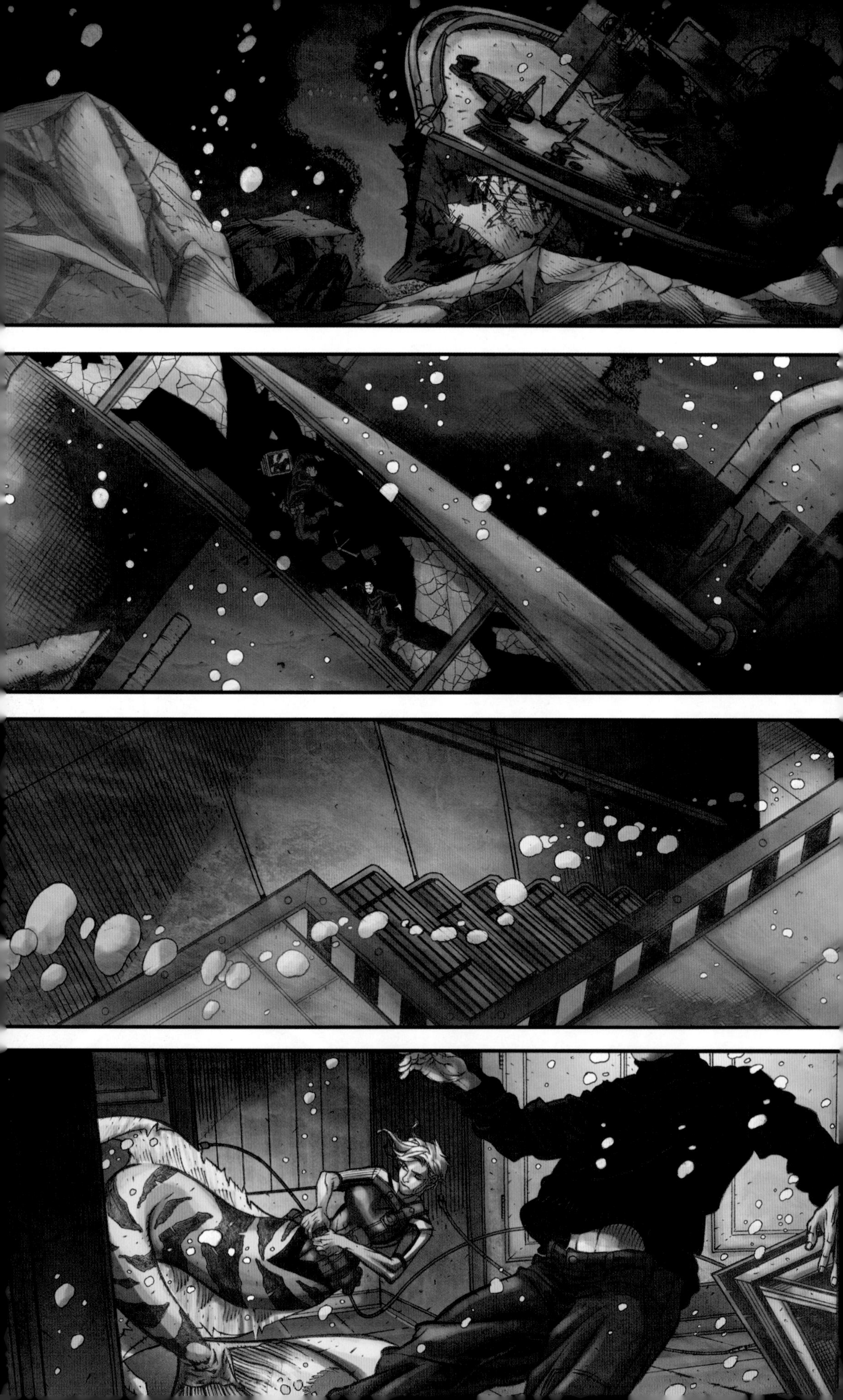

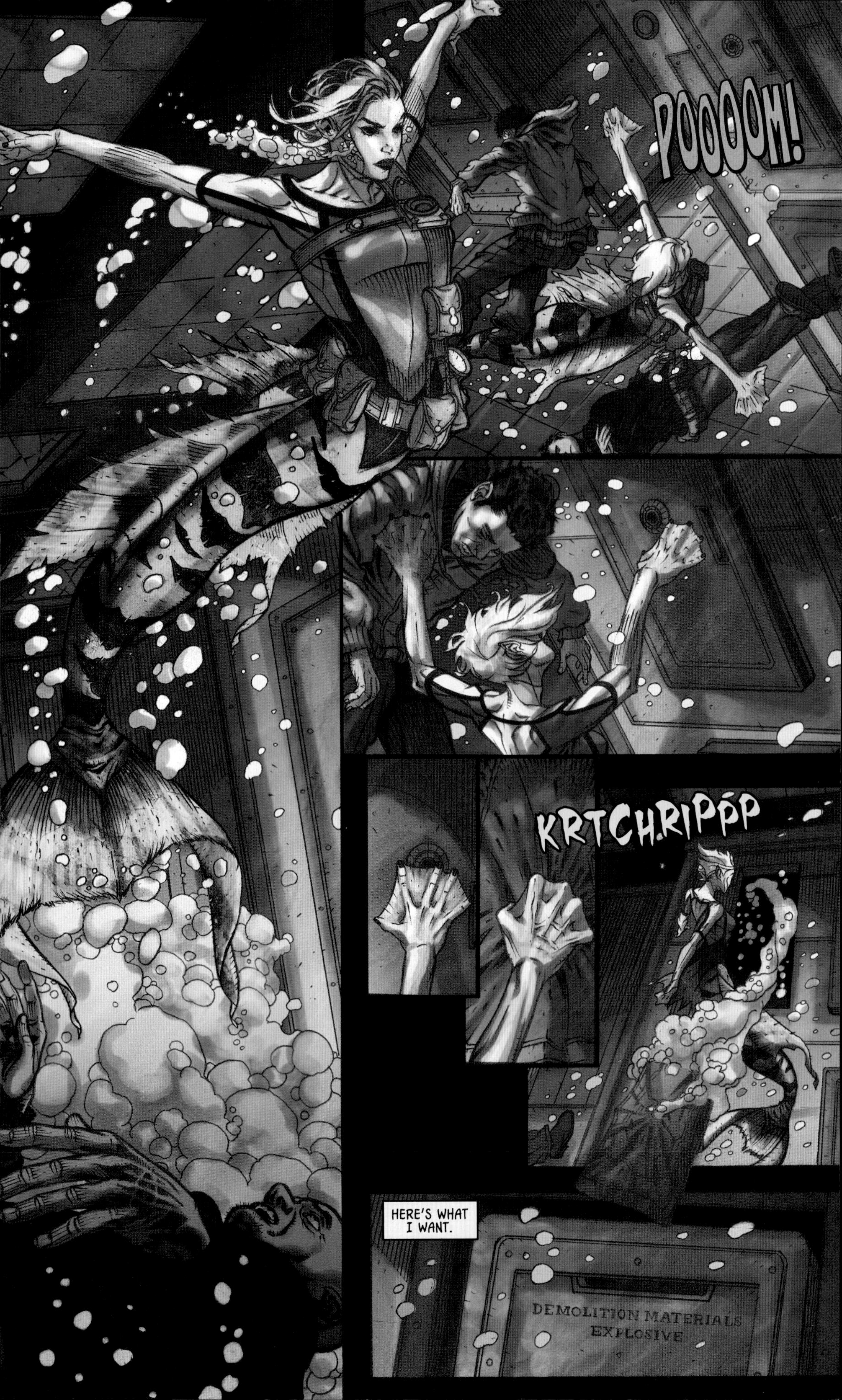
POOOOM!
KRTCHRIPPP
HERE'S WHAT I WANT.
DEMOLITION MATERIALS
EXPLOSIVE

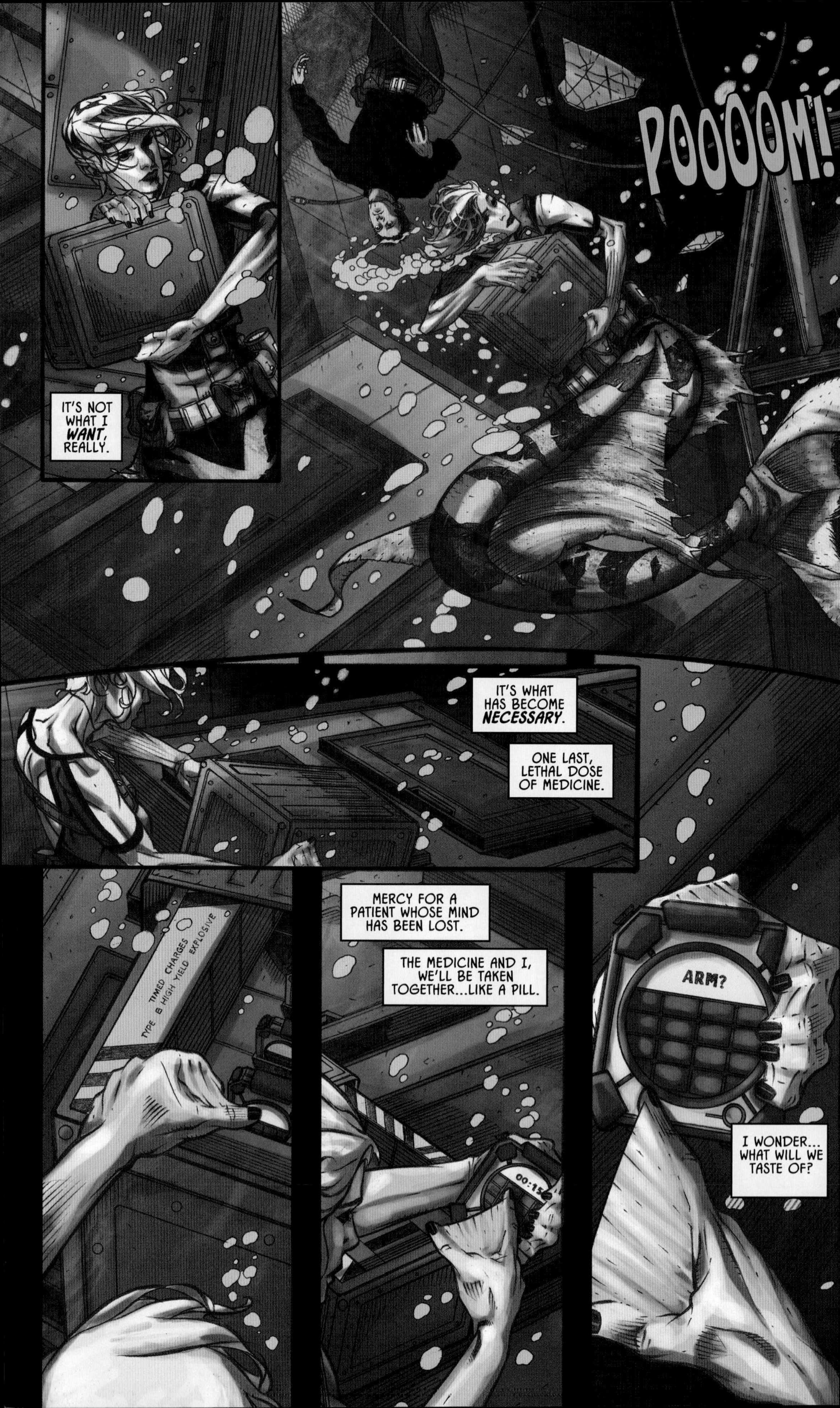
IT'S NOT WHAT I *WANT*, REALLY.
POOOOM!
IT'S WHAT HAS BECOME *NECESSARY*.
ONE LAST, LETHAL DOSE OF MEDICINE.
TIMED CHARGES
TYPE B HIGH YIELD EXPLOSIVE
MERCY FOR A PATIENT WHOSE MIND HAS BEEN LOST.
THE MEDICINE AND I, WE'LL BE TAKEN TOGETHER...LIKE A PILL.
00:15
ARM?
I WONDER... WHAT WILL WE TASTE OF?

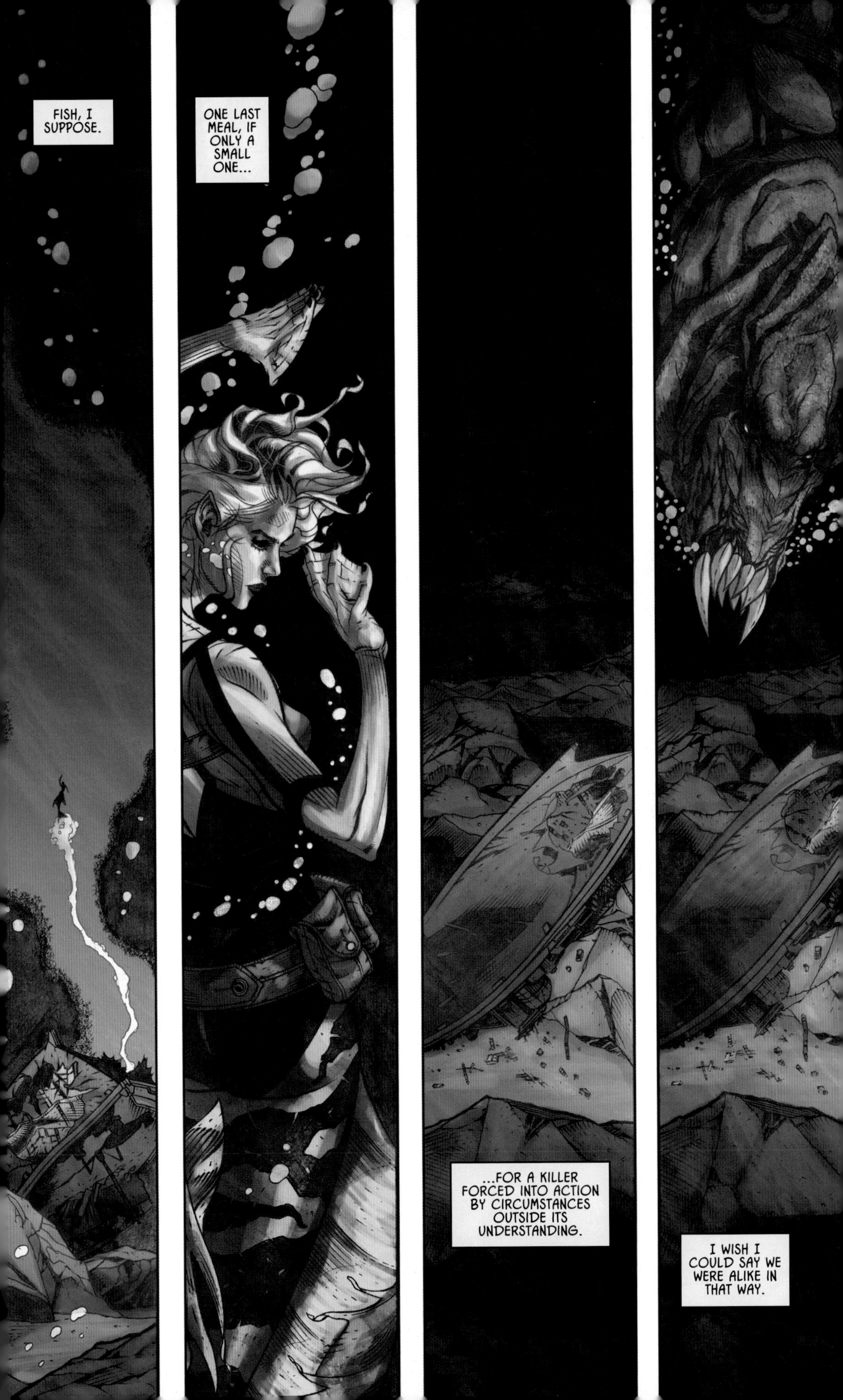
FISH, I SUPPOSE.
ONE LAST MEAL, IF ONLY A SMALL ONE...
...FOR A KILLER FORCED INTO ACTION BY CIRCUMSTANCES OUTSIDE ITS UNDERSTANDING.
I WISH I COULD SAY WE WERE ALIKE IN THAT WAY.

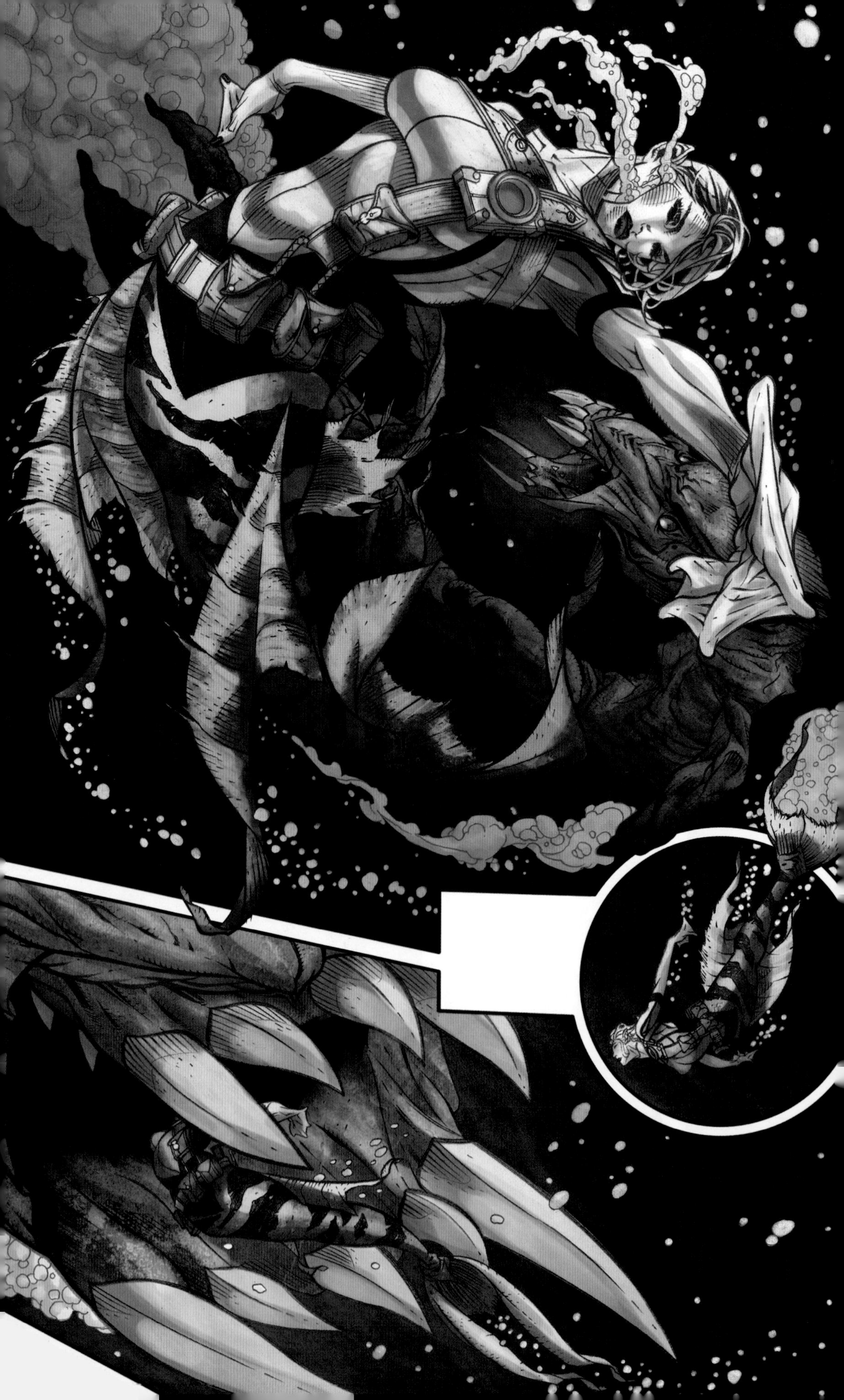

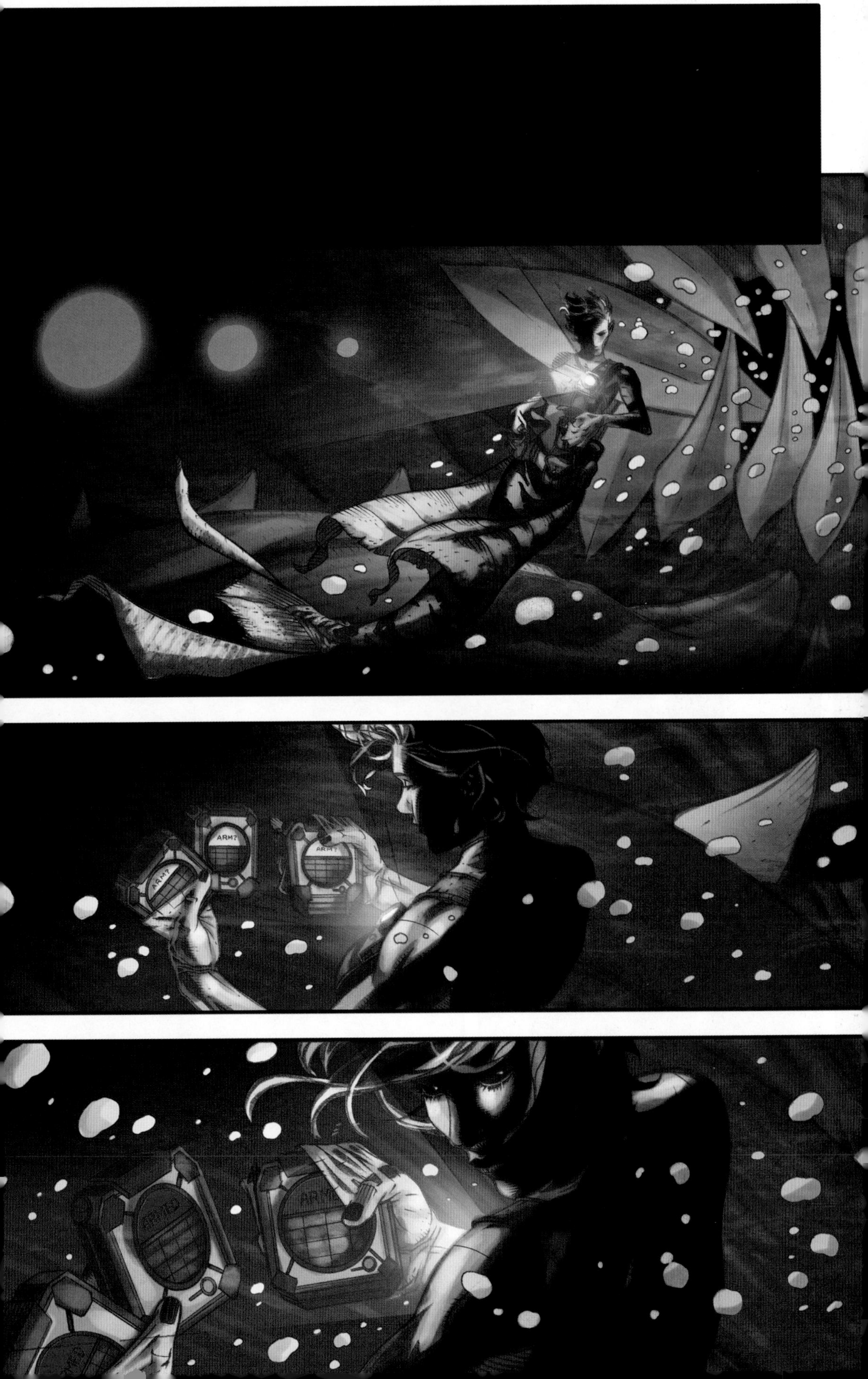
ARM?
ARM?
ARM?

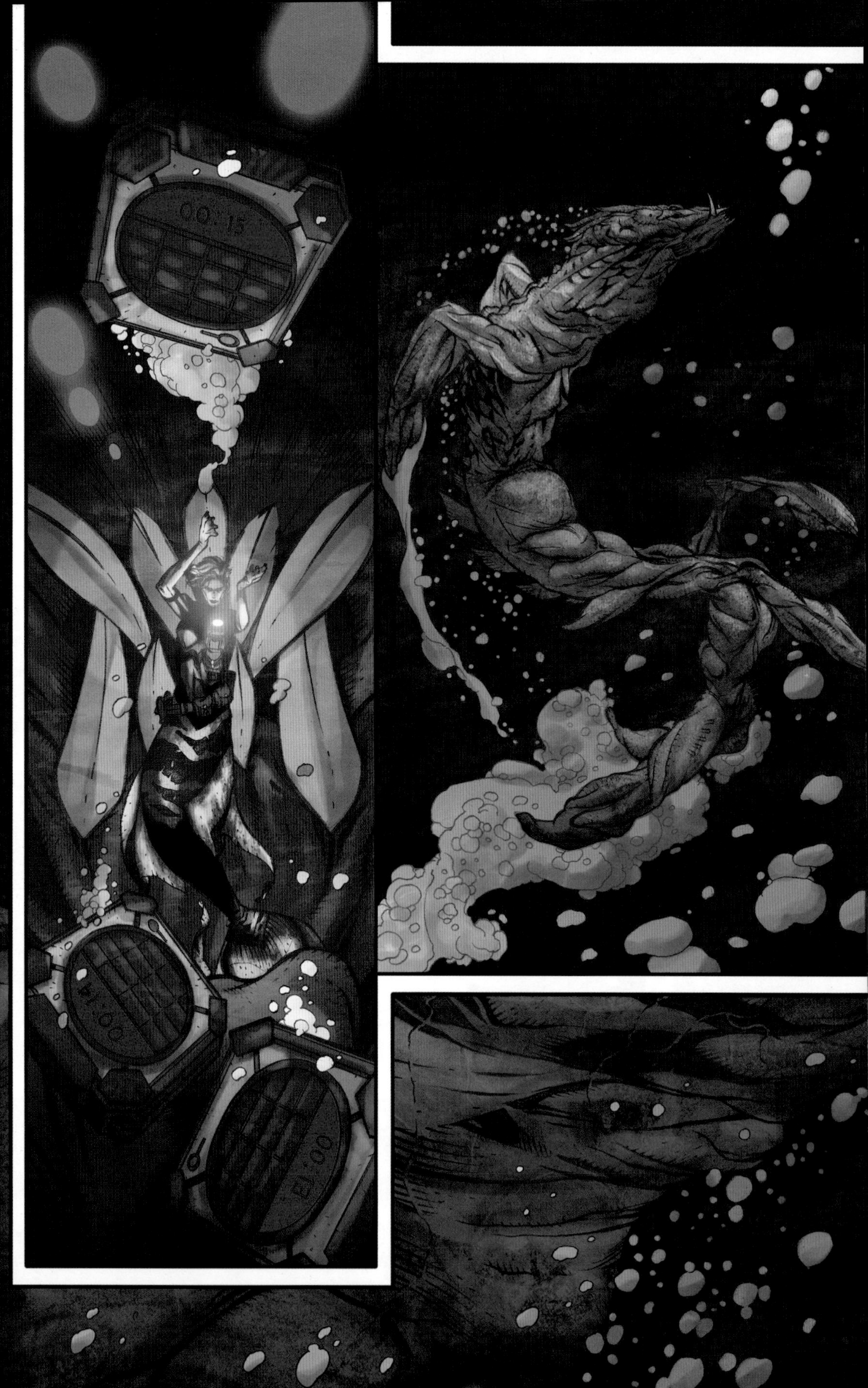
00:15

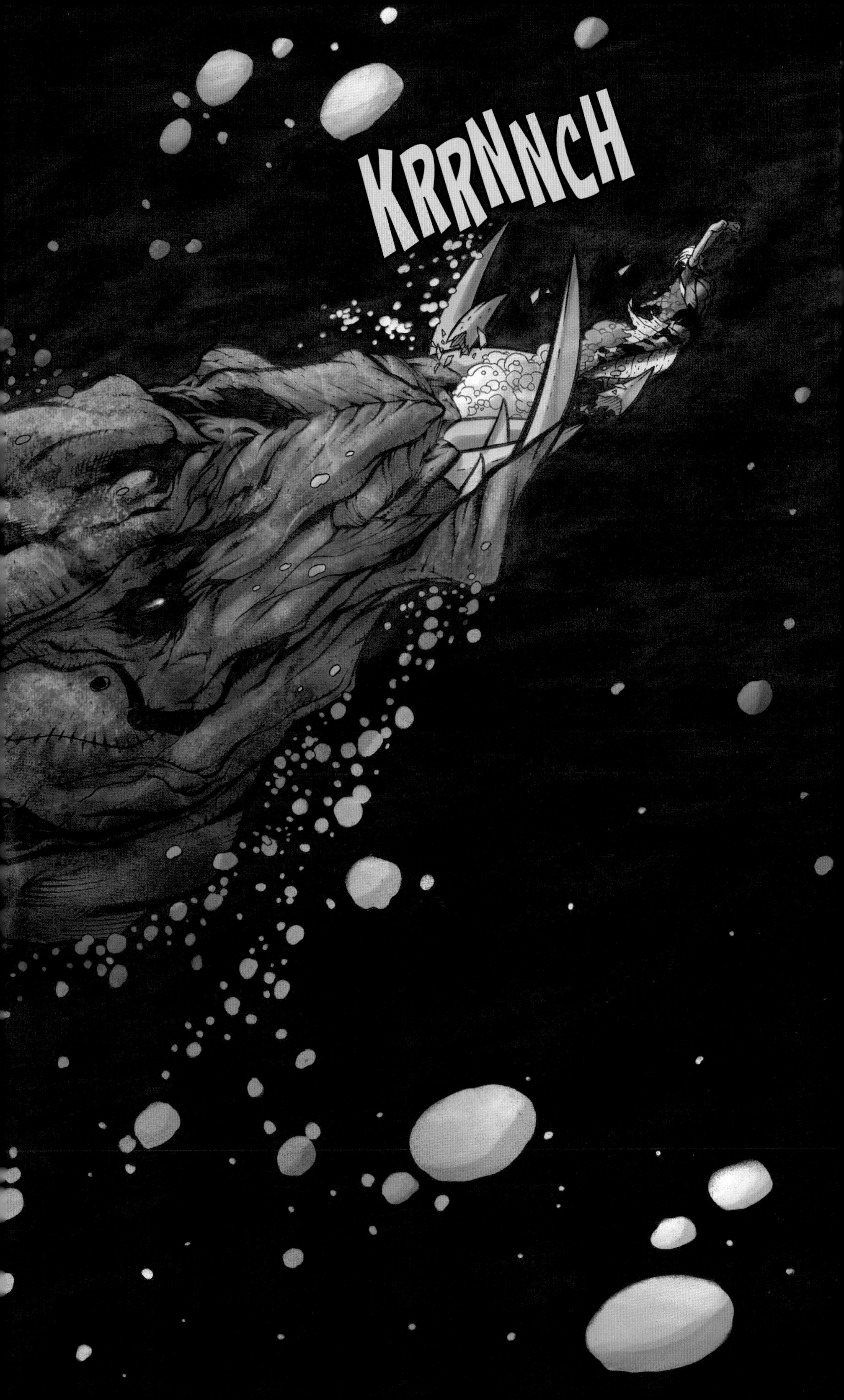
KRRNNCH

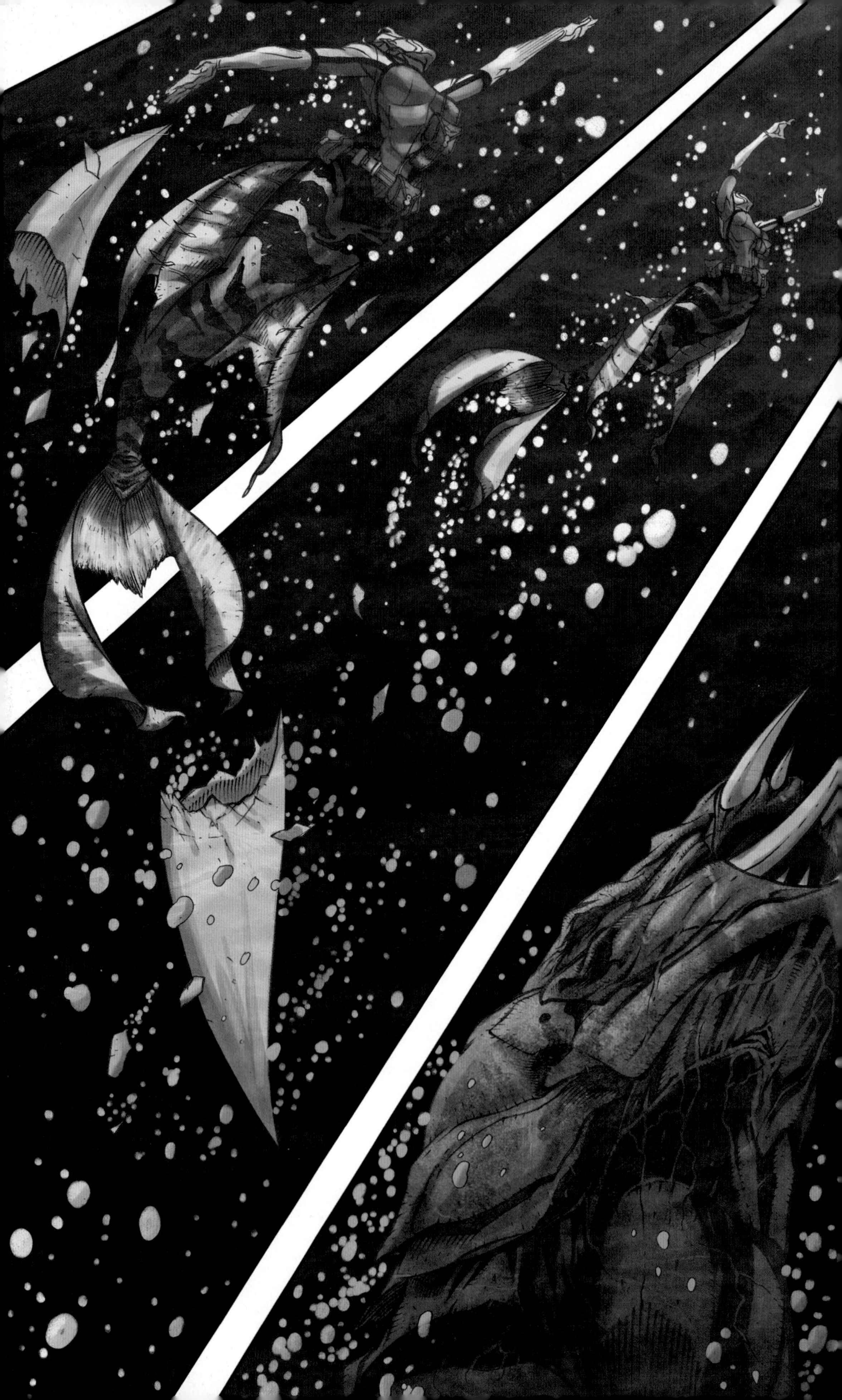

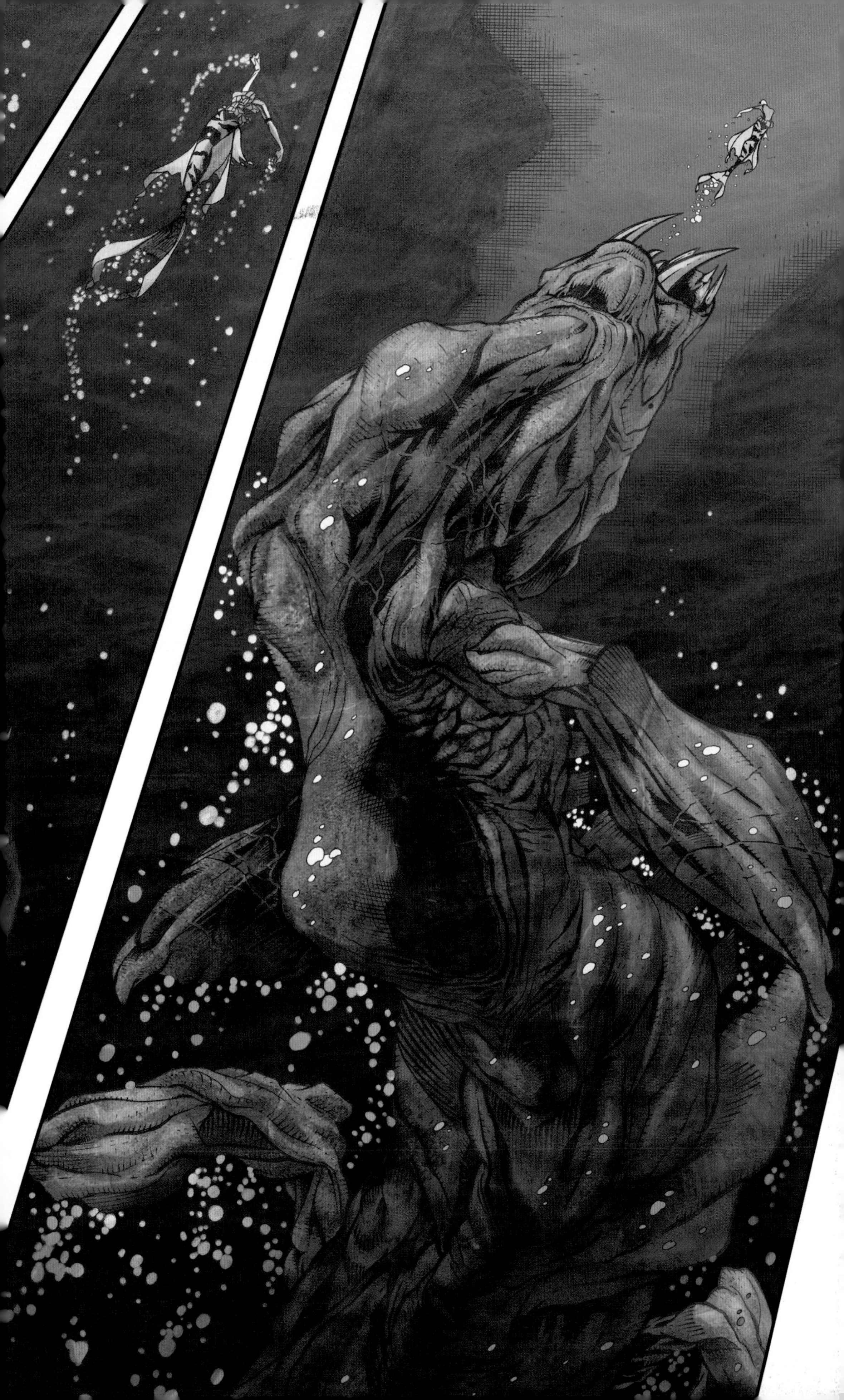

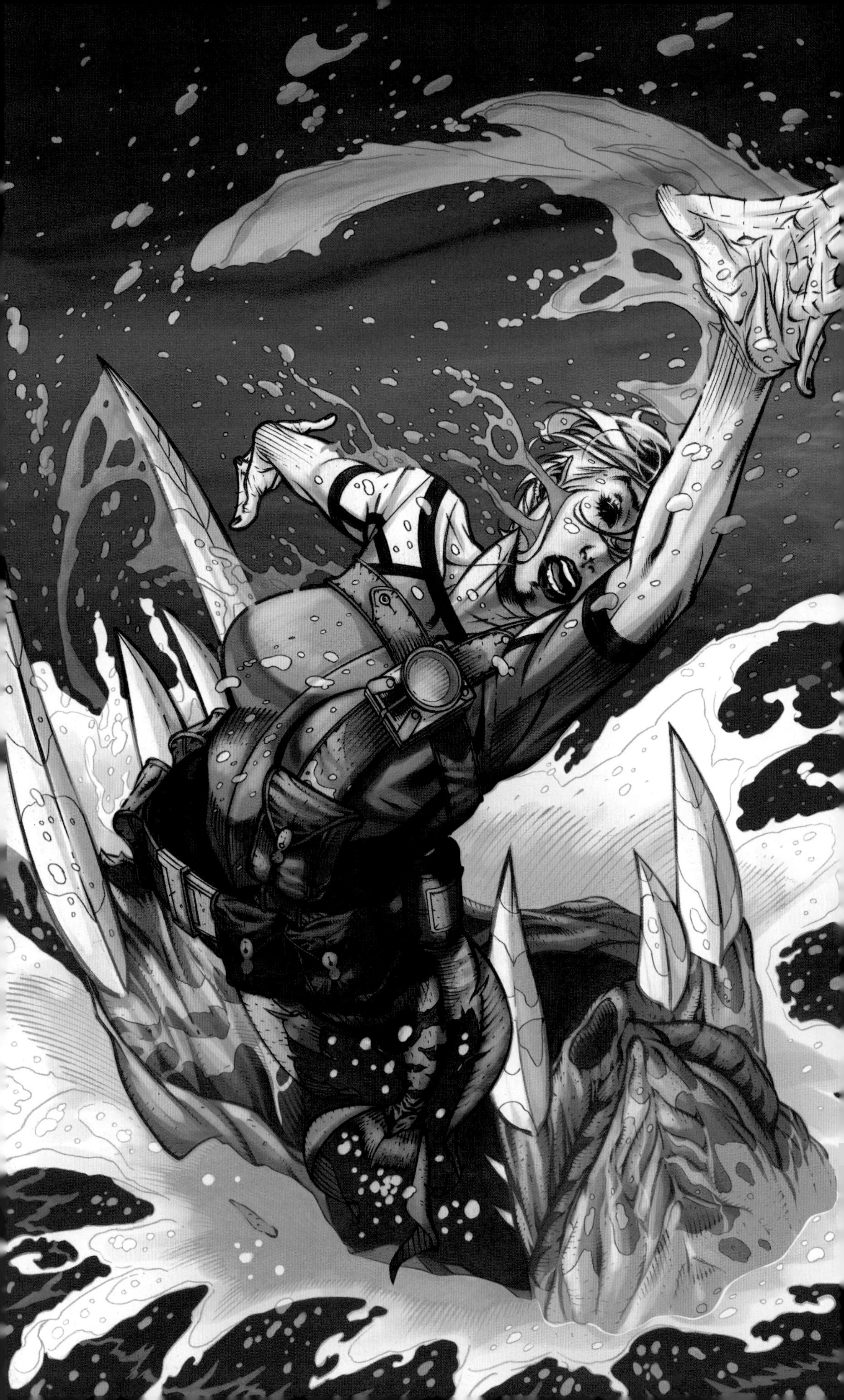

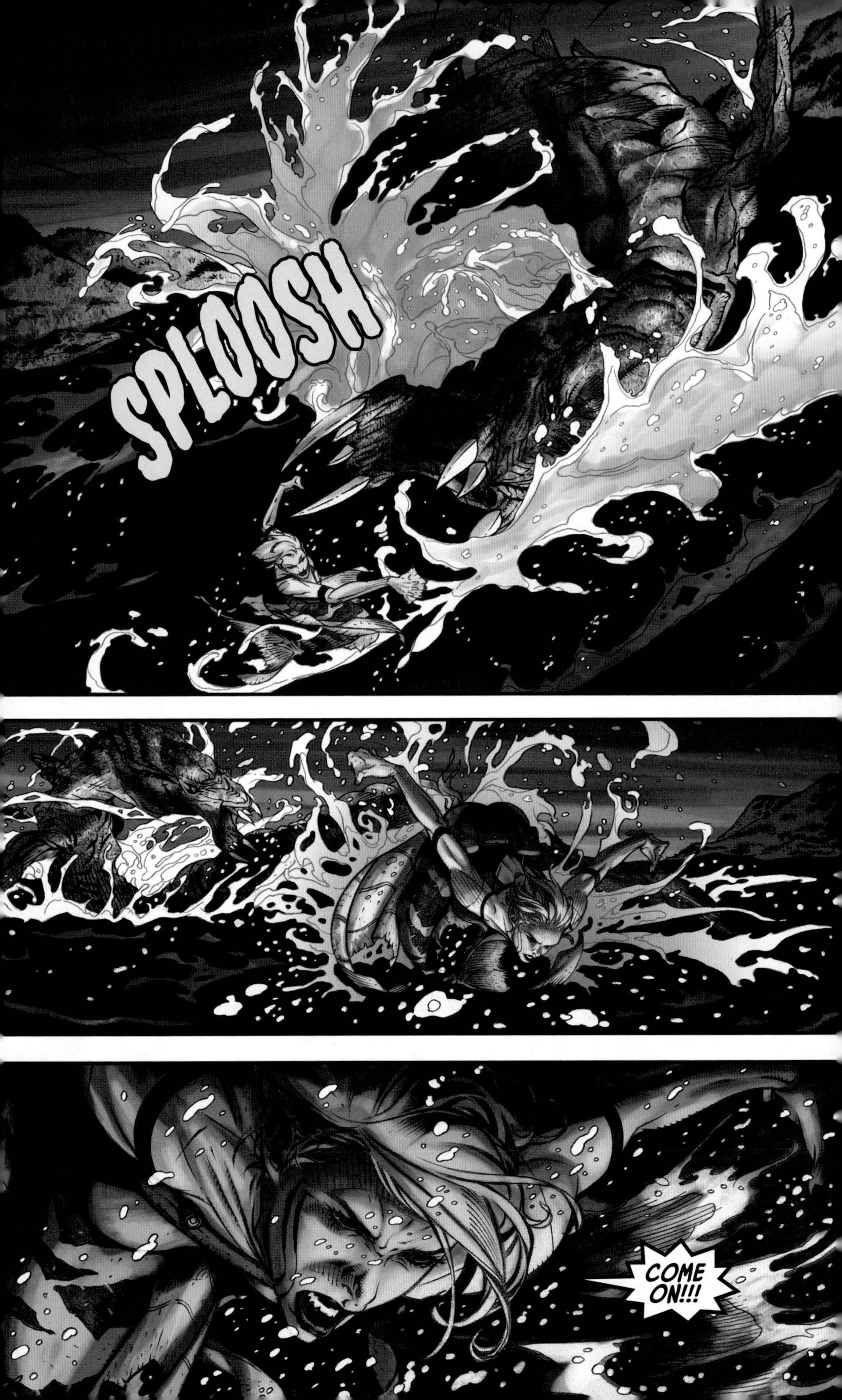
SPLOOSH
COME ON!!!

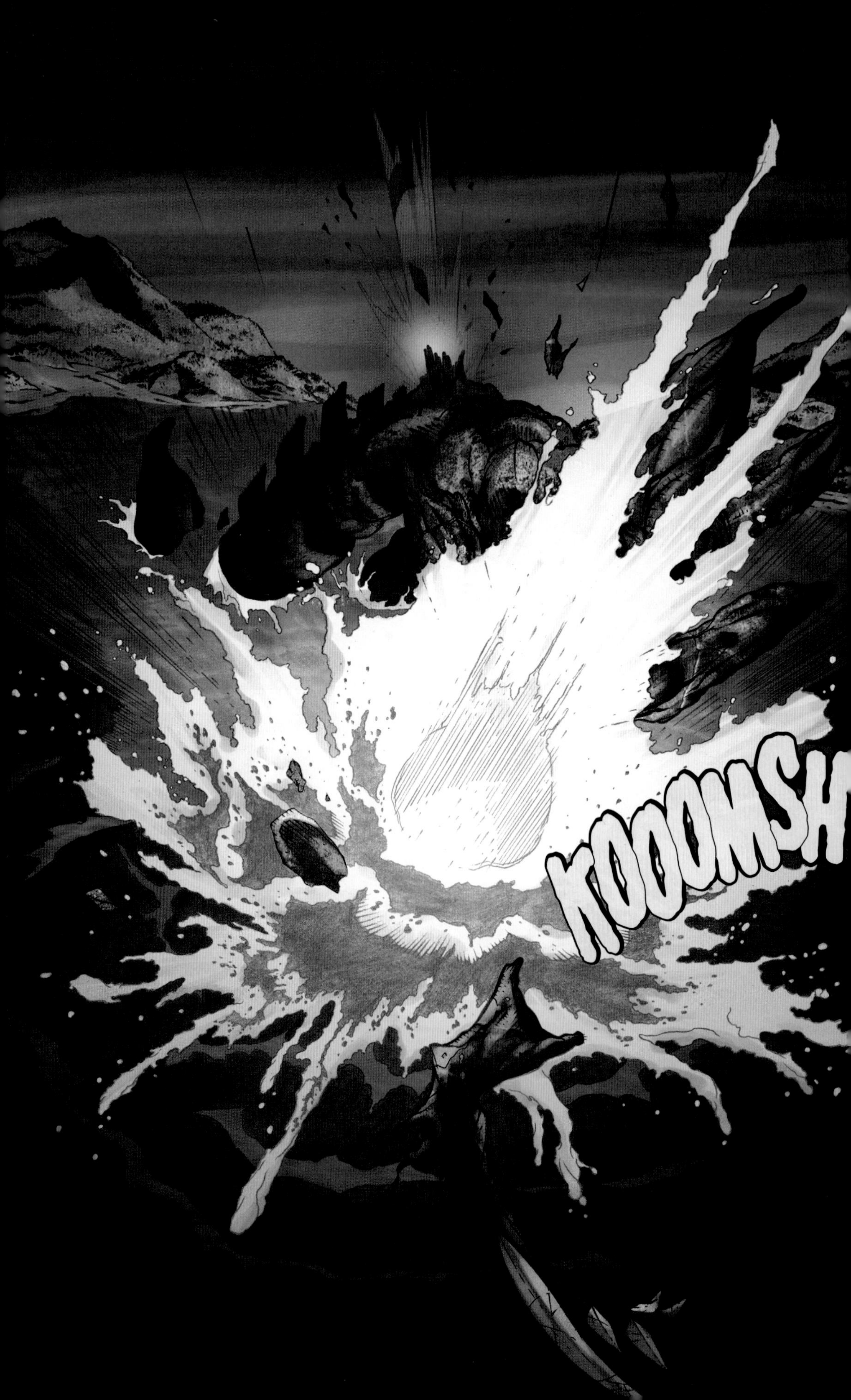
KOOOMSH

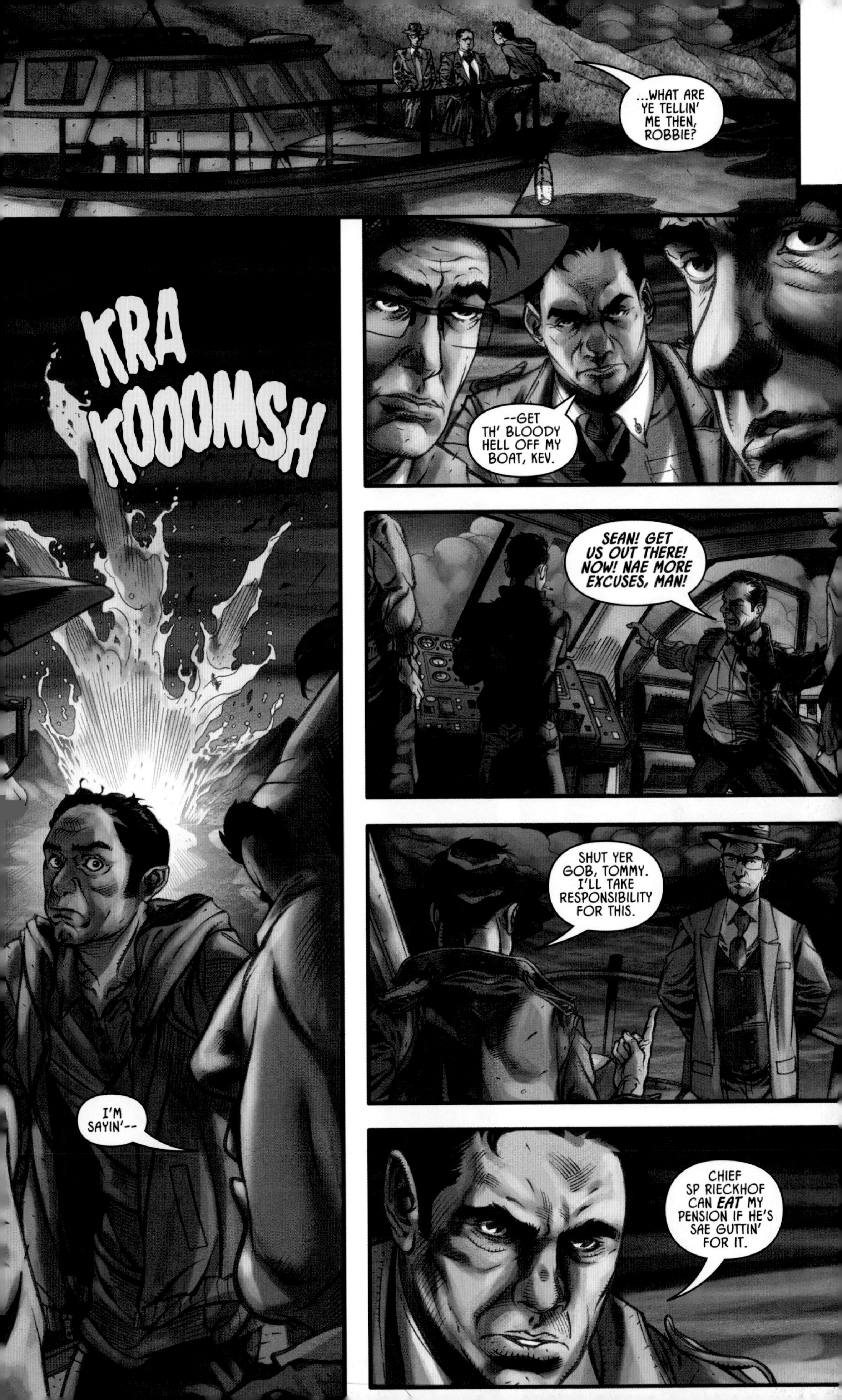
...WHAT ARE YE TELLIN' ME THEN, ROBBIE?
KRA KOOOMSH
I'M SAYIN'--
--GET TH' BLOODY HELL OFF MY BOAT, KEV.
SEAN! GET US OUT THERE! NOW! NAE MORE EXCUSES, MAN!
SHUT YER GOB, TOMMY. I'LL TAKE RESPONSIBILITY FOR THIS.
CHIEF SP RIECKHOF CAN EAT MY PENSION IF HE'S SAE GUTTIN' FOR IT.

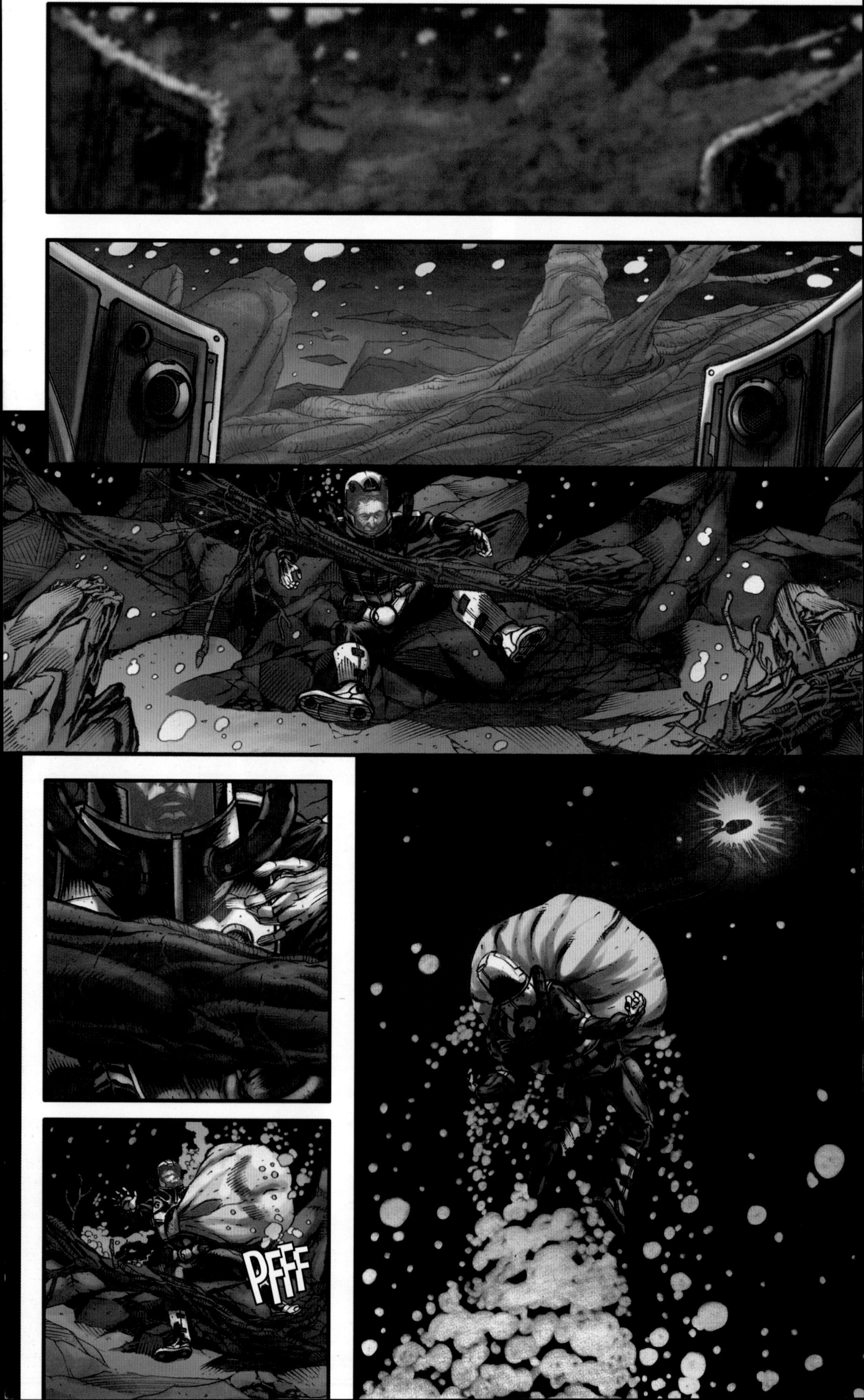
PFFF

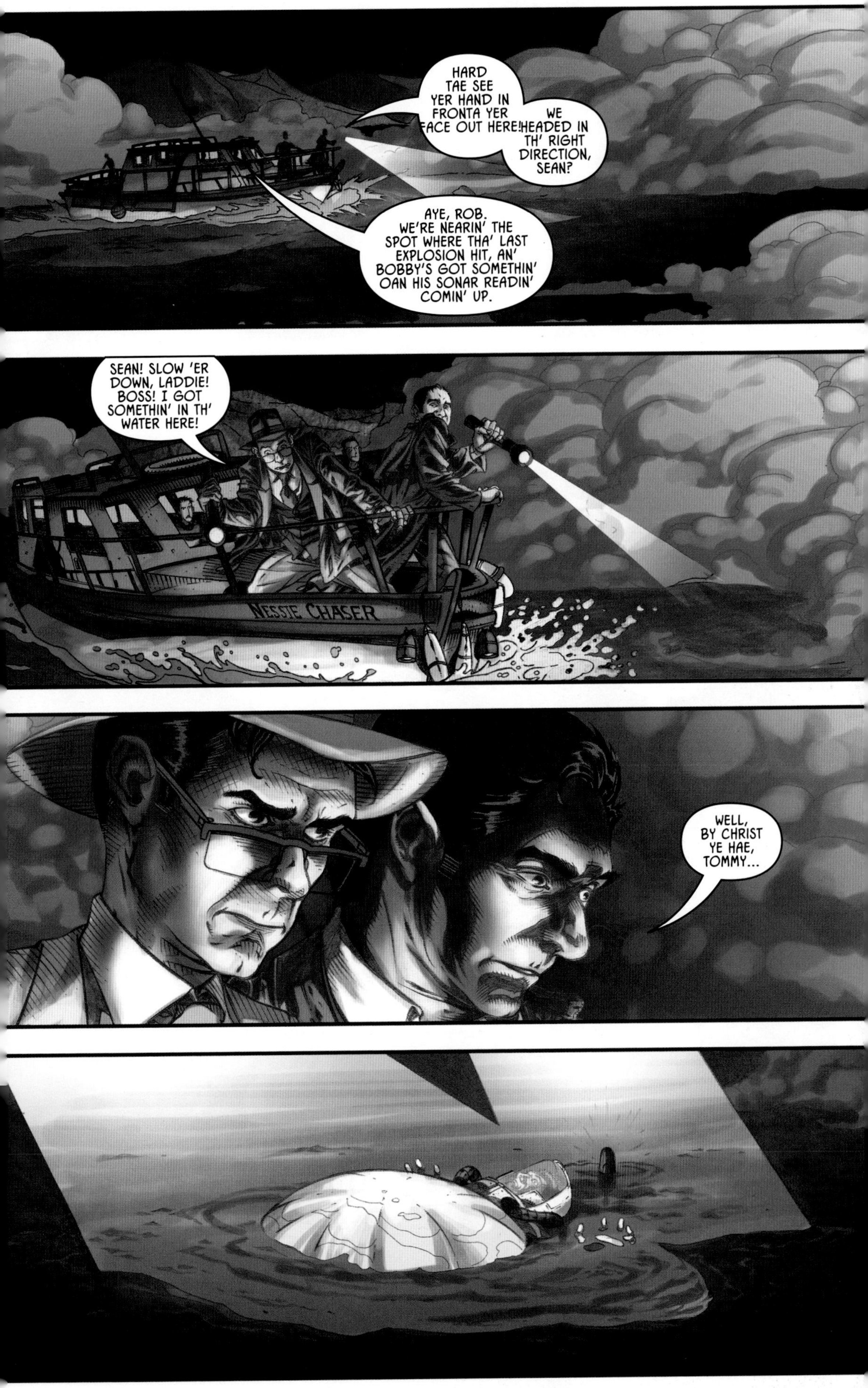
HARD TAE SEE YER HAND IN FRONTA YER FACE OUT HERE!
WE HEADED IN TH' RIGHT DIRECTION, SEAN?
AYE, ROB. WE'RE NEARIN' THE SPOT WHERE THA' LAST EXPLOSION HIT, AN' BOBBY'S GOT SOMETHIN' OAN HIS SONAR READIN' COMIN' UP.
SEAN! SLOW 'ER DOWN, LADDIE! BOSS! I GOT SOMETHIN' IN TH' WATER HERE!
NESSIE CHASER
WELL, BY CHRIST YE HAE, TOMMY...

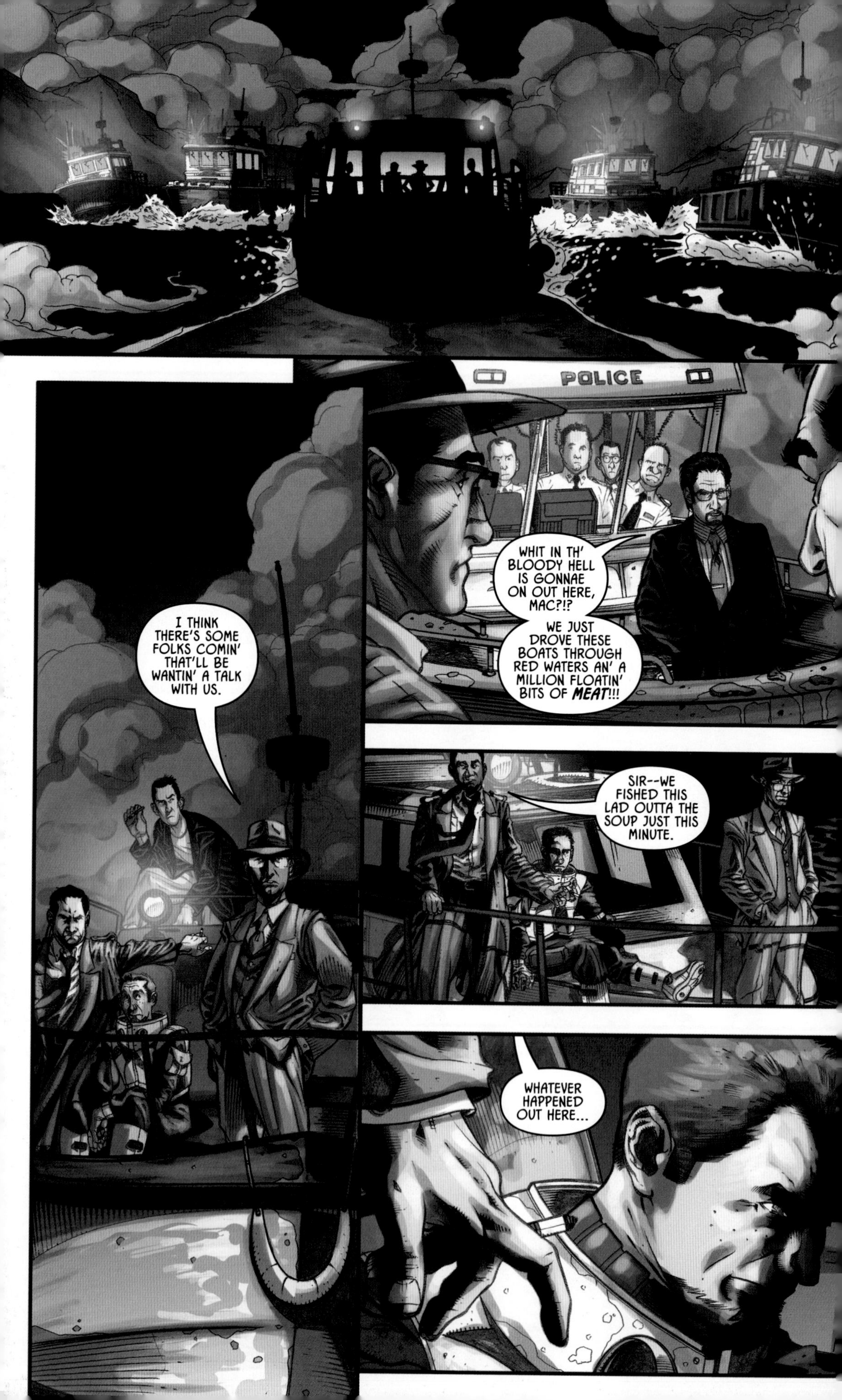
POLICE
I THINK THERE'S SOME FOLKS COMIN' THAT'LL BE WANTIN' A TALK WITH US.
WHIT IN TH' BLOODY HELL IS GONNAE ON OUT HERE, MAC?!?
WE JUST DROVE THESE BOATS THROUGH RED WATERS AN' A MILLION FLOATIN' BITS OF *MEAT*!!!
SIR--WE FISHED THIS LAD OUTTA THE SOUP JUST THIS MINUTE.
WHATEVER HAPPENED OUT HERE...

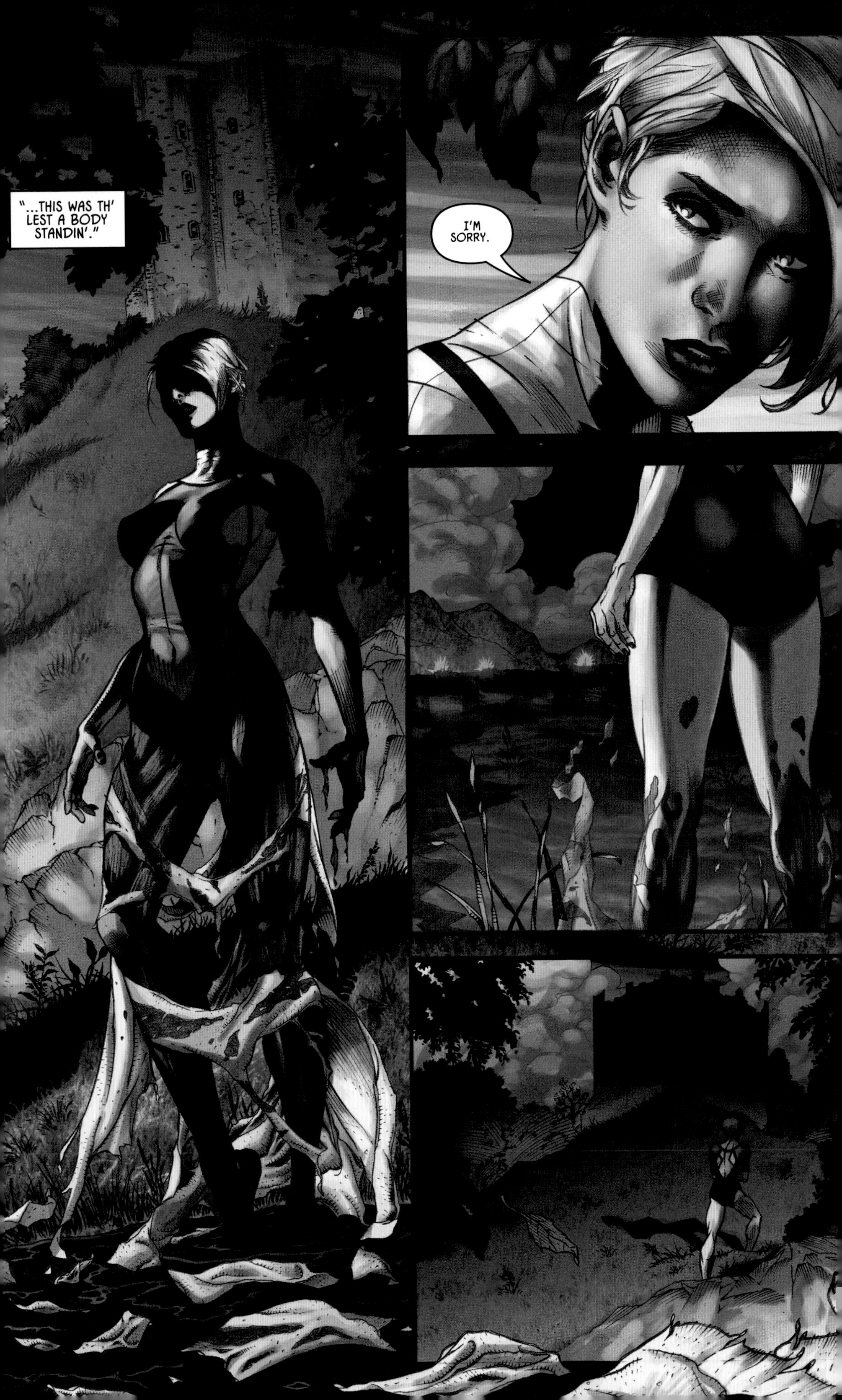
"...THIS WAS TH' LEST A BODY STANDIN'."
I'M SORRY.

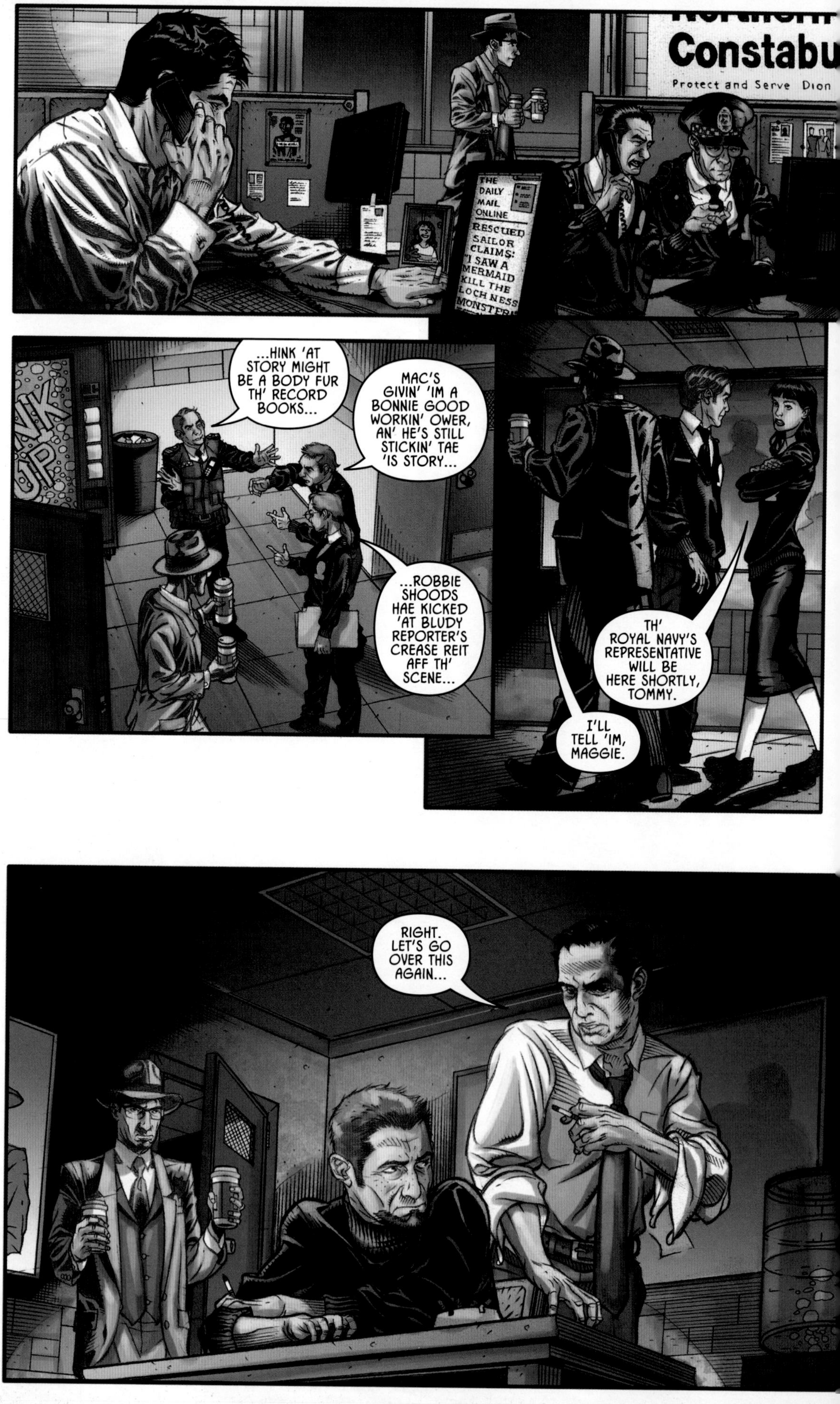

Constabu
Protect and Serve Dion
THE DAILY MAIL ONLINE
RESCUED SAILOR CLAIMS: "I SAW A MERMAID KILL THE LOCH NESS MONSTER
...HINK 'AT STORY MIGHT BE A BODY FUR TH' RECORD BOOKS...
MAC'S GIVIN' 'IM A BONNIE GOOD WORKIN' OWER, AN' HE'S STILL STICKIN' TAE 'IS STORY...
...ROBBIE SHOODS HAE KICKED 'AT BLUDY REPORTER'S CREASE REIT AFF TH' SCENE...
TH' ROYAL NAVY'S REPRESENTATIVE WILL BE HERE SHORTLY, TOMMY.
I'LL TELL 'IM, MAGGIE.
RIGHT. LET'S GO OVER THIS AGAIN...

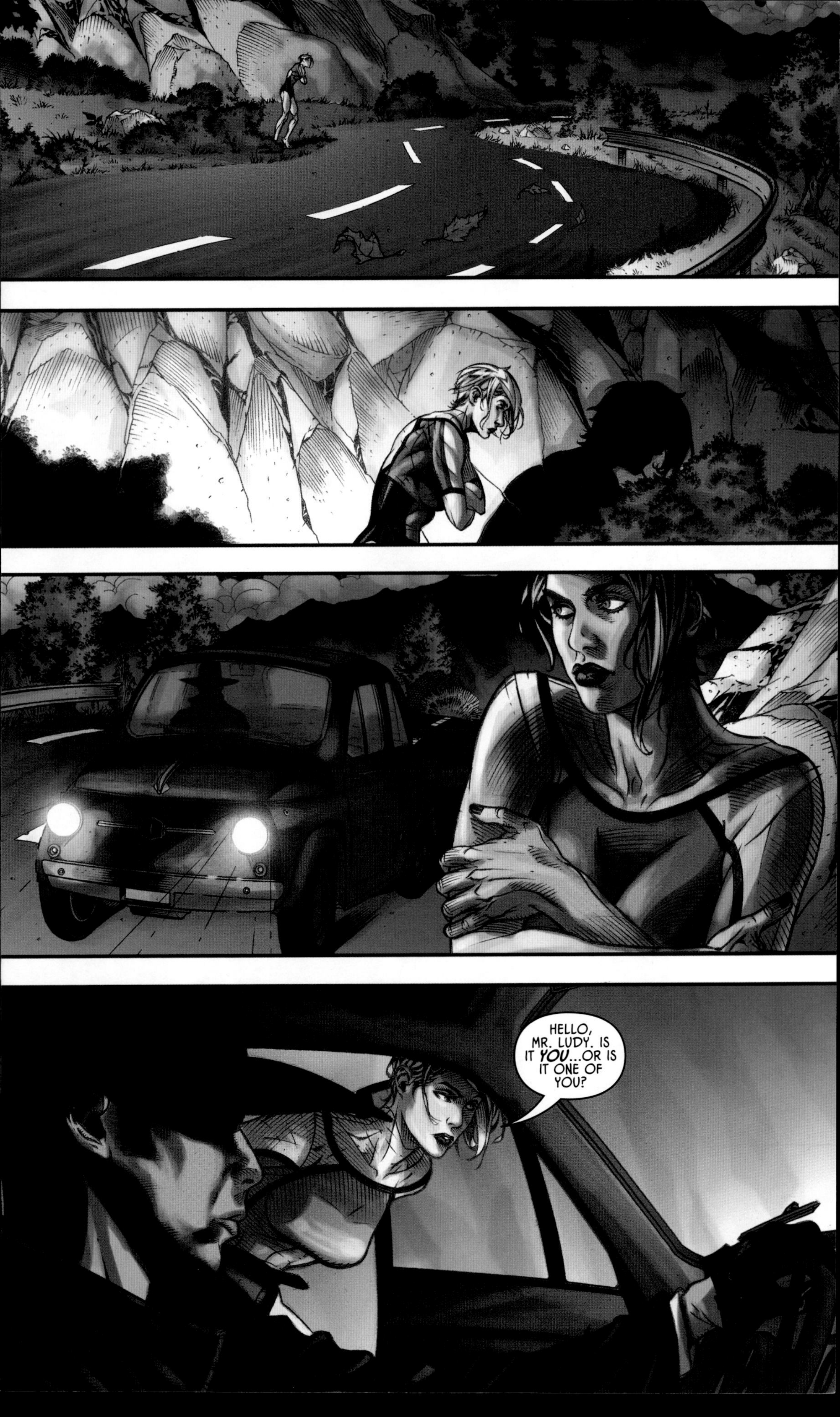
HELLO, MR. LUDY. IS IT YOU...OR IS IT ONE OF YOU?

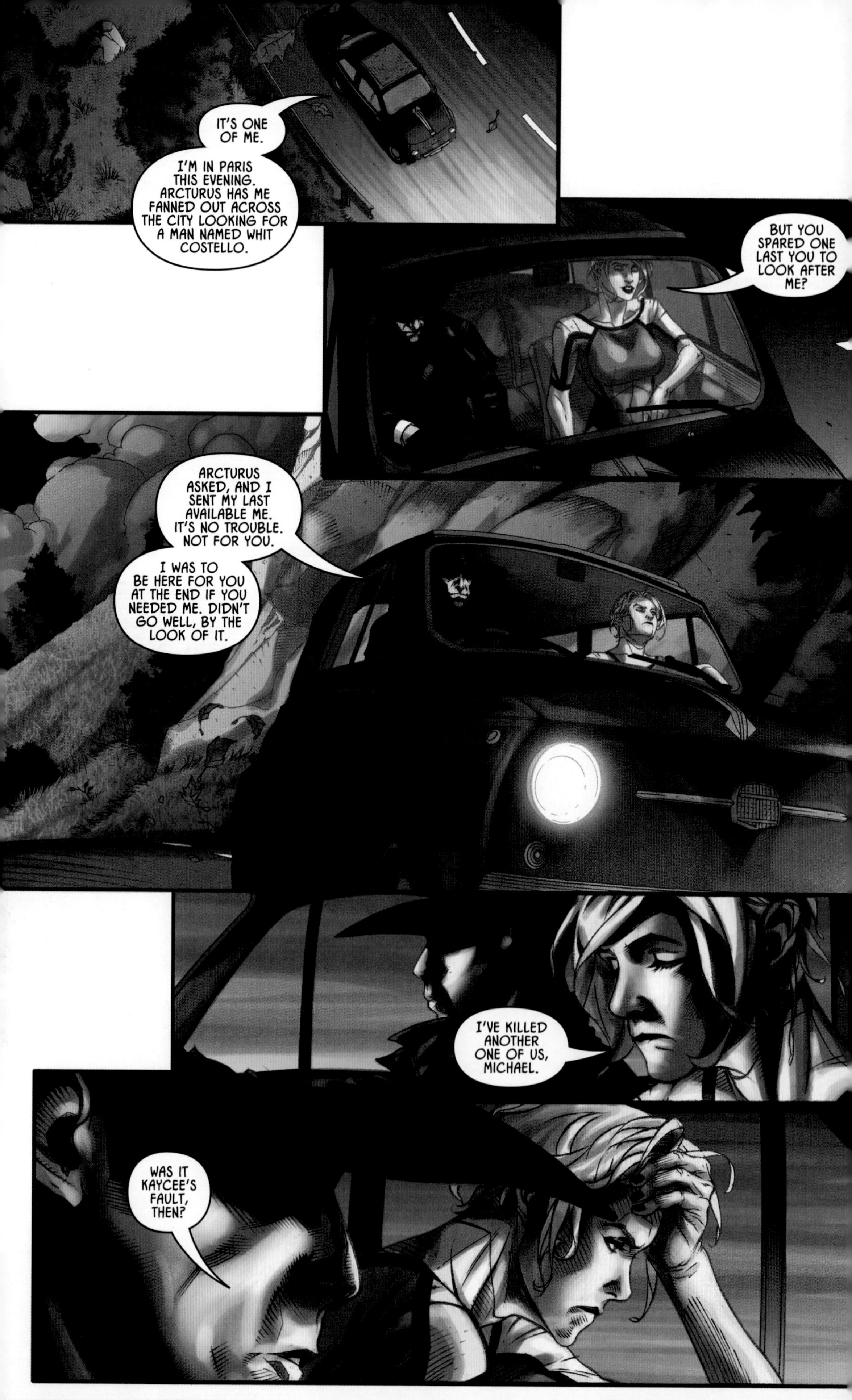
IT'S ONE OF ME.
I'M IN PARIS THIS EVENING. ARCTURUS HAS ME FANNED OUT ACROSS THE CITY LOOKING FOR A MAN NAMED WHIT COSTELLO.
BUT YOU SPARED ONE LAST YOU TO LOOK AFTER ME?
ARCTURUS ASKED, AND I SENT MY LAST AVAILABLE ME. IT'S NO TROUBLE. NOT FOR YOU.
I WAS TO BE HERE FOR YOU AT THE END IF YOU NEEDED ME. DIDN'T GO WELL, BY THE LOOK OF IT.
I'VE KILLED ANOTHER ONE OF US, MICHAEL.
WAS IT KAYCEE'S FAULT, THEN?

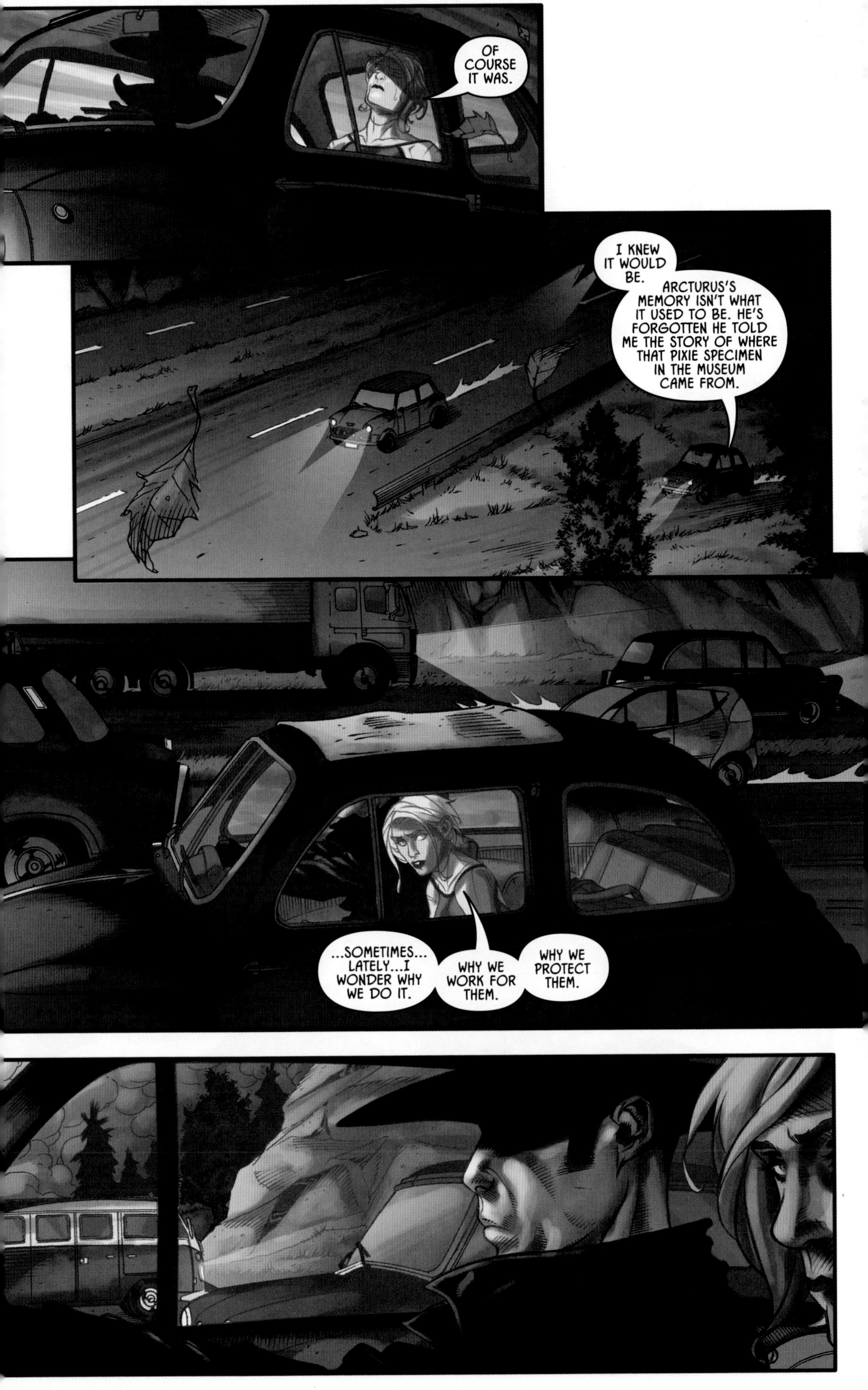
OF COURSE IT WAS.
I KNEW IT WOULD BE.
ARCTURUS'S MEMORY ISN'T WHAT IT USED TO BE. HE'S FORGOTTEN HE TOLD ME THE STORY OF WHERE THAT PIXIE SPECIMEN IN THE MUSEUM CAME FROM.
...SOMETIMES... LATELY...I WONDER WHY WE DO IT.
WHY WE WORK FOR THEM.
WHY WE PROTECT THEM.

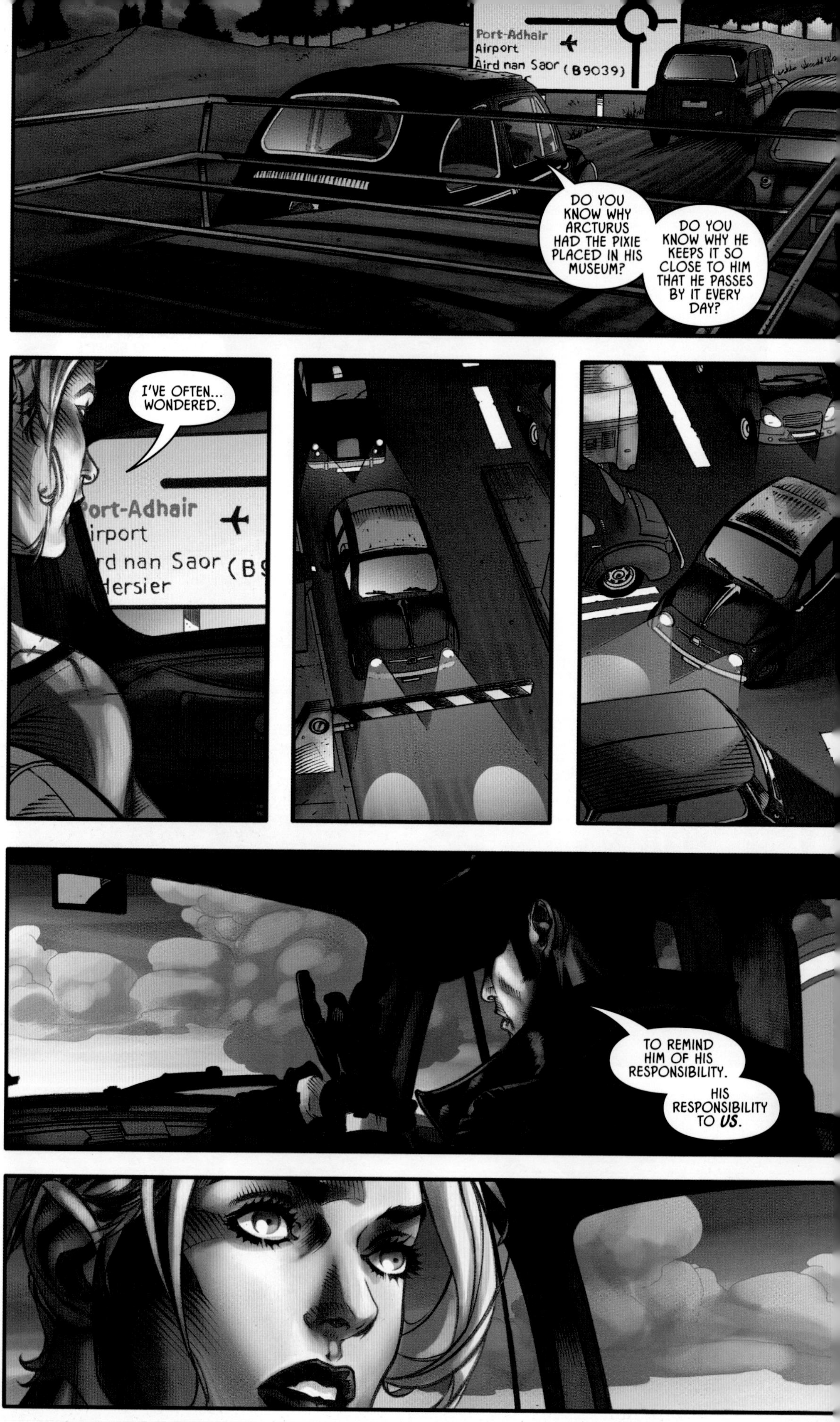
Port-Adhair
Airport
Àird nan Saor (B9039)
DO YOU KNOW WHY ARCTURUS HAD THE PIXIE PLACED IN HIS MUSEUM?
DO YOU KNOW WHY HE KEEPS IT SO CLOSE TO HIM THAT HE PASSES BY IT EVERY DAY?
I'VE OFTEN... WONDERED.
TO REMIND HIM OF HIS RESPONSIBILITY.
HIS RESPONSIBILITY TO *US*.

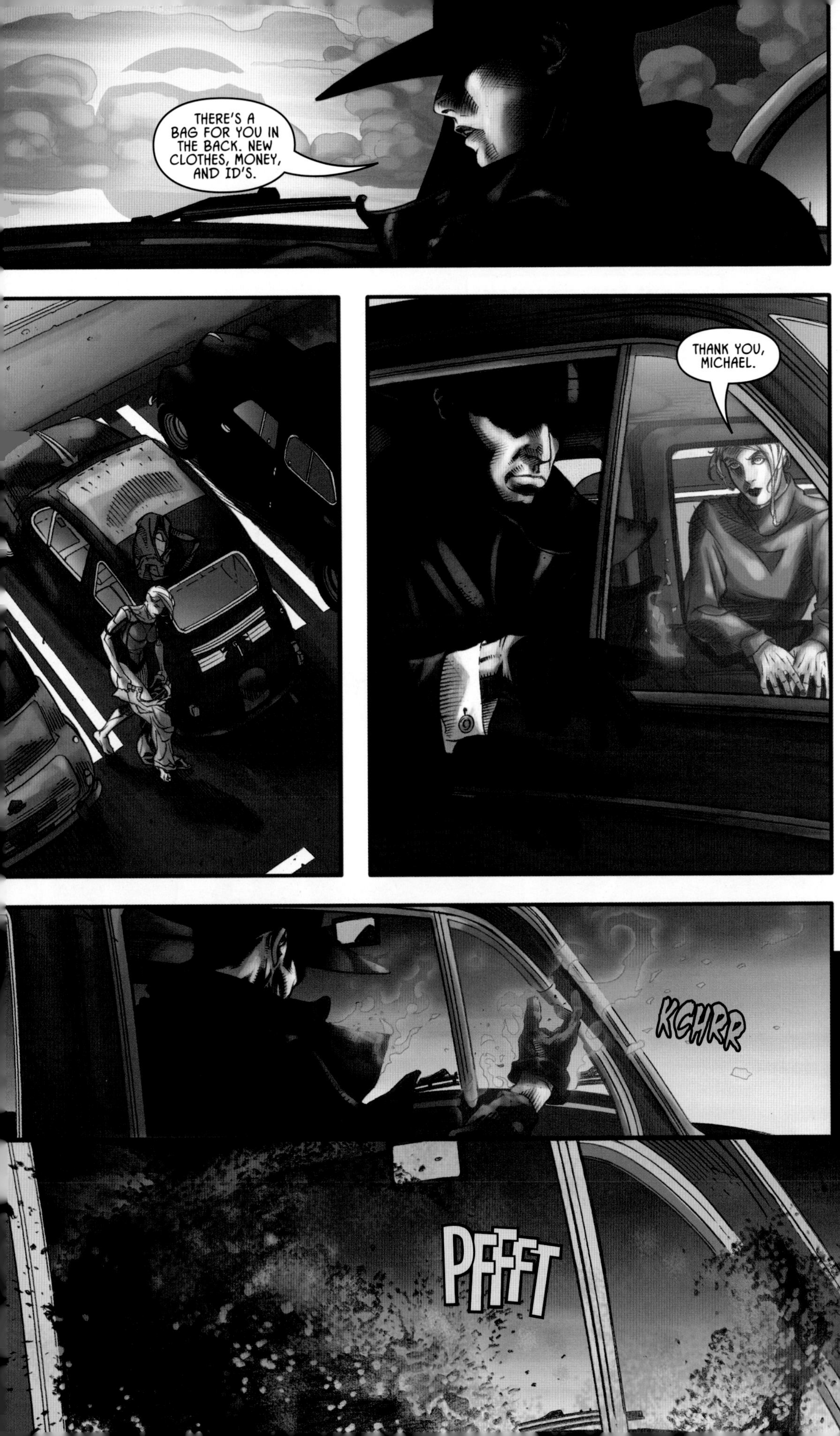
THERE'S A BAG FOR YOU IN THE BACK. NEW CLOTHES, MONEY, AND ID'S.
THANK YOU, MICHAEL.
KCHRR
PFFFT

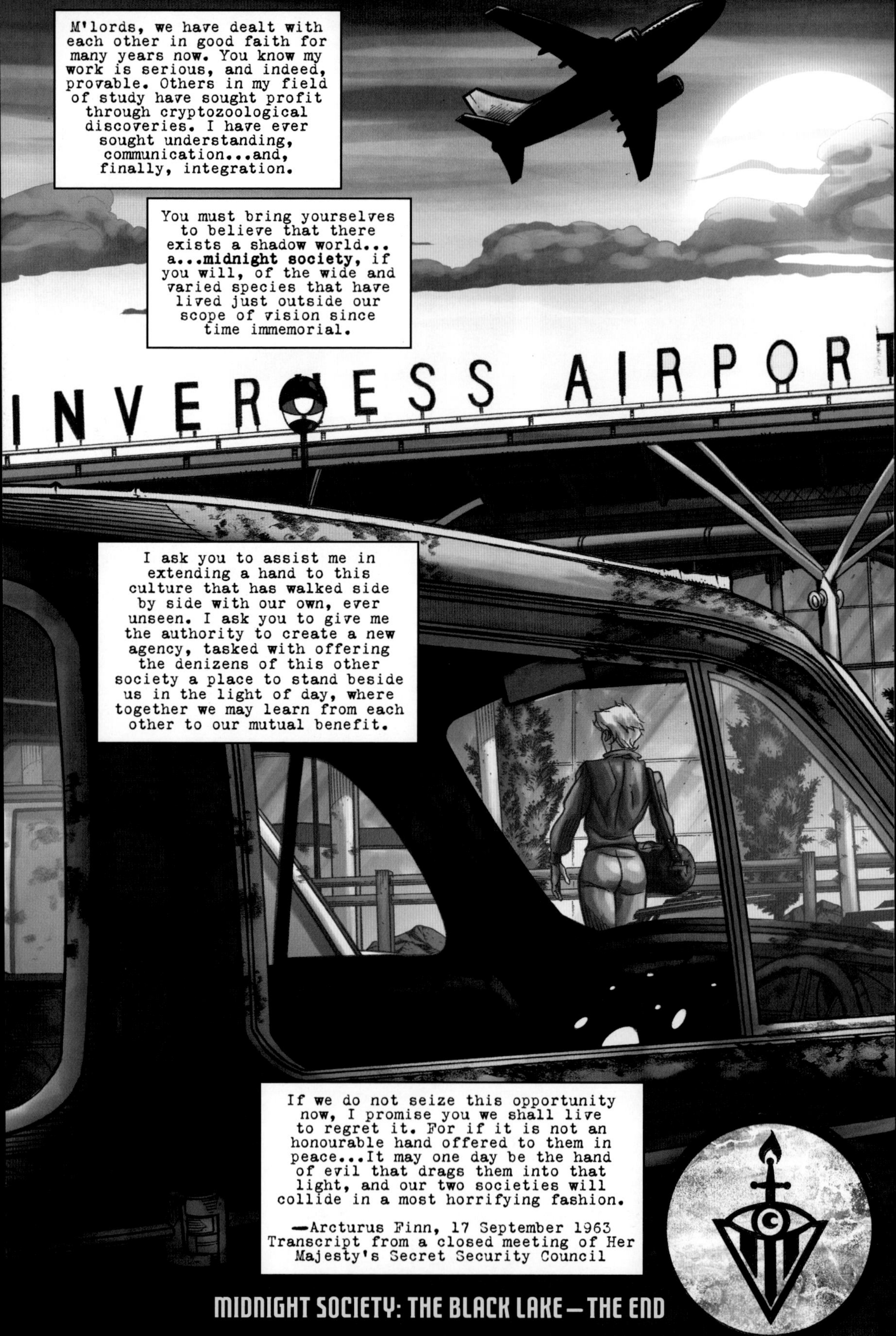
M'lords, we have dealt with each other in good faith for many years now. You know my work is serious, and indeed, provable. Others in my field of study have sought profit through cryptozoological discoveries. I have ever sought understanding, communication...and, finally, integration.
You must bring yourselves to believe that there exists a shadow world... a...**midnight society,** if you will, of the wide and varied species that have lived just outside our scope of vision since time immemorial.
INVERNESS AIRPORT
I ask you to assist me in extending a hand to this culture that has walked side by side with our own, ever unseen. I ask you to give me the authority to create a new agency, tasked with offering the denizens of this other society a place to stand beside us in the light of day, where together we may learn from each other to our mutual benefit.
If we do not seize this opportunity now, I promise you we shall live to regret it. For if it is not an honourable hand offered to them in peace...It may one day be the hand of evil that drags them into that light, and our two societies will collide in a most horrifying fashion.
—Arcturus Finn, 17 September 1963 Transcript from a closed meeting of Her Majesty's Secret Security Council
MIDNIGHT SOCIETY: THE BLACK LAKE — THE END

I love the pulp era.

Adventurers, mystery men and women, pseudo-science—darkness and horror colliding with invention and magic—these things crank the gears of my imagination. I've wondered for a while . . . Could pulp stories told in a modern setting reignite the fire of wonder and breathless excitement once found blazing on newsprint, under a glossy cover?

I put pen to paper and got to work one night, figuring I'd try to find out. This is how my first effort was realized. Here's my spark. I hope it catches fire for you.

—**Drew Edward Johnson**
Burbank, California, 2015

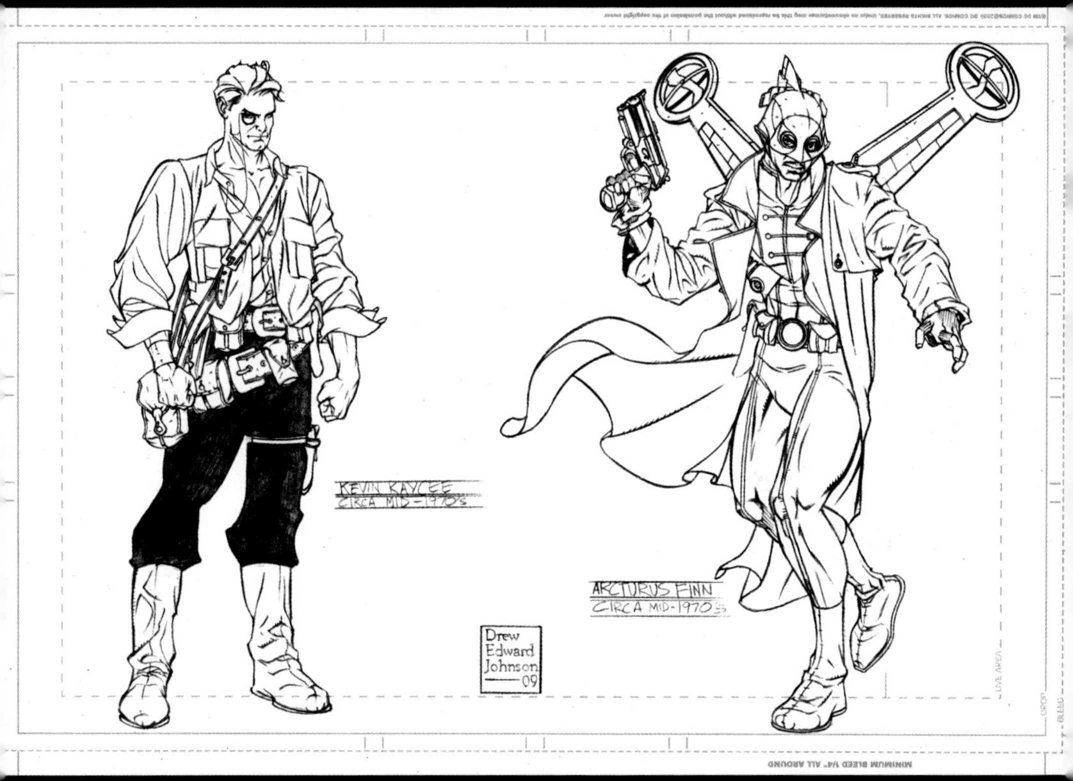
KEVIN KAYCEE
CIRCA MID-1970's
ARCTURUS FINN
CIRCA MID-1970's
Drew Edward Johnson 09

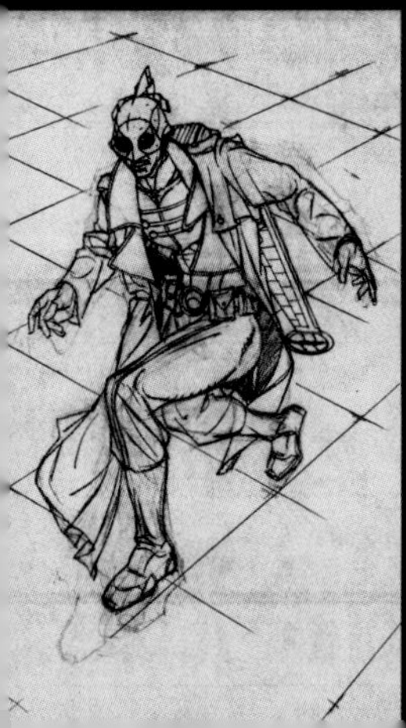

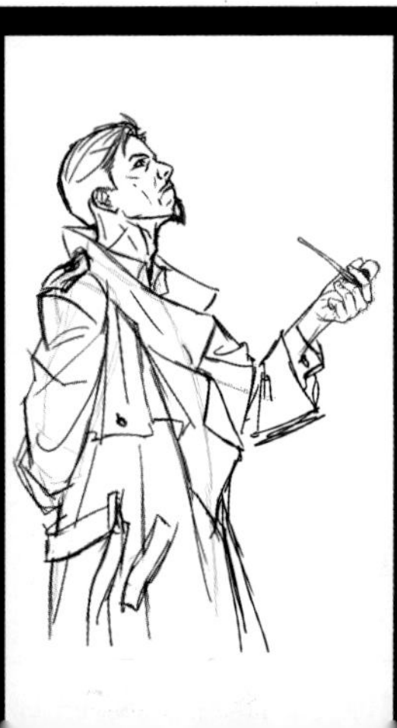

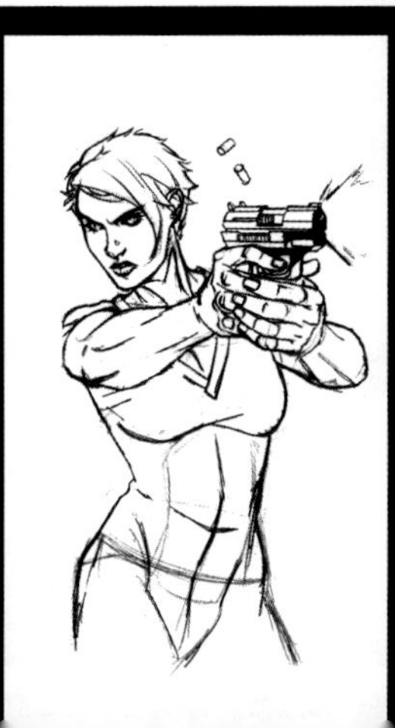

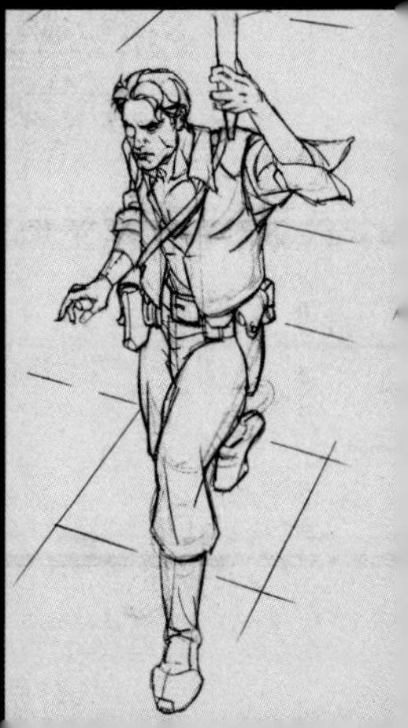

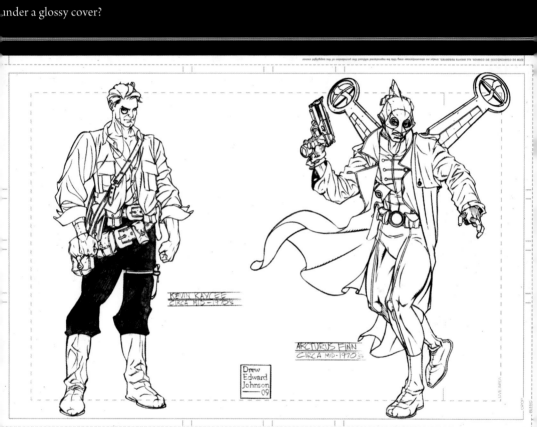

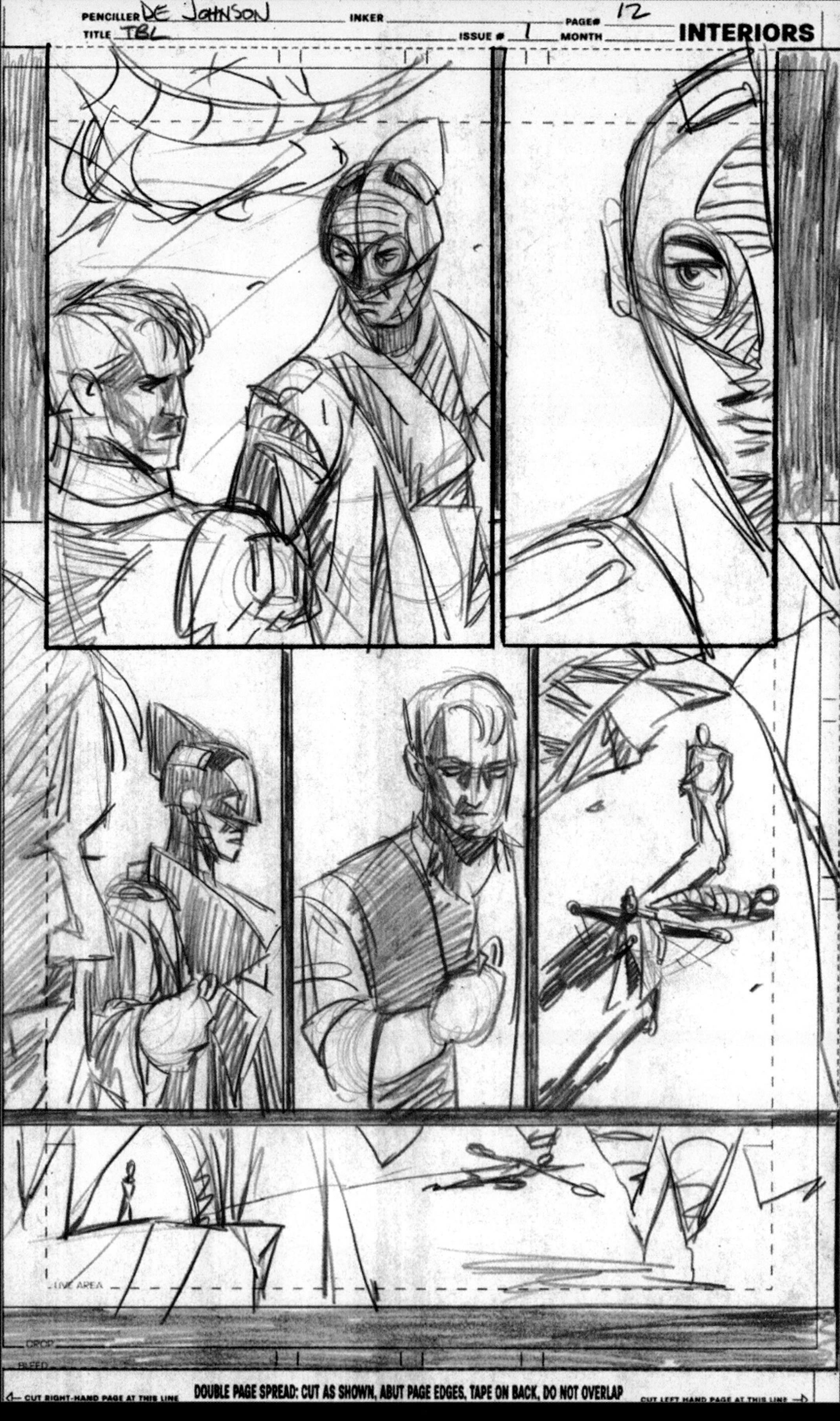
PENCILLER DE JOHNSON
INKER
PAGE# 12
TITLE TBL
ISSUE # 1
MONTH
INTERIORS
LIVE AREA
CROP
BLEED
CUT RIGHT-HAND PAGE AT THIS LINE
DOUBLE PAGE SPREAD: CUT AS SHOWN, ABUT PAGE EDGES, TAPE ON BACK, DO NOT OVERLAP
CUT LEFT HAND PAGE AT THIS LINE

A look at Drew's early layout process.

3

Initial *Midnight Society* icon designs by Hart Reickhoff.

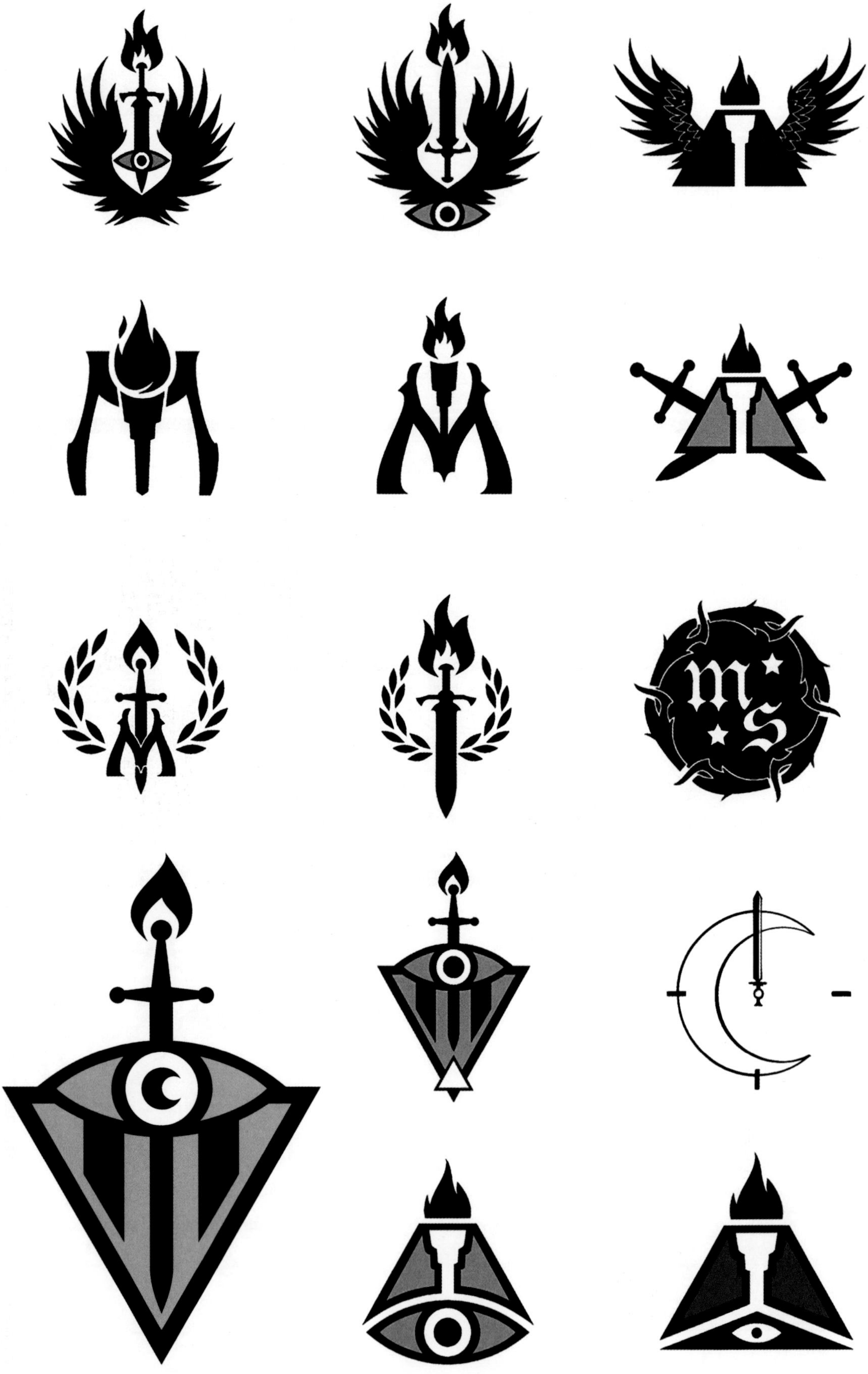

The final incarnation of the *Midnight Society* icon.

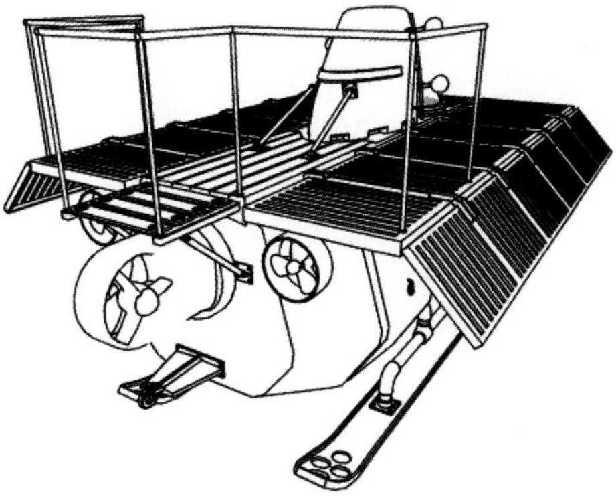
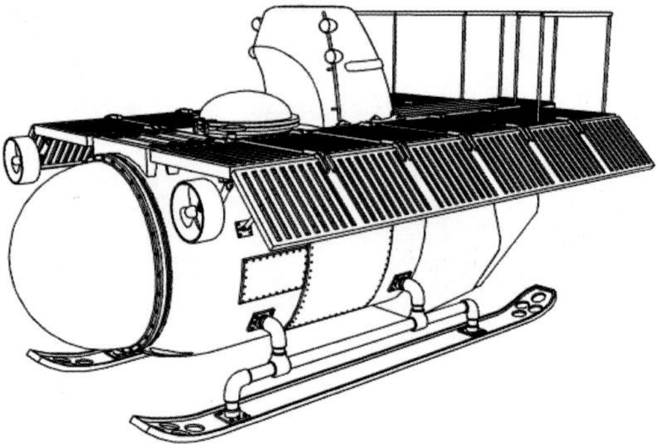
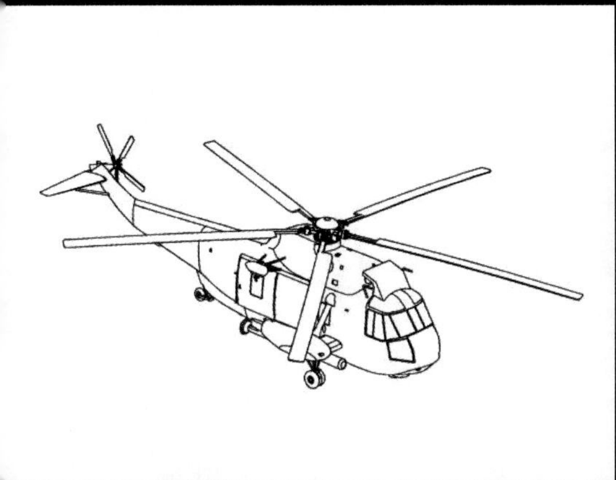
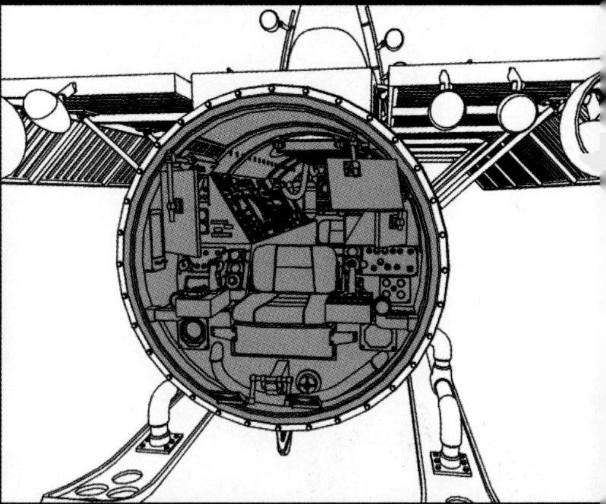
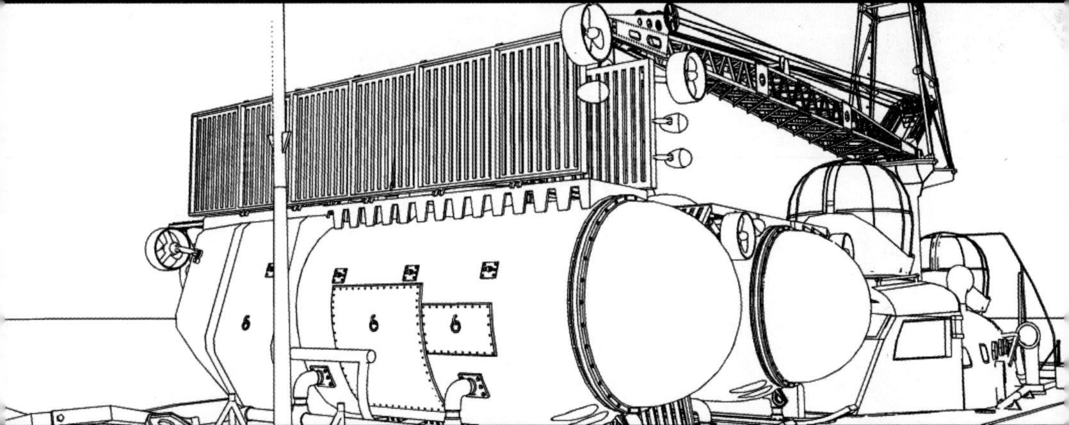
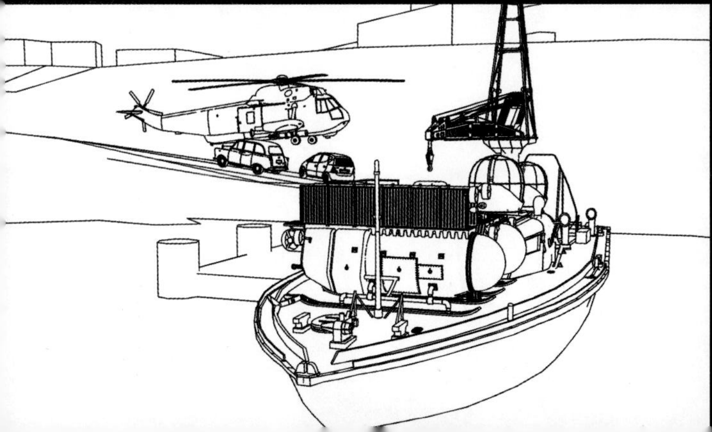
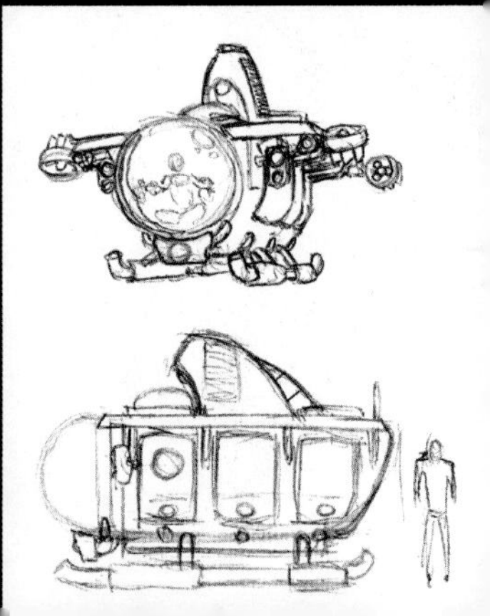

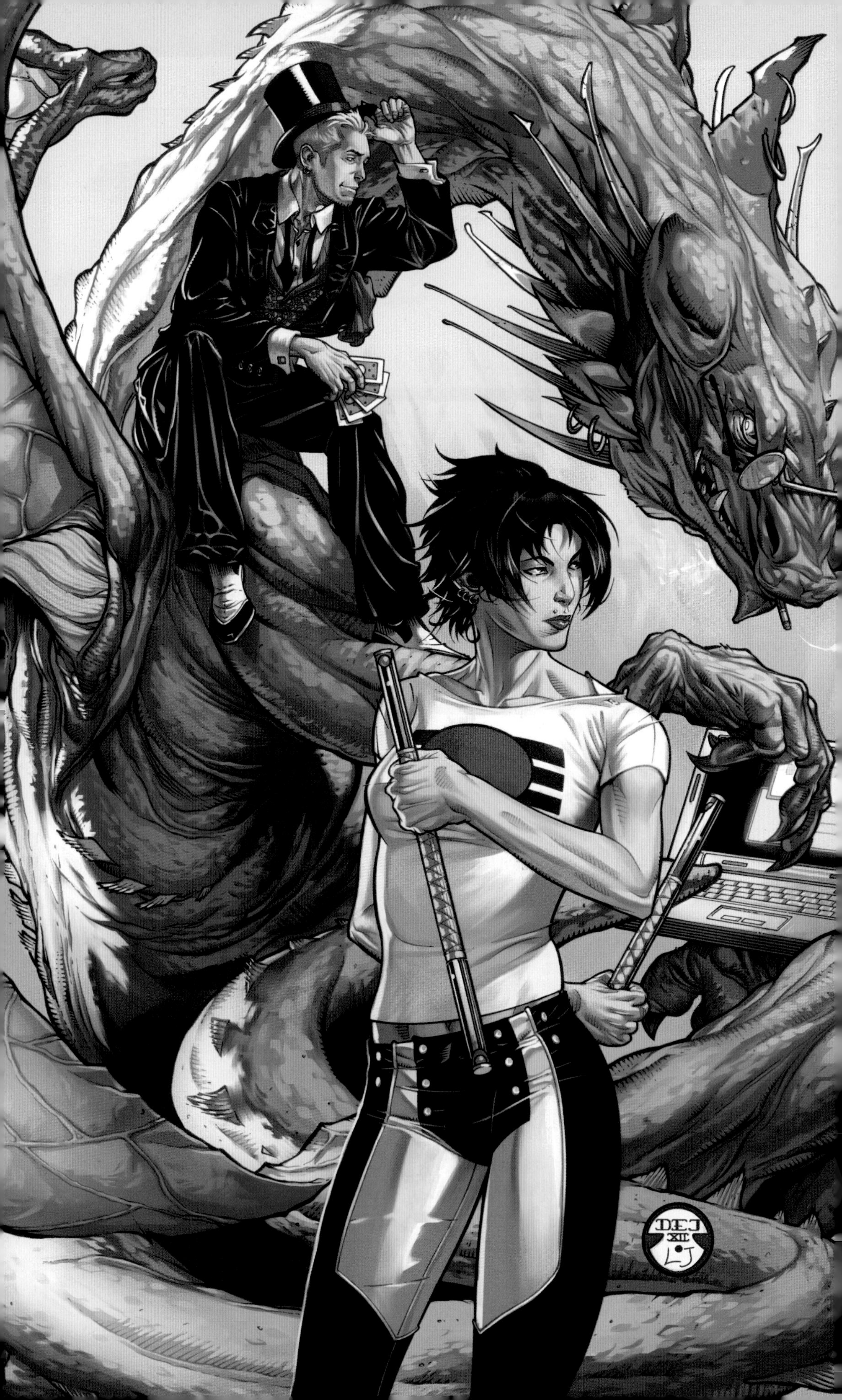

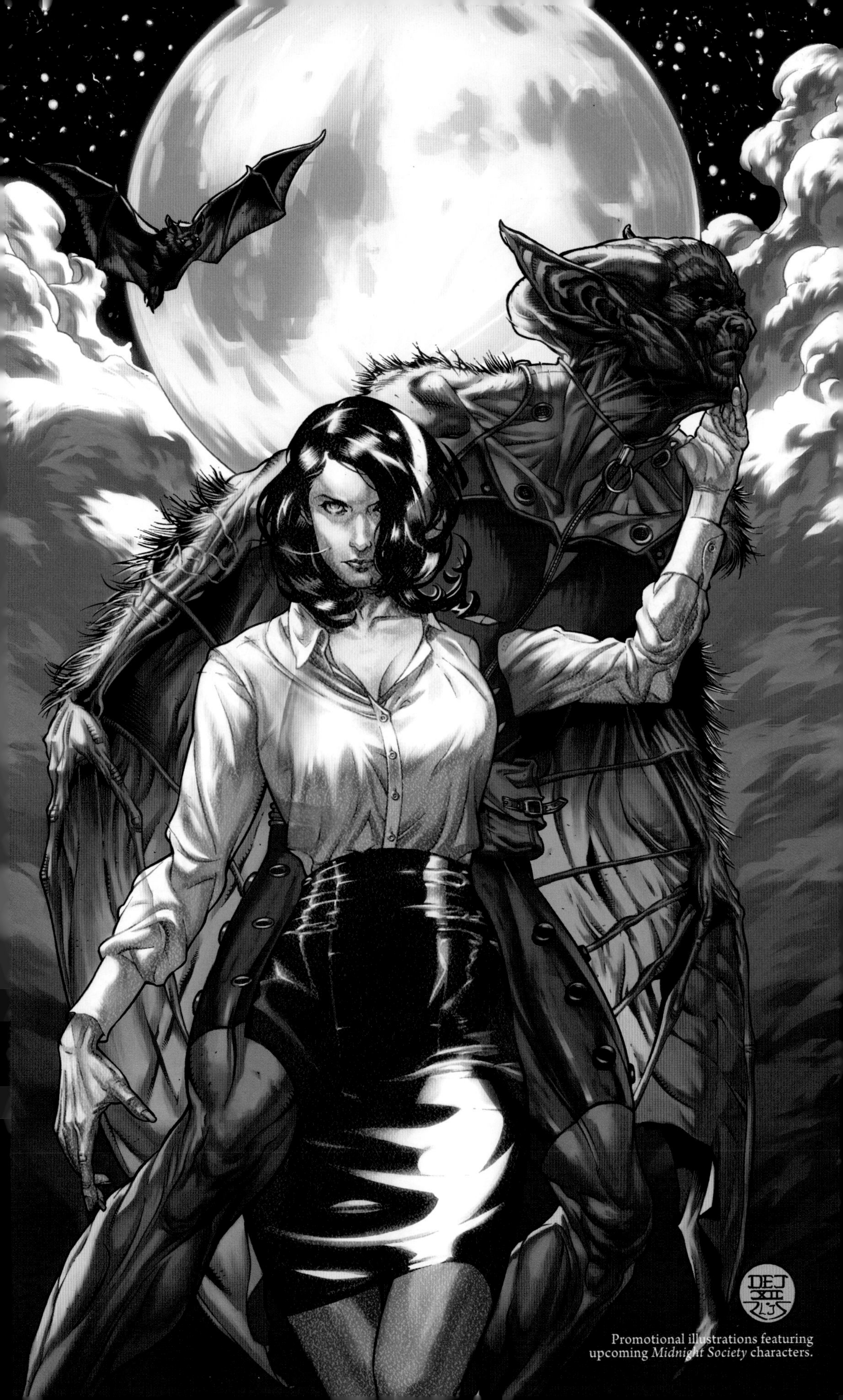

Promotional illustrations featuring upcoming *Midnight Society* characters.

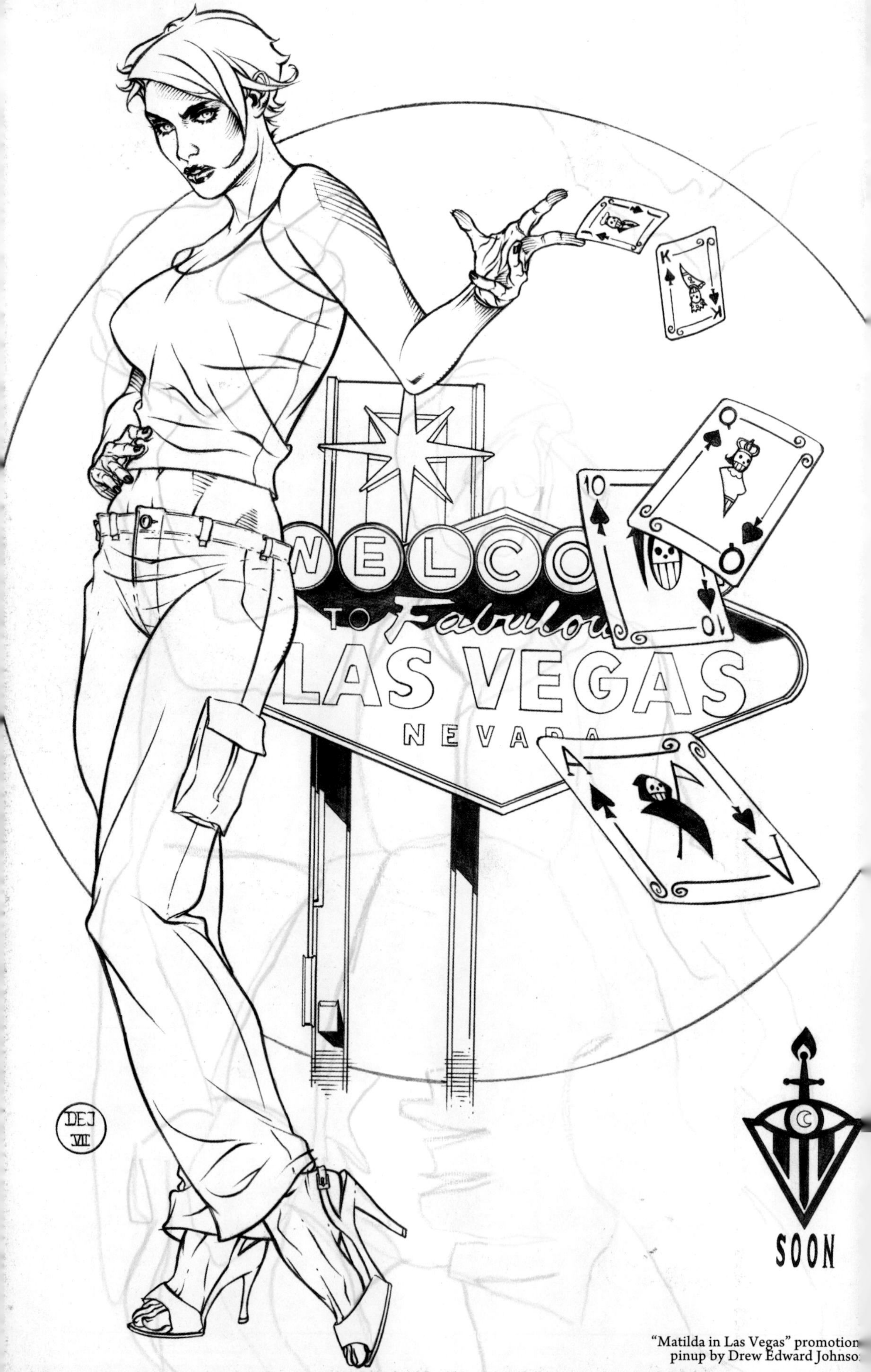
WELCO
TO Fabulou
LAS VEGAS
NEVADA
DEJ
VII
SOON
"Matilda in Las Vegas" promotion
pinup by Drew Edward Johnso

More great

NOIR AND ESPIONAGE

from Dark Horse Books

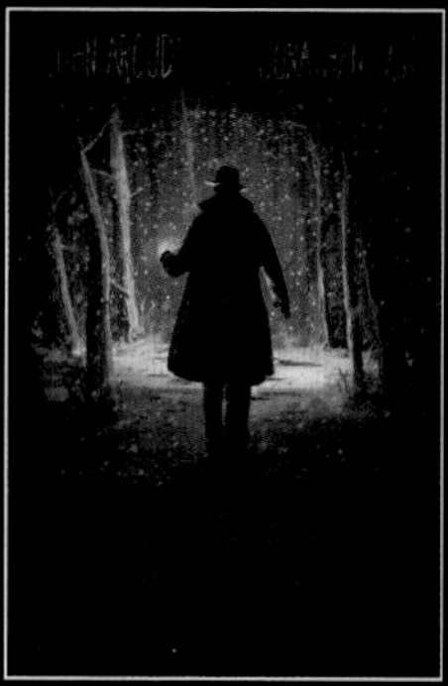

THE CREEP

JOHN ARCUDI, JONATHAN CASE, AND TONCI ZONJIC

A young boy puts a gun in his mouth and pulls the trigger. The police don't care—not about his death or the death of his best friend two months earlier. The dead boy's mom seeks help from an old flame that's employed as a detective. Will the detective's freakish appearance get in the way of uncovering the terrible secrets of these two teenagers?

ISBN 978-1-61655-061-5
$19.99

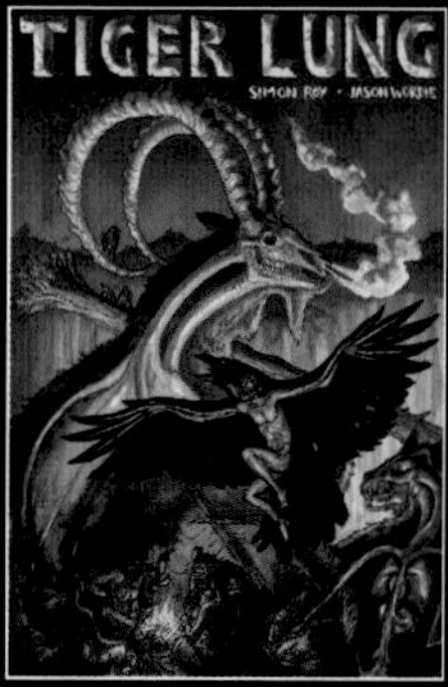
TIGER LUNG
SIMON ROY • JASON WORDIE

TIGER LUNG

SIMON ROY AND JASON WORDIE

Thirty-five thousand years ago, the world was ruled by strange beasts and ancient gods! For some Paleolithic tribes, hope lay in the shaman warriors who stood between them and the unknown. *Tiger Lung* follows the struggle of one of these shamans to keep his people alive in a vast, hostile universe!

ISBN 978-1-61655-543-6
$15.99

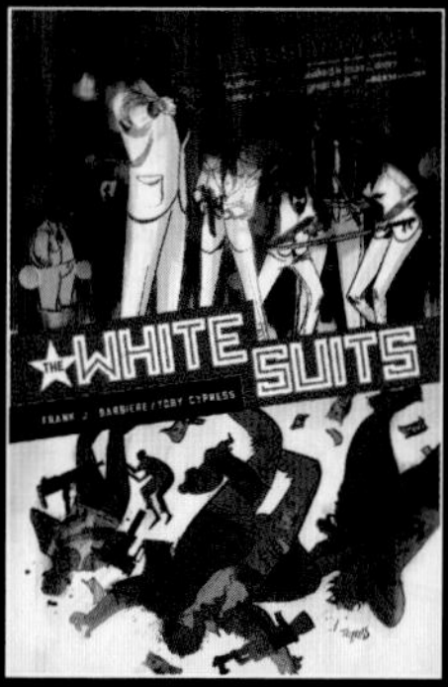
WHITE SUITS

THE WHITE SUITS VOLUME 1: DRESSED TO KILL

FRANK BARBIERE AND TOBY CYPRESS

They savaged the Cold War Russian underworld—then disappeared. When they resurface, leaving a trail of dead mobsters in their wake, an amnesiac and an FBI agent seek to answer a single question: Who are the White Suits?

ISBN 978-1-61655-493-4
$17.99

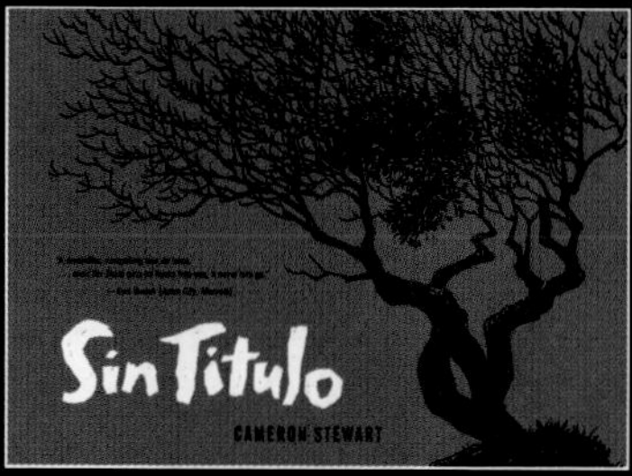
Sin Titulo
CAMERON STEWART

SIN TITULO

CAMERON STEWART

The Eisner Award–winning web comic! Following the death of his grandfather, young Alex Mackay discovers a mysterious photograph in the old man's belongings that sets him on an adventure like no other—where dreams and reality merge, family secrets are laid bare, and lives are irrevocably altered.

ISBN 978-1-61655-248-0
$19.99

AVAILABLE AT YOUR LOCAL COMICS SHOP OR BOOKSTORE • TO FIND A COMICS SHOP IN YOUR AREA, CALL 1-888-266-4226
For more information or to order direct: • On the web: DarkHorse.com • E-mail: mailorder@darkhorse.com • Phone: 1-800-862-0052 Mon.–Fri. 9 AM to 5 PM Pacific Time.

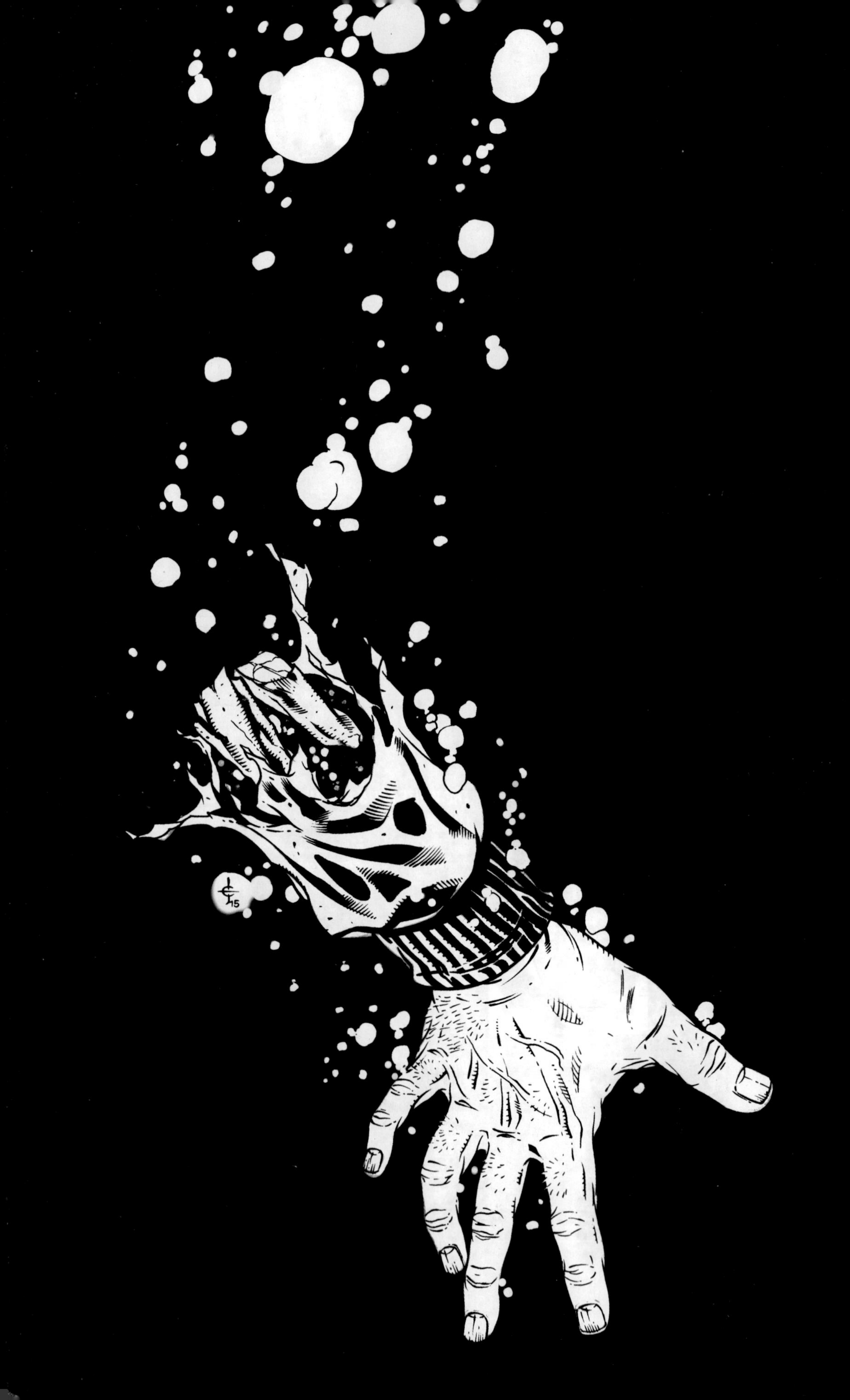